Market-Based Interest Rate Reform in China

T0331350

The market-based interest rate reform remains a core part of China's financial reforms, and an important topic of both theoretical and policy studies. This book presents a comprehensive analysis of the process and logic of China's interest rate reform from a historical perspective. It is structured along three lines, i.e. loosening interest rate controls, establishing market-based interest rates, and building an effective interest rate adjustment mechanism, and systematically reviews the characteristics and evolvement of the reform process. The book further explores the lessons and challenges of the reform by examining China's development stage and auxiliary reforms needed, and offers policy recommendations on how to further push forward the reform.

China Finance 40 Forum (CF40) is a leading independent think tank dedicated to policy research in the fields of macroeconomics and finance. In addition, it is a platform with over 300 members from governmental agencies, financial institutions, and academia. The core membership consists of about 40 influential experts around the age of 40.

CF40 Research Group members:
Lu Lei, Liu Xiangyun, Niu Muhong, Li Hongjin, Mo Wangui, Zhang Huaiqing, Ma Zhiyang, Chen Jun, Yao Jingchao, Wang Jinhui, Guo Qi, Zhang Zhaoyan

Main translators:
Tao Mengying, Xie Yuelan, Qu Qiang, Hu Bing, Gao Zheng, Sam Overholt, Niu Muyao

中国金融四十人论坛书系
CHINA FINANCE 40 FORUM BOOKS

The "China Finance 40 Forum Books" focus on the macroeconomic and financial field with a special emphasis on financial policy studies to facilitate innovations in financial thinking and inspire breakthroughs, while building a high-end, authentic brand for think tank books with top academic quality and policy value.

The "China Finance 40 Forum Books" has published more than 100 monographs since 2009. Through its rigorous and cutting-edge research, this book series has a remarkable reputation in the industry and a broad influence overall.

Market-Based Interest Rate Reform in China

China Finance 40 Forum Research Group

Routledge
Taylor & Francis Group

LONDON AND NEW YORK

First published in English 2019
by Routledge
2 Park Square, Milton Park, Abingdon, Oxon OX14 4RN

and by Routledge
52 Vanderbilt Avenue, New York, NY 10017

First issued in paperback 2020

Routledge is an imprint of the Taylor & Francis Group, an informa business

Translated by Tao Mengying, Xie Yuelan, et al.

British Library Cataloguing-in-Publication Data
A catalogue record for this book is available from the British Library

Library of Congress Cataloging-in-Publication Data
A catalog record has been requested for this book

ISBN 13: 978-0-367-58245-6 (pbk)
ISBN 13: 978-1-138-60307-3 (hbk)

Typeset in Times New Roman
by Apex CoVantage, LLC

Contents

Illustrations

Figures

Tables

Preface

Market-based interest rate reform, one of the key areas of China's financial reforms, has consistently been the focus of academic research and policy studies. The reform has sparked numerous debates and analyses over the last few decades.

Discussions and studies on China's interest rate reform have gone through several stages. In the early stage of the reform and opening-up, research on interest rate reform focused on its necessity, prerequisite, and path selection. After the country joined the WTO, researchers analyzed the reform on the basis of the possible impact of WTO accession and the poor performance of the nation's banking system. Some studies also looked into the risks of interest rate reform. During the global financial crisis, when China's economic imbalance was becoming a noticeable problem, many argued that the structural imbalance was caused by interest rate controls and the low interest rate policy, and several studies called for the liberalization of interest rates. In recent years, with the financial reform making progress, China is moving into a critical stage of liberalizing its deposit and lending interest rates. Heated discussions have taken place on furthering interest rate reform and the relationship between interest rate liberalization and financial openness, as well as the influence of liberalized deposit and lending rates on the banking system, the financial sector, economic development, and SME financing. Meanwhile, the interest rate adjustment mechanism is becoming an important subject.

Current research has reached a broad consensus on the necessity, prerequisite, path selection, risk, and influence of the market-based interest rate reform, and many of the findings are mutually verifiable and complementary. However, evaluations of the reform process vary greatly. One school of thought holds that China's interest rate reform lags behind economic development. Nicholas Lardy (2013) argues that the long time control on interest rates has led to low real deposit rates. Particularly after 2004, the low rate policy has severely hampered the increase of income and consumption and led to an imbalance in economic growth; low interest rates, Lardy says, have also led to excess demand for bank credit, forcing the People's Bank of China (PBOC) to take quantity control measures. However, such arguments are challenged by others, as evidence shows that China's consumption rate has been underestimated and that low interest rate policies have benefited the banking sector and the consumers (Yi, 2013). Some argue that it is unreasonable to claim that China's financial system is a failure when the country's economic reform and development is a widely acknowledged success (Xia and Chen, 2011). Basically, the past reforms of the financial system have not impeded China's economic growth (Perkins and Rawski, 2007).

Opinions also differ on the next step of interest rate reform, and disagreements mainly center on how to further loosen up interest rate controls and expand the areas for market-set prices. Opinions can be categorized into three camps: First is the indirect approach, which suggests pushing forward the interest rate reform by improving external conditions, such as developing direct financing to encourage competition in the financial market; developing the money market as the core market of the financial system to form short-term benchmark rates; and developing shadow banking to create market-based interest rates through various financing channels (Wang, 2014).

The second is the direct approach, which recommends that the PBOC gradually remove the upper limit of deposit rates and the lower limit of loan rates. This method believes that forcing interest rate reform by fostering external conditions when bank interest rates are regulated will push up risks in the banking sector. The crisis in the US banking system in the 1980s is an example. The direct approach proposes that the reform should be gradual and be coordinated with comprehensive measures to balance inflation expectation and assisted by credit regulations (Lu, 2011). Former IMF resident representative in China Tarhan Feyzioğlu with others (2009) argue that China should remove the upper limit of deposit rates and suggest that long-term, large deposit rates should be liberalized before short-term, small deposit rates. Jun Ma (2010) argues that deposit rates could be targeted in the short run, gradually removing the upper limit of rates on long-term deposits and then on short-term deposits. For example, the central bank can first allow the two-year or longer-term deposit rates to rise 20 percent above the benchmark and the three-month to one-year rates to increase 10 percent above the benchmark while leaving the rates of current deposit unchanged. Current deposit accounts for 50 percent of total deposit, and a change in its rates is likely to bring unpredictable changes. In the medium to long run, further actions will depend on the feedback of banks and enterprises.

The third method is the integrated approach. Ruoyu Li (2013) suggests that future interest rate reform should include the following: 1. Prudently pushing forward the reform of deposit rates and completely liberalizing deposit rates in five years; 2. Improving the benchmark rate system; 3. Establishing targeted policy rates and the basic framework for interest rate adjustment; and 4. Improving the complementary policies.

Further research is needed to evaluate and push forward China's interest rate reform. An accurate evaluation of past reforms is crucial as it will influence the direction of future reforms.

It should be noted that China's interest rate reform took place against the backdrop of the country's economic reforms and the thriving domestic economy and financial sector. Interest rate reform not only constitutes a key step in constructing the socialist market economy but also reflects the achievement of China's economic reform and development. In the past 30 years, the nation has been exploring a path of reform and development with Chinese characteristics. The interest rate reform also bears these characteristics. Different from the reforms in developed countries that have a relatively mature financial system, China's interest rate reform is being carried out in a constantly evolving economic and financial environment that has just transformed from a planned economy.

Different from the shock therapy adopted by former Soviet Union and Eastern European countries, China is taking the approach of gradual reform. It starts from the easy parts and moves to the hard ones, from separate sectors to the whole system and from the surface to the root. Interest rate reform as an important part of comprehensive reforms should be considered and pushed forward along with reforms in other areas. Moreover, the various aspects of the reform should be gradual and coordinated. Therefore, China's interest rate reform should be viewed as part of the country's overall reforms and dynamic economic development. This research aims to analyze the background and evolution of China's interest rate reform from a historical perspective in order to facilitate a better understanding of the process.

If we take into account other nations' experience and theories on interest rate reform as well as China's economic and financial condition, the country's reform emphasizes steady progress. It aims to first liberalize the interest rates in the money market and bond market and then move to reform the deposit and loan rates. Liberalization of deposit/loan rates will be carried out in a gradual manner – from foreign currency to domestic currency; from loans to deposits; from long-term, large loan/deposit to short-term, small loan/deposit. The PBOC has gradually loosened the control on interest rates to push forward the liberalization process. At the same time, it is also set on improving the market interest rate system and establishing an adjustment mechanism.

With the development of diversified financial institutions and the increase in commercial banks' autonomy, the interbank financial market has developed substantially. From 1996 to 1999, the interbank rates had been mostly liberalized. In the new century, reforms of state-owned commercial banks and state-owned enterprises (SOEs) focusing on improving corporate governance have laid a solid foundation for the liberalization of deposit/loan rates on the micro-level. And China's entry into the WTO and the ensuing economic growth created a good environment for interest rate reform on the macro-level. In October 2004, China achieved the goal of reserving only a lower limit on loan rates and an upper limit on deposit rates. After that, the PBOC focused on developing the pricing ability of financial institutions by strengthening their pricing mechanisms. With the development of the interbank bond market since 2005, the PBOC set up the Shanghai Interbank Offered Rate (Shibor) in 2007 to build a better environment for interest rate reform.

In recent years, with the rapid development of financial innovation and financial disintermediation as well as the transformation of the economic structure, China's economy and financial markets have undergone fundamental changes. Determination of interest rates by market forces has become not only a goal of policymakers but also a demand and a reality. In response to market trends, the lower limit of loan rates was loosened up and eventually removed, and the upper limit of deposit rates has been eased as well.

To meet the demand of China's economic and financial transformation, the 3rd Plenum of the 18th CPCCC reached a decision to comprehensively deepen reforms. The principle for interest rate reform has changed from steady progress to speeding up the market-oriented reform. On October 24, 2015, the PBOC removed the upper limit of deposit rates imposed on commercial banks and rural cooperative financial institutions, which signaled the removal of control on interest rates. However, interest rate reform is a complicated and systemic project and does not end with the liberalization of deposit rates. In addition, apart from liberalizing interest rates, the reform also aims to develop the benchmark rate system, establish market-based interest rate adjustment and transmission mechanisms, improve the deposit insurance system, and develop tools to manage interest rate risks. As a result, in the 12th Five-Year Plan for the Development and Reform of the Finance Industry, interest rate reform was given priority, and the principle for the reform was set as "loosening rate controls, establishing market-based interest rates and building an effective adjustment mechanism", which also set the tone for current and future reform measures.

Based on this principle, this study offers a systemic review of the achievements and weakness of China's interest rate reform, analyzes the challenges, and proposes some policy advice. The key to accelerating interest rate reform is to apply concentrated efforts in tackling the obstacles and limitations in the liberalization process. Whether China can successfully achieve its goals is highly dependent on the condition of the market and the economic and financial environment. As stated above, interest rate reform has been carried out against the backdrop of the progressive reforms and development of China's economy and the financial sector. When evaluating past reforms and planning for the future, we need to take into consideration this background. Based on this, this research conducts a systemic review of the characteristics and progress of the interest rate reform, discusses the problems and challenges faced by the process, and offers a set of comprehensive policy suggestions.

The book is divided into six chapters. In response to loosening the control, Chapter 1 looks back at the history of deregulating interest rates and analyzes the rationale, path, and characteristics of China's interest rate reform by referring to international practices. In terms of establishing the market-based interest rate system, Chapter 2 focuses on how China strengthens the market-based interest rate formation mechanism by elaborating on the characteristics and performance of the dual-track system and analyzing the transmission of interest rates. In terms of developing the adjustment mechanism, Chapter 3 reviews the adjustment of interest rates and analyzes the necessity, environment, and conditions of strengthening the central bank's adjustment mechanism and summarizes the experience with interest rate adjustment of major countries. Based on this, the chapter further proposes policy suggestions on how to improve the PBOC's adjustment mechanism. Chapter 4 goes on to analyze the impact that different economic and financial development stages have on the interest rate reform. Chapter 5 analyzes the relationships between the interest rate reform and a number of crucial issues, including budget constraint on microeconomic entities, degree of competition in the banking sector, the bankruptcy system, financial regulation, exchange rate formation mechanisms, and capital account liberalization. Chapter 6 reviews past reforms and looks ahead at the future process.

It should be noted that this study was completed in October 2015, when the cap on deposit rates had not been lifted. The liberalization of deposit rates marks a milestone in China's interest rate reform. This book can be seen as a summary and an analysis of the reforms prior to this. Lifting the cap on deposit rates is not the end but rather a beginning. The interest rate reform needs to be further pushed forward. We hope that this study can provide some insight for the research and implementation of future reforms.

1　Interest rate deregulation

China's path

Relaxing interest rate controls is a key part and an important goal of interest rate liberalization in both the Chinese and global context. Different countries have different approaches to interest rate liberalization; some liberalize the interest rate quickly, while others do it gradually after taking certain steps. China has adopted a measured approach. After removing controls on its money market rates, bond market rates, and foreign currency deposit and loan rates, it relaxed control of lending rates in July 2013 and lifted the cap on deposit rates in October 2015. Therefore, China has basically removed regulation on interest rates, marking an important milestone in the process of market-based interest rate reform. This chapter provides a comprehensive and systematic review of China's practice in relaxing interest rate controls to provide an understanding of the principles, approach, sequence, and pace of the reform measures.

I Path selection of interest rate deregulation: theoretical basis and international experiences

A Theoretical analysis: regulation and liberalization of interest rates

Judging from a historical perspective, most countries have undergone "free–controlled–free" stages in their interest rate systems. This process is a reflection of the development of economic theory. Before the 1930s, the "laissez-faire" theory played a dominant role and most nations did not regulate interest rates. For instance, the US embraced a free banking system before the establishment of the Federal Reserve System in 1913. And from then until the Great Depression, the US government and the Federal Reserve did not intervene strongly in the financial market, and interest rates were decided by supply and demand. The Great Depression from 1929 to 1933 weakened the dominance of the free market theory and Keynesianism became the mainstream. Many countries began to emphasize the importance of the government's role in economic activities, and interest rate regulation became a crucial part of government intervention. The US passed Regulation Q in 1933, which prohibited banks from paying interest on demand deposits and imposed maximum interest rates on savings and fixed deposit. Germany started to regulate interest rates in 1932 and continued to do so long after the Second World War; France imposed regulations on deposit and lending rates during the war and strengthened credit regulation afterward to boost economic growth, with the State Credit Commission setting the maximum interest rates of bank deposit and loans and keeping the rates at a low level; Japan in 1947 imposed regulation on deposit rates, short-term lending rates, long-term loan preferential interest rates, and bond issuance interest rates. However, many western countries experienced stagflation in the 1970s, and Keynesianism began to be challenged. Liberal thinking represented by neoclassical economics became popular, and some major nations started to relax control on the economy with liberalizing interest rates as the main focus.

From the perspective of financial theory, the term financial deepening, coined by Ronald McKinnon and Edward Shaw, laid the foundation for interest rate liberalization. McKinnon and Shaw felt that interest rate and credit regulation were restraining financial development in developing countries. The low interest rate was leading to low savings, and the government was forced to conduct credit allocation due to strong investment demand. This reduced accumulation of capital led to misallocation of financial resources and affected the channeling of savings to investment, hindered economic growth, and eventually resulted in a vicious cycle of financial repression and economic distress. In developing countries, money and physical capital are to a large extent complementary rather than substitutional as suggested by traditional theory, and the real interest rate is to a degree in positive correlation with savings and investment. Therefore, developing countries should reduce intervention in the financial system and remove regulation of the interest rate to let it reflect the real supply and demand of capital in the market, increase the interest rate to an equilibrium level, and allow the financial system to be the intermediator, thus achieving a virtuous cycle between the financial system and economic development. The theory of financial deepening caught widespread attention in academic and policy circles; empirical research on developing countries had confirmed its conclusions. The policy recommendation was adopted by most developing nations.

However, financial liberalization with interest rate reform as the prime focus has caused some countries severe economic and financial problems. The theory of financial restraint brought forward by Thomas Hellmann, Kevin Murdock, and Joseph Stiglitz (1997) argues about issues such as moral hazard and adverse selection in the context of information asymmetry. According to them, laissez-faire financial policies often lead to market failure or economic crisis if there's not enough prudential regulation. Therefore, for developing countries with weak market infrastructure, financial repression, a monopolistic financial institutional arrangement set by the government, works better than financial liberalization and a competitive institutional arrangement in terms of financial deepening and economic growth. By implementing financial repression policies, the government can, on the one hand, maintain a positive but lower than equilibrium deposit rate and reduce the financing cost for banks; on the other hand, the government can put a cap on the lending rate to minimize default risks for borrowers and financing costs for companies and help boost economic growth.

Though Hellmann, Murdock, and Stiglitz (1997) believe that financial restraint is good for developing countries, they do not reject the possibility of liberalization.

They further point out that financial restraint is not a static financial instrument. Rather, it should be adjusted as the economy matures. So, the policy options provided by this theory are not a static comparison between laissez-faire and financial restraint, but a dynamic process following financial market development. The arguments set forth in this paper are not designed to claim that there exists a single optimal level of financial restraint that should be implemented by all governments identically, regardless of the state of financial development. Rather, financial restraint should be a dynamic policy regime, adjusting as the economy develops, and moving in the general direction of freer and more competitive financial markets. The policy trade-off is not a static one between laissez-faire and government intervention; the relevant question is over the proper order of financial market development.

The comparison of the two theories shows that financial deepening theory points out the necessity of financial liberalization but fails to take into account the conditions of developing countries and the risks involved in the process, whereas financial restraint provides a thorough analysis of the conditions and approaches for liberalization and is more in line with the reality of developing nations. In fact, Ronald McKinnon (1991) also proposed the sequence of financial liberalization for developing countries in his book *The Order of Economic Liberalization: Financial Control in the Transition to a Market Economy*.

For reasons such as financial information asymmetry and the particularity of financial conduct, it's debatable if complete financial liberalization is even good for developed countries. Some economists have reflected on the direction of interest rate reform after the recent financial crisis; Professor Amar Bhide, among others, pointed out that it's necessary to put a cap on demand deposit interest rates to reduce excess competition among financial institutions and ensure financial stability. And Stiglitz argued that a well-functioning market economy is in itself neither stable nor effective. He further said that the only time in modern capitalism that did not see reoccurring financial crises was the short period when strong financial regulation was exercised after the Great Depression, and it was also a period when the fruit of economic growth was widely shared. Of course, there are those who argue against Stiglitz.

In short, the various theories on interest rate liberalization reflect different views on the role of market and government in financial resource allocation. The relation between the government and the market is an abiding theme in economic and financial research. With the development of the economy and financial sector, people's understanding is also evolving and deepening, and the views of experts vary. But one thing is certain: The allocation of resources should not be completely handed over to the market, nor be completely dependent on the government, and the boundary between the market and the government often relies on a lot of factors. Relaxing interest rate controls is inevitable, but there's no absolute truth as to how to do it and how much liberalization should be allowed.

B   *International experience: radical or incremental*

Countries all over the world usually choose one of two paths for interest rate liberalization: Complete liberalization carried out over a short period or incremental reform.

4 *Interest rate deregulation*

a Deregulate interest rates entirely over a short time

Of all the developing countries, Latin American nations are the best examples of this model of liberalization. Argentina in 1975 totally deregulated all interest rates except for the upper limit for the deposit rate and lifted the cap on the deposit rate in June 1977. Chile started to liberalize interest rates in May 1974 and lifted restrictions on deposit rates by November the same year, and all regulations by April the next year. However, since these nations had less developed financial systems, poor corporate governance, and insufficient supervision, this led to moral hazard in the banking sector. The nominal interest rate and inflation rose, real interest rate began experiencing volatility, and bad loans increased. The governments were forced to intervene. Argentina set the upper limit back for the deposit rate and Chile halted liberalization by releasing guiding rates.

The former Soviet Union and Eastern European countries adopted the same model under the shock therapy prescribed by the west. Russia initiated reform on interest rates in 1993 and finished it in 1995. The process improved the interest rate transmission mechanism, but it was so radical that the other aspects of the system couldn't keep up. The stability of the financial system was adversely affected.

Developed countries such as the UK, Germany, and other European nations also deregulated their interest rates over a short time. The Federal Republic of Germany removed restrictions on interest rates of fixed deposits longer than two and a half years in March 1965, and restrictions on interest rates of large deposits of more than one million Deutsche Marks and longer than three and a half months in July 1966. The government rolled out a liberalization plan in February 1967 and completely let go of control of interest rates in April the same year. But the government kept its guidance on the deposit and lending rates of financial institutions until October 1973.

The Bank of England abolished the regulation on interbank deposit and lending rates in one go in September 1971, allowing financial institutions to decide their own interest rates. But due to the pressure of high inflation, economic recession, and a weak currency, the central bank forbade banks to pay an interest rate above 9.5 percent on deposits of less than 10,000 pounds in September 1973, which lasted until February 1975. To control short-term interest rates, it announced the lowest loans rate every week. The UK did not achieve full liberalization of interest rates until August 1981.

b Incremental liberalization

Among developed economies, the US, Japan, France, and Australia adopted the model of incremental liberalization. The US liberalized interest rates on long-term, large-amount loans and deposits, and then moved to liberalize rates for short-term, small-amount loans and deposits. Since 1970, the US has gradually relaxed regulations on large-denomination negotiable certificates of deposit and fixed deposits. The Depository Institutions Liberalization and Monetary Control Act in 1980 marked the official beginning of interest rate liberalization, and by 1986 the US had basically achieved full liberalization.

Japan's reform followed the sequence of "Treasury bonds first and other categories later, interbank business first and bank customers later, long-term large deposits first and short-term small deposits later". Japan liberalized the issuing rate and trading rate of government bonds from 1975 to 1978. The central bank allowed some flexibility to the interbank offered rate in April 1978 and liberalized the interbank note rate that June. Meanwhile, it lowered the threshold for fixed deposit interest control and increased the variety and term structure of liberalized fixed deposits. By April 1991, Japan had basically liberalized fixed deposit rates and by October 1994 demand deposit rates. The liberalization of lending rates went hand in hand with deposit rates.

France lifted the cap on the rates of fixed deposit longer than six years in April 1965 and deregulated rates on deposits over 250,000 francs and with a two-year term in July 1976. The French central bank revised its regulation on deposit rates three times, in 1969, 1976, and 1979, and by then all deposit rates had been deregulated except for fixed deposits of less than six months and of less than one year but not over 500,000 francs. According to the 1984 Banking Act, demand deposits were not interest-bearing, and banks were allowed to issue certificates of deposit with independent pricing.

Australia was more cautious about the liberalization of interest rates, but the reformers took an upper hand after a heated debate. It launched the process in the 1970s and removed regulation on large deposits in 1973. But the authority didn't cede control completely. The Campbell Committee was established in 1979 to study the efficiency of financial regulation and offer policy advice. Ever since 1981, the liberalization of interest rates has been implemented in a measured way against the background of all-rounded financial reforms. From 1981 to 1985, Australia removed the limits on deposit and lending rates, deposit terms, and borrowing amounts one after another, and implemented a public bidding system for short-term treasury issuances in 1979 first and later for long-term treasury issuances in 1982.

Most developing countries adopted the model of incremental liberalization based on their specific conditions. South Korea started to liberalize interest rates in 1981 by first deregulating deposit and lending rates and then interbank rates. Liberalization was basically in place by 1988, but the country's economy was facing downside pressure at that time with rising inflation and interest rates, and the central bank had to provide window guidance on interest rates in 1989. When South Korea restarted the reform in 1991, it followed the order of lending rates first and deposit rates later, long-term large deposits first and short-term small deposits later. And by 1997, it had liberalized most interest rates except for demand deposit rates.

Thailand also followed the sequence of deposit rates first and lending rates later from 1989 to 1992. However, the strong bargaining power of major borrowers pushed the lending rates to fall quickly. To avoid a large gap between the lending rates for major borrowers and other bank customers, the Thai authority required its commercial banks to announce minimum retail rates in October 1993, and therefore strengthened regulation on lending rates.

As early as 1985, India allowed banks to set interest rates freely with an 8 percent ceiling for deposits of 15 days to one year, but this rule only lasted for a month. The country restarted liberalization in 1992 and removed restriction for loans above 200,000 rupees in 1994. It was not until July 2010 that India fully liberalized lending rates by removing regulation on small loans less than 200,000 rupees and export credit loans in rupees. In terms of deposit rates, India allowed the rates of deposit above 46 days to fluctuate below a 13 percent ceiling in 1992, and removed restriction for deposit of more than two years in 1995, deposit of one to two years in 1996, and deposit below one year in 1997. The deposit rate was not fully liberalized until October 25, 2011.

Taiwan's central bank maintained regulations on commercial banks' deposit and lending rates before 1975 and started to allow a wide floating band for lending rates from then on. The authority issued the Essentials of Interest Rate Adjustment to officially start interest rate liberalization. The interest rates of money market instruments would be freely set by market forces; the banks could independently set deposit rates as long as they were below the upper limit set by the monetary authority; the upper and lower limits of lending rates would be reviewed by the Interest Rate Review Committee established by major banks and approved by the central bank. From 1984 to 1986, the authority further increased the degree of pricing by the market by expanding the floating band of interest rates and streamlining the categories of deposits, and achieved liberalization of interest rates in 1989.

C   The key to path selection of interest rate liberalization: market-driven or government-dominated

Although decisions regarding interest rate liberalization are made by the government, the decision-making process varies: It could be based on practical conditions or out of some economic ideology. There's great distinction among different countries.

a   The interest rate liberalization process in developed countries is mostly driven by the market

Though the process of interest rate liberalization in developed countries is to some degree influenced by neoliberalism, it's mainly a product of economic and financial evolution, a choice made by the market with or without the intervention of the government.

In the case of the US, with inflation rising in the late 1960s, the rigid Regulation Q often led to negative real interest rates. Regulation Q and the limitation of separation of business lines had put banks at a disadvantage, with development of the securities market, internationalization of financing, and investment diversification causing capital flow to non-banking institutions. The development of the euro-dollar market also led to the large-scale outflow of dollar deposits. Deposit-taking financial institutions created a large number of financial products to prevent outflows, such as negotiable order of withdrawal (NOW) accounts, automatic transfer service (ATS), TTS, and Credit Union Share Draft Account (CUSDA). These new types of products combined deposits and investment, thus breaking the upper limit of interest rates set by Regulation Q. Financial institutions were trying all possible ways to bypass the regulation and were calling for liberalization, making interest rate liberalization inevitable.

Japan was pushed by domestic and foreign conditions to start interest rate liberalization. In the 1970s, to deal with stagnation and the need to finance fiscal deficits, Japan was forced to remove controls of the rates of Treasury bonds to increase their volume and liquidity. But because of very low real interest rates, other financing channels took away funds from banks. Given this disintermediation process, banks involuntarily decided to support interest rate liberalization. On the other hand, the US and some European countries were actively deregulating their interest rates, leading to higher rates than in Japan, which led to capital outflows and large purchase of dollar bonds. With limited foreign investment, Japan's capital account saw huge deficits, and the Japanese yen weakened. An overvalued dollar and undervalued yen created a large trade surplus with the US. Pressured by the domestic situation and urged by other countries, Japan finally set out to liberalize its financial sector and open up the market.

Though the UK and Germany liberalized interest rates over a short time, these two countries were also pushed by market forces to reform. For Germany, there were domestic and international factors. The country resumed free convertibility of the Deutsche Mark in 1958 and achieved the liberalization of capital account the next year. The free flow of capital enhanced the influence of other countries' interest rates on the domestic market. The private sector shifted its deposits to the European money market for higher yields, causing large-scale capital outflows. Domestic banks then tried to avoid capital outflows caused by the regulation. With the advantage of their universal banking business model, they were able to offer depositors other preferential terms, creating de facto high real interest rates. For instance, banks which also engaged in securities business would sell securities to clients at a low price and then buy them back at a higher price, thus offering higher yields to the clients. Under domestic and external pressure, interest rate liberalization became a foregone conclusion for Germany.

The UK, one of the oldest capitalist countries, boasts a very developed financial market. Even at times of regulation, its interest rates were considered highly liberalized with rate arrangements among banks as the means for regulation. In the 1960s and 1970s, real interest rates were negative due to rising inflation, making it difficult for monetary policies to reach their goals with the interest rate tool; therefore, the authority switched to money supply as the intermediate target. But at the same time, control of the interest rate also weakened the competitive edge of banks, leading to the outflow of bank deposits. At the end of the 1960s, the UK loosened the requirements for entering the City of London; foreign banks quickly went in and intensified competition. With increasing international capital flows and an expanding euro dollar market, capital outflows were largely increased and the pound plunged in November 1967. Under such circumstances, the Bank of England brought forward a financial reform plan, and one key component was to let the banks set their own interest rates.

In general, interest rate liberalization in developed countries was the natural result of financial innovation, development of the securities market, and financial opening-up. The reform was mostly driven by financial innovation of banks for the purpose of bypassing interest rate regulation. When reaching a certain stage, the innovation was legalized by the government, which further pushed forward the process of interest rate liberalization.

b   Radical interest rate liberalization in developing countries mainly led by the government

Before interest rate liberalization, developing countries usually experienced financial repression, such as low deposit and lending rates, credit rationing, and repressed development of direct financing. When most developing countries set out to liberalize their interest rates, their financial markets were far less mature than those in the developed economies and monetization was at a very preliminary stage. Though many developing countries, to a degree, were forced to liberalize interest rates due to worsening economic and financial situations, the ideology of financial liberalization and the moves taken by developed nations were the more important driving forces.

In the 1970s, countries ruled by military governments such as Chile, Argentina, and Uruguay adopted liberal policies to tackle economic crisis. Chile's military government supported a market economy, free enterprises, and private ownership. Argentina's economic reform aimed to decrease and eventually remove state control on prices, the exchange rate, interest rates, rents, and wages. The goal of financial reforms was particularly eye-catching in its grand plan to stabilize and liberalize the economy, including removing restrictions on interest rates and capital flows, removing credit guidance, privatizing state-owned banks, and reducing registry barriers for domestic and foreign banks.

Though economic liberalization in Latin American countries was not ideal, neoliberalism, the so-called Washington Consensus, which advocates privatization and liberalization to prevent government failure and raise economic efficiency, was the dominant ideology for a considerable time in developing nations. It's under the influence of the Washington Consensus and some specific guidelines proposed by western experts that the former Soviet Union and Eastern European countries adopted a radical model of reform, the so-called shock therapy, hoping to see the core system of developed countries take effect overnight.

Take Russia as an example. Around the time of dissolution of the Soviet Union, the drawbacks of the planned economy began to unravel and the situation took a turn for the worse with stagnant economic growth and inflation going out of control. At the beginning of 1992, the Yeltsin government initiated shock therapy: Deregulating prices in one go, privatizing state-owned enterprises, and letting go of commercial bank rates all at once. It shows that radical interest rate liberalization was mainly led by the government.

D   *The core of path selection: a trade-off between benefit and risk*

Theoretically, the liberalization of interest rates has both pros and cons. The reward of interest rate liberalization includes the effective mobilization of savings, relieving financing restraints on enterprises and households, increased capital allocation efficiency and more reasonable income distribution. The cons include greater volatility of interest rates, bigger risks for financial institutions, higher financing cost for enterprises, and threats to financial stability. How each country selects its path of interest rate liberalization depends on its assessment of the pros and cons. For example, some countries emphasize how interest rate liberalization can improve efficiency while others worry about the potential risks. This influenced the path selection of different countries.

The experiences of many countries show that interest rate liberalization, particularly the reform of deposit and lending rates, is a double-edged sword. It could help enhance efficiency of financial resource allocation, but also cause great financial risks, and many countries have experienced substantial bank losses and bankruptcies during and after the reform. A World Bank survey found that of the 44 countries that went through interest rate liberalization, almost half underwent a financial crisis during the process.

In the US, 14 banks went bankrupt in 1975, and the number rose to 42 in 1982 and 184 in 1987. From 1987 to 1991, on average 200 banks went under. In Argentina, about 15 percent of financial institutions went through bankruptcy and liquidation during interest rate reform from 1980 to 1983. Chile's banking system was hit hard, with eight financial institutions suffering bankruptcy and liquidation in 1981, accounting for 35 percent of the total assets of the financial system. From 1987 to 1988, among the 12 private commercial banks in Bolivia, two were liquidated and seven suffered huge losses; in 1988, the value of accounts receivable took up 92 percent of the banks' net value. Columbia's banking system collapsed in 1985 with losses exceeding 140 percent of banks' capital and reserves. The central bank of Columbia intervened in six banks whose assets accounted for 24 percent of total financial assets from 1982 to 1987; five of the six banks had losses over 202 percent of their capital and reserves in 1985.

Table 1-1 Interest rate liberalization and bank crises

Country	Interest rate liberalization	Bank crisis
US	1970–1986	1980–1992
Japan	1977–1994	1992–1994
Germany	1962–1976	1974–1976
Argentina	1975–1977	1980–1982
Chile	1974–1975	1981–1987
Mexico	1988–1989	1994–1997
South Korea	1981–1997	1985–1988
Thailand	1985–1992	1983–1987, 1997–2002

Source: Endowment and Path: International experiences for interest rate liberalization, Hongyuan Securities, September 2013

Table 1-2 The impact of interest rate liberalization on macro-economy and finance in major countries and regions

Country and time period for interest rate liberalization	GDP	CPI	Market rate	Interest rate spread of deposit and lending	Impact on financial institutions	Credit supply	Asset price	Exchange rate
US 1970–1986	Fluctuation in GDP	Rising inflation from 1973 to 1975 and from 1979 to 1983	Deposit and lending rates rose at the early stage of liberalization; peaked at 15.91% and 18.87% in 1981; fell and stabilized thereafter (affected by oil crisis)	The average spread of deposit and lending rates from 1986 to 1990 was 54 basis points lower than that from 1980 to 1985	Savings and loan crisis in the 1980s, large amount of long-term loans could not cover cost of deposits	The average growth rate of credit and money supply from 1980 to 1986 rose 1.05 and 1.89 percentage points, respectively, from that between 1980 and 1990	NYSE composite rose from over 800 in 1980 to over 1900 in 1990	
Japan 1977–1994	Recovery in 1975 from the economic recession after the oil crisis	High inflation from 1973 to 1977 and steady decline thereafter	Relatively stable with slight fluctuations	The average spread of deposit and lending rates in 1994 dropped 82 basis points from that in 1984	Many banks went under from 1992 to 1994	The average growth rate of M2 from 1984 to 1990 was 3.4 percentage points higher than that from 1984 to 1994	Nikkei 225 Index hit the record high in 1989; housing market boomed	The yen appreciated 87.3% against the dollar from 1984 to 1990

South Korea 1981–1997	Poor profit for enterprises, economic slowdown, and rising social conflict from the end of the 1980s to the 1990s	Slight fluctuation and relatively stable price	Deposit and lending rates rose after reform; rates on corporate bonds increased from 4.4% to 16.3% from 1988 to June 1989; non-bank interest rates rose from 11.6% to 17.5%	The average spread of deposit and lending rates dropped from around 4% in early 1980s to less than 3% in late 1980s		The average growth rate of M2 from 1990 to 1996 was 2.7% higher than that from 1990 to 2000	KOSPI rose from 700 in 1990 to over 1000 in 1994, followed by gradual drop	The won appreciated 21.7% against the dollar during the first interest rate reform and depreciated during the second round of reform
Latin American countries 1970–1980	5.9% growth rate for the whole region from 1960 to 1973, and 4.5% from 1973 to 1981		Market rate rose first then fell to 3.7% in 1990	Interest rate spread increased slightly at the early stage of reform and lowered later on	Bank crisis hit the region; about 15% of Argentinean financial institutions went through bankruptcy and liquidation		Price level grew at double-digit rate in the 1970s and 1980s	Monetary crisis at the end of 1970s and the beginning of 1980: Currency depreciation, capital outflow, and even economic crisis

In addition, some countries also saw interest rate fluctuation, exchange rate appreciation, and expansion of credit and money supply and asset bubbles, putting downside pressure on the economy or making it more volatile. Therefore, it's important to consider how to avoid the negative impact of interest rate liberalization on the macro-economy.

In conclusion, though interest rate liberalization can improve the efficiency of resource allocation, it also carries great risks. At the early stage of interest rate reform, the overshooting and wild swings of interest rates will overburden enterprises and threaten the economy; on the other hand, interest rate liberalization can reduce financing restraints on enterprises and households, but the private sector is prone to depend more on debt and banks are more likely to indulge in risky behaviors. For commercial banks that were once under protection but are now completely exposed to market risks, the lack of a coping mechanism could possibly lead to crisis. Therefore, it's important to weigh the benefits and risks when implementing interest rate reform. Domestic situations, such as the depth of economic and financial development and the level of financial regulation, should also be taken into account. With a comprehensive study of the effects of interest rate liberalization, we can choose the right approach that minimizes the risks.

II   China's road to interest rate liberalization

China's market-based interest rate reform is commonly believed to have started in 1996, when the interbank offered rates were liberalized. However, the process can be further traced back to the initial stage of the reform and opening-up in 1978, when the development of the commodity economy and the use of more technical measures in managing the economy put the market in an increasingly important position for resource allocation. The liberalization of interest rate controls in China in general has gone through the following stages.

A   The initial step

Since 1978, China has been raising the deposit and loan rates after they remained low for a considerable period of time. More types of deposit accounts and rates were created and more variety was added to interest-bearing deposits, which reignited interests for corporate deposits and membership fees for trade union and the Party. The standards for interest rates were unified and the management of interest rates was enhanced. In 1981, the People's Bank of China (PBOC) released the *Report on Adjusting the Deposit and Loan Interest Rates of Banks* approved by the State Council. The report stated that the interest rates should strictly come under the control of the PBOC, and non-financial institutions shall not set the interest rates independently; specialized banks and other financial institutions must adopt the unified interest rates approved by the State Council and may not set the interest rates themselves unless authorized by the State Council or the PBOC; the PBOC can set different interest rates within the range approved by the State Council.

The report laid the foundation for interest rate management and the introduction of market forces in interest rate determination.

a Loan rates

In the document *Provisions for Implementing the Report on Adjusting the Loan and Deposit Interest Rates of Banks* released by the PBOC in February 1982, it was stated that the interest rates for trust companies' business, such as absorbing trust funds and offering loans and investments, can fluctuate around rates set by the banks but within the range of 20 percent. Entrusted loan rates can be negotiated between the trustee bank and the entrusting entity but within the range set by the authority.

In 1983, the State Council approved and released a report on transferring the liquidity management of state-owned enterprises (SOEs) to the PBOC. The report allowed the loan rates of the PBOC to float by up to 20 percent above or below the benchmark loan rates, which marked the beginning of loosening regulation on loan rates. In January 1987, the PBOC announced that it would delegate the power of determining lending rates to specialized banks. It stated in the announcement that, in order to facilitate the reform of the economic system and to utilize the interest rates to leverage the economy, specialized banks could have the right to adjust loan rates within a 20 percent range. Specialized banks could raise rates on liquidity loans according to national economic policies by up to 20 percent above the benchmark rates. The specialized banks could also adjust preferential interest rates except for those for loans to the food system and welfare factories set up by the Ministry of Civil Affairs.

In 1988, the PBOC further empowered financial institutions to adjust the loan rates. The upper fluctuation limit for loan rates was increased from 20 percent to 30 percent, and its application was expanded from liquidity loans to almost all types of loans, including fixed assets loans.

However, chaos and confusion were inevitable in the early stage of the reform, causing the authorities to swing between tightening and loosening regulation on interest rates. In 1990, the PBOC revoked the power of its branches to decide on the degree of floating allowed to lending rates of specialized banks and other financial institutions. It also required that the commercial banks, urban credit cooperatives, and other non-banking financial institutions strictly abide by the deposit and loan rates set by the PBOC.

b Deposit rates

In order to boost rural finance and enhance the efficiency of financing as stated in the *No.1 Document of the Central Committee of the Communist Party of China (CCCPC)* in 1985, the PBOC published the *Announcement on Strengthening the Regulation on Savings Deposit Rates*, which stated that the credit cooperatives in rural areas (not including the credit cooperatives in cities, towns, counties, and major industrial and mining areas) can adopt floating interest rates after being approved by the provincial branches of the PBOC. In the PBOC's *Announcement of Regulation on Savings Deposit Rates* released in April 1987, the deposit rates of rural credit cooperatives in rural areas can float between the lower limit of benchmark rates and upper limit of market interest rates. Those within a floating range of 20 percent must be approved by the local branches of the Agricultural Bank of China; those above 20 percent must be approved by the provincial branches of the PBOC.

c   Interbank offered rates

In 1981, the document *Responsibility for Credit Balance* first proposed the development of interbank offered rates. But the interbank lending market did not take off until 1984, when China established a financial system comprising the PBOC, the specialized banks, and other financial institutions. The interbank lending was first limited to specialized banks and then gradually expanded to other financial institutions. In 1986, the PBOC clarified the term, scope, and operation of interbank lending and stated that the interbank offered rates and terms should be negotiated by the lender and the borrower.

In its early stage, the interbank lending market was marked by misconduct. In response, the *Interim Regulation on Interbank Lending* was introduced in 1990, which specified rules on the management of the interbank market and the terms of interbank lending: PBOC shall determine and adjust the maturity and interest rate cap for interbank borrowing according to capital supply and demand; the interbank offered rates should not exceed the PBOC's overnight rates set on specialized banks by 30 percent; the lenders and the borrowers can negotiate the specific terms and rates within a prescribed limit. The term for interbank lending usually is one month; and for loans from financial institutions to specialized banks, the term usually does not exceed four months; no kick-back was allowed in the transactions except for the interest and service fee.

In 1993, faced with an overheated economy, the government rolled out policies to improve the interbank lending market and to enhance regulation on the terms and rates in the interbank lending market. It was stipulated that overnight lending should be the major form of interbank lending, and the term should be no more than one month unless in special cases where the term can be extended to up to seven days. It was also stated that interest spreads and service fees should not be charged at the same time. The interest spreads cannot exceed 0.3 percent of the interbank bid rates, and the service fees should not exceed the interest spreads for the same period.

B   The takeoff stage

The progress of gradual reform has deepened the Chinese authority's understanding of reform. In 1993, the 3rd Plenum of the 14th CPC Central Committee announced the *Decisions on Issues Concerning the Establishment of a Socialist Market Economy*, which brought forward the basic concept of market-based interest rate reform. With the progress of various reforms, the market-based interest rate reform was also advancing gradually.

a   The liberalization of interbank offered rates accomplished

In June 1993, the PBOC released the *Announcement on Further Regulating the Interbank Lending Market*, which called for the establishment of a unified interbank lending market. After several years of experimenting, the national interbank lending market was set up in 1996, and the control on the upper limit of interbank rates was removed.

In 1996, the Ministry of Finance achieved the market-oriented issuance of treasury bonds through securities exchange. In 1997, the interbank repo rates and spot trading rates were deregulated. And in 1998 and 1999, the issuance rates for policy bank financial bonds and treasury bonds in the interbank market were liberalized, respectively.

b   The rapid development of interest rate liberalization for
*   foreign currencies*

In September 2000, the deposit rates for large foreign currency deposits (no less than US\$3 million) and the loan rates for foreign currency were liberalized. In July 2003, the deposit rates of small foreign currency deposits within China were liberalized for British Pound, Swiss Franc, and Canadian Dollar. In November 2003, the lower limit of the deposit rates for small foreign currency deposits was lifted.

c   The experiment with RMB loan and deposit rate liberalization

In 1994, commercial banks and other financial institutions were again given some autonomy in setting interest rates, but only rates for liquidity loans were allowed to float with a band of 10 percent below and 20 percent above the benchmark rates. The commercial banks were required to manage interest rate fluctuations according to the industry policies, the credit ratings of enterprises, and the principle of limiting the low-quality loans. The commercial banks were required to submit proposals for managing the interest rates to the PBOC for approval. In May 1996, in order to reduce interest payment for enterprises, the upper limit of loan rates was reduced from 20 percent to 10 percent.

On October 31, 1998, to address the difficulties for small and medium-sized enterprises (SMEs) to access loans and encourage banks to provide SMEs loans, the rates for loans from financial institutions to SMEs were allowed to fluctuate 20 percent maximum above the benchmark as opposed to 10 percent before, and the rates for loans from rural credit cooperatives were permitted to fluctuate 50 percent maximum above the benchmark as opposed to 40 percent before. The cap on loan rates for large and medium enterprises remained at 10 percent above the benchmark. In 1999, the rates for loans from financial institutions in counties and villages to SMEs were permitted to float above the benchmark rate by up to 30 percent, while the floating cap of loan rates for big enterprises remained the same. In August 2003, the loan rates for rural credit cooperatives in pilot regions were allowed to float up to 100 percent above the benchmark.

C   The consolidation stage

a   Steady progress of deposit and loan rate liberalization

In 2002, the report of the 16th National Congress of the CPC pointed out that the market-based interest rate reform must be pushed forward to improve the efficiency of financial resource allocation. In 2003, the 3rd Plenum of the 16th CCCPC issued the document *Decisions on Improving the Socialist Market Economic System*, which set the framework and goals of interest rate liberalization, marking a breakthrough in the market-based interest rate reform.

In January 2004, the cap of loan rates for commercial banks and urban credit cooperatives was raised to 1.7 times the benchmark rate, while that for rural credit cooperatives increased to 2 times the benchmark rate. On October 29, 2004, the PBOC decided to remove the cap on loan rates for financial institutions (except for credit cooperatives). The cap on loan rates for credit cooperatives remained 2.3 times the benchmark rate, while the floor of loan rates for all financial institutions stayed at 0.9 times the benchmark rate. However, the deposit rates were permitted to fluctuate below the benchmark but not above. By then, the cap on loan rates and the lower limit for deposit rates were basically lifted.

b   Interest rates for foreign currency loans and deposits were basically liberalized

In November 2004, while adjusting the rates for small domestic deposits in foreign currencies, the PBOC decided to liberalize the rates for such deposits with terms longer than one year.

c   Enhancing the price-setting mechanism of financial institutions

The goal of interest rate liberalization is to have the market replace the monetary authorities and play the decisive role in determining interest rates, with the banks setting deposit and loan rates. Before the reform, China's interest rates had been under government control. The loan and deposit rates were determined by the PBOC instead of commercial banks, and the interest spreads between deposits and loans were fixed. The commercial banks were unable and did not need to set the price. As a result, they lacked the ability for price-setting. After the interest rates were liberalized, the price-setting ability of commercial banks became the key to the progression and success of the interest rate reform.

Throughout the process of interest rate liberalization, China has always emphasized the improvement of the price-setting ability of financial institutions. In 1998, the PBOC researched the banks' practice of managing floating interest rates and selected a few national and regional banks as role models for other banks. The PBOC asked banks to develop price-setting models and software and to establish the price-setting authorization system. When the banks were granted more autonomy in managing floating loan rates in 2003, the PBOC once again urged the commercial banks and credit cooperatives to build up the pricing system on loan rates, and provided the rural credit cooperatives with four templates for setting the floating range of loan rates. Under the guidance of the PBOC, the four major commercial banks (Industrial and Commercial Bank of China, Agricultural Bank of China, Bank of China, and China Construction Bank) and other large commercial banks established a standardized interest rate management system and pricing policies. The joint-equity commercial banks set up a pricing management mechanism comprised of the asset and liability management committee and the financial planning department. They also established unified pricing policies and a graded pricing authorization system.

d   Improving the benchmark rate system

Benchmark rates play a fundamental role in the interest rate system and act as a reference for the pricing of other financial products. As the pricing basis for fixed-income instruments and other financial products, and as a reference for monetary policies, benchmark rates are essential to many areas of reforms, such as interest rate liberalization, the monetary policy transmission mechanism, the pricing mechanism, innovation in the financial market, internal funds transfer pricing for financial institutions, exchange rate reform, and RMB internationalization. They are also important for the healthy, stable, and orderly development of the financial system (Yi, 2008). From 1996, when China deregulated the interbank offered rates, to 1999, when the treasury bonds began to be issued by tender, the interbank interest rates had been market-determined, and the methods, variety, and scale of transactions had greatly improved. However, China had not formed a comprehensive benchmark rate system in the money market. As interest rate liberalization moved forward, the establishment of an effective benchmark rate system became increasingly important. In October 2006, the benchmark rate for money market – Shanghai Interbank Offered Rate, or Shibor – was put on a test run and officially launched on January 4, 2007. In recent years, the benchmark rate system has been developing fast and the status of Shibor has been rising. A benchmark rate system based on Shibor and government bond yield curves has started to take shape.

D   *The crucial stage*

With the regulatory framework which controlled the lower limit of loan rates and the upper limit of deposit rates, the pricing ability of financial institutions has increased greatly. The commercial banks have preliminarily established a market-based incentive and restraint mechanism. In addition, the financial markets, including the money market, capital market, foreign exchange market, gold market, and insurance market, have further developed. All this provided favorable conditions on both the macro- and micro-levels for further interest rate reform. At the same time, financial innovation (e.g. bank's wealth-management products, trusts, and Internet finance) and financial disintermediation have developed rapidly, and China's economic growth model and economic structure have been going through transition, which in turn has made interest rate liberalization the intrinsic demand of market entities. With demand and policy support coming together, the reform of loan and deposit rates was further promoted in 2012. The 3rd Plenum of the 18th CCCPC made the decision to comprehensively deepen the reform, changing the wording from "steadily push forward interest rate liberalization" to "accelerate interest rate liberalization". This marked a milestone for the liberalization of deposit and loan rates.

a   Complete liberalization of loan rates

On June 7, 2012, the PBOC announced that the lower limit for loan rates for financial institutions had been adjusted from 90 percent of the benchmark rates to 80 percent, and the floor was further adjusted to 70 percent on July 5.

On July 19, 2013, the PBOC released the document *On Pushing Forward the Market-Based Interest Rate Reform*, which removed the lower limit for loan rates (except for individual commercial housing loans) and the regulation on discount rates. Meanwhile, the upper limit for loan rates of rural credit cooperatives was lifted. In this regard, the regulation on loan rates was basically removed.

b   Establishment of a self-discipline pricing mechanism for market interest rates

On September 24, 2013, a conference was held on the establishment of a self-discipline pricing mechanism for market interest rates. The mechanism aimed to maintain fair competition and healthy development in the financial market by managing interest rates on money and credit markets.

In order to further improve the interest rate pricing mechanism, China drew from international experience and established a centralized mechanism for quoting and publishing loan prime rates (LPR), and this mechanism was officially launched on October 25, 2013, after a month of pilot run. The LPR is what commercial banks offer to their best customers. It is also the basis for other loan rates. Under the LPR centralized quoting and publishing mechanism, the weighted average of LPR quoted by each commercial bank was published. The mechanism is an extension of the Shibor system in the credit market. It can help enhance the benchmark rate system in the financial market and smooth the transition from a government-controlled interest rate system to a market-based system. It can also raise the efficiency and transparency of credit product pricing and reduce irrational pricing. In addition, the mechanism serves to improve the regulation of the PBOC and lay the foundation for future interest rate liberalization.

c   Adjustment of the cap on the deposit rates

On June 7, 2012, the PBOC announced its decision to adjust the upper limit of deposit rates to 1.1 times of the benchmark rates, the first time it had allowed the deposit rates to float above the benchmark rates. The adjustment of the rate cap received positive reactions. After the announcement, many banks adjusted their deposit rates accordingly. A diversification in deposit pricing started to emerge, with state-owned banks, joint-equity banks and urban commercial banks setting up their own rates.

d   Steady progress of the issuance and trading of interbank certificate of deposits

Interim Measures on Managing Interbank Certificate of Deposits was published on December 8, 2013 by the PBOC and was put into operation on December 9, 2013. On December 12 and 13, ten financial institutions, including Bank of China, China Construction Bank, and China Development Bank, issued their first batch of such products and later traded on the secondary market, establishing a bilateral quoting system with interbank certificate of deposits. The interbank certificate of deposits is priced by the market and is electronic, standardized, liquid, and transparent. It can provide mid- and long-term Shibor with more transparent and marketized pricing reference, which will solidify the benchmark status of Shibor rates, enlarge the financing channels for deposit-taking financial institutions, and standardize the interbank transactions. Meanwhile, it can help accumulate experiences in issuing large certificates of deposits to enterprises and individuals and can bring valuable insights for the advancement of interest rate liberalization.

e   Removal of the cap on deposit rates

After allowing the deposit rates to float above the benchmark rates, the PBOC further raised the cap. In November 2014, March 2015, and May 2015, the caps for deposit rates of financial institutions were adjusted to 1.2, 1.3, and 1.5 times the benchmark rates, respectively. On October 23, 2015, the PBOC published *Announcement on Lowering the RMB Benchmark Rates for Deposits and Loans and Advancing the Market-based Interest Rate Reform*, which stated that from October 24, 2015, the cap for deposit rates of commercial banks and rural credit cooperatives would be removed. By then, the deposit rates were liberalized.

III   Characteristics of interest rate deregulation in China

A   China's interest rate liberalization is incremental

The deregulation of interest rates in China was incremental. One characteristic is the long duration, as this process has been going on for more than 30 years since the reform was first started, or more than 20 years since 1993 when China clearly formulated the blueprint for market-based interest rate reform, or 19 years since 1996 when China liberalized the interbank offered rates. Compared with other countries that adopted an incremental approach, the process in China has taken a long time.

The second characteristic is that incremental liberalization of interest rates follows a certain sequence though the sequence may vary among countries. The US first

Table 1-3 Timeframe of interest rate liberalization in major countries

Countries	Duration
US	1970–1986
France	1965–1985
Japan	1977–1994
Australia	1973–1985
South Korea	1981–1997
India	1992–2011

liberalized rates for large deposits, then rates for small deposits, and rates between non-banking institutions before interbank rates. Japan started with liberalization of rates on Treasury bonds before expanding to other products, from the rates in the interbank market to the retail market, from long-term interest rates to short-term rates, and from large transactions to small ones. South Korea began from non-bank financial institutions and then moved to banks and from lending rates to deposit rates. China liberalized money market rates and bond market rates first, then gradually pushed forward the liberalization of deposit and lending rates, which followed the order from foreign currency to domestic currency, from loans to deposit, and from long-term and large-amount deposits/loans to short-term and small-amount ones.

B   The process of interest rate liberalization reflects the characteristics of China's reforms

a   The reform is incremental and complementary

China had no holistic blueprint or clear target at the beginning of the economic reform. Deng Xiaoping coined the saying "crossing the river by groping for stones" to describe China's reform process. It shows that China was doing it step and step and learning by experimenting.

This model of incremental reform means the process was easier at the early stage and became harder along the way. The economic system comprises many sectors with different priorities and conditions. And the costs and benefits of reforms for different sectors also vary. Therefore, the process often starts from sectors with the easiest breakthroughs and lowest costs.

Another important characteristic of incremental reform is maintaining the interest rate structure and allocation mechanism for the existing financial sector and adopting a market mechanism for newly developed businesses. As the reform and development take hold, the proportion of market economy increases and eventually dominates.

However, the different sectors of the economic system are closely related, and a slight move in one part would affect the entire system. Therefore, incremental reform should follow a certain order. The reform of one sector should be complemented by reform of other sectors, and the reforms of the various sectors should be mutually beneficial.

Incremental reform is an ever-improving process. Constrained by institutional conditions, the reform of one or a few sectors might not progress as expected; even when the process has reached an ideal state, it might regress. For example, China implemented a household contract responsibility system in the rural area and rolled out reform of state-owned enterprises in the cities. However, even today the property and the associated management rights of farmers remain a problem, and reform of state-owned enterprises remains a key issue. Therefore, reform is a dynamic and ever-evolving process.

Interest rate reform as a subset of systemic reform is connected with reform of other sectors. As interest rate reform involves a lot of stakeholders and risks, it should be carried out after less risky and less difficult reforms, and when the reforms of other sectors have set the right conditions. As interest rate reform itself is a huge undertaking, its implementation should start from the easy part before moving onto the difficult part and from the newly developed market to the existing market. For example, interest rates that have less impact, such as the money market rates, bond market rates, and foreign currency market rates, should be liberalized first, followed by RMB deposit and loan rates; and the infrastructure of the financial market should be solidified first before liberalization of interest rates. Acceleration of reforms of other sectors that could serve as the basis for interest rate reform can also speed up the latter, while the stagnation of the former could delay the latter. The decision-making process on whether to push forward the reform can also influence the process.

*b   Interest rate liberalization goes hand in hand with financial
development*

Compared with developed economies or some emerging economies that deregulated their interest rates in a relatively mature financial system, China's interest rate liberalization went hand in hand with the development of its financial system. Different from former Soviet Union and Eastern European countries that liberalized their interest rates before development of the financial sector, China gradually deregulated interest rates based on specific needs and circumstances while developing the financial sector.

I   THE LIBERALIZATION OF DEPOSIT AND LENDING RATES UNDERTAKEN ALONGSIDE
    THE DEVELOPMENT OF THE BANKING SECTOR

The PBOC was the one and only financial institution in China during the planned economy period. The economic reform triggered development of the financial sector. In February 1979, the government tasked the Agricultural Bank of China (ABC) to support economic development in the rural area, and rural banking business was handed over from the PBOC to the ABC. And in March 1979, the Bank of China was spun off from the PBOC to specialize in foreign exchange business to cater to the demand of opening-up and international economic exchange. China Construction Bank was separated from the Ministry of Finance in 1979, and in 1982 it was established as a national financial institution to operate general banking business in addition to allocation of funds. The Industrial and Commercial Bank of China was set up in January 1984, taking over all industrial and commercial credit business and savings business from the PBOC. Since then the PBOC has been functioning solely as the central bank. The Bank of Communications was re-established in 1986, followed by the establishment of more than ten joint-equity commercial banks. In the meantime, many non-bank financial institutions were set up, including credit cooperatives, insurance companies, trust and investment corporations, securities companies, finance companies for enterprise groups, financial leasing companies, and investment funds, while many foreign financial institutions were introduced. As these specialized banks were performing the dual role of commercial banks and national policy tasks, three policy banks – China Development Bank, the Export–Import Bank of China, and Agricultural Development Bank of China – were established in 1994 to streamline their responsibilities. A financial system comprising commercial banks, policy banks, and non-bank financial institutions was established with the central bank at the center.

During this development process, China had simplified the business operation of the banking sector and was looking to grant more rights to banks on interest rate pricing. With the reform and development of commercial banks, the liberalization of deposit and lending rates are also moving forward, as they are closely connected: Only when there are commercial banks can there be interest rate liberalization; and only when commercial banks are developing well can the liberalization of interest rates progress rapidly. And when commercial banks are not doing well, the liberalization of interest rates would also face difficulties.

II INTEREST RATE LIBERALIZATION MAKES BREAKTHROUGH ALONGSIDE THE
DEVELOPMENT OF THE FINANCIAL MARKET

Ever since 1984, with the economic reform in full swing, all kinds of market financing activities have been emerging and developing. First, the expansion and standardization of commercial credit helped create the market for bankers' acceptance. From February 1984, the PBOC started to carry out discounting business of bankers' acceptance nationwide.

Second, the government adopted a new credit management system in 1985, and since then specialized banks could borrow funds from each other. The quota for interbank borrowing was increased in 1986 with the development of financial institutions. By the end of 1987, major cities and regions in China had opened up interbank markets, and in March 1990, the PBOC announced tentative management measures for interbank borrowing, which stipulated the rules and requirements for this business.

Third, the foreign exchange market also expanded with the deepening of institutional reform and opening-up. Shenzhen established China's first foreign exchange swap center in December 1985, and by 1988, all provinces, autonomous regions, municipalities directly under the central government, and special economic zones had set up such centers, further opening up the foreign exchange market to more market participants while allowing the price of foreign exchange to fluctuate according to market demand and supply. In September 1988, Shanghai launched open transactions of foreign exchange and gradually set up several foreign exchange open markets in the following years.

Fourth, the government first issued treasury bills in 1981, and by 1984, the treasury bills were widely held with the demand for trading. Trans-regional and standardized trading of treasury bonds started to take off in 1991, and the Ministry of Finance and the PBOC started a tryout of repo business the same year.

Fifth, with the development of reform on enterprise ownership systems, the capital market and new types of financial intermediary were introduced. A new wave of direct financing emerged in 1984, with many companies issuing stocks and bonds. The Shanghai Stock Exchange was launched on December 19, 1990, and Shenzhen Stock Exchange on July 30, 1991. The establishment of the two stock exchanges marked the standardization of China's stock market. Important financial intermediaries such as securities firms and securities investment funds were also founded.

With the banks as the backbone of the financial sector, interest rate liberalization in the financial market will not have a fundamental effect on the stability of the financial system, nor on the financing cost for enterprises. It's for this reason that China first carried out interest rate liberalization in the financial market. Moreover, China had always put institutional improvement first, which created positive institutional settings conductive to the liberalization of interest rates.

III INTEREST RATE LIBERALIZATION GOES HAND IN HAND WITH MONETIZATION
     AND THE PROLIFERATION OF FINANCIAL PRODUCTS

As the modern financial framework came into being, the allocation of social capital went through fundamental changes. The share of fiscal spending declined rapidly while that of financial capital took the dominant place. Economic monetization also sped up, with broad money increasing 19 times from 1978 to 1992 and GDP growing seven times during the same period. "The ratio of broad money to real GNP rose steadily from 0.32 to above 1.0, which reflected the monetization effect of institutional reform" (Yi, 2008). There came the problem of how to better control and regulate the flow of financial resources after the financial sector had become essential to the economy, and it's in this context that the liberalization of interest rates was put on the agenda.

Along with the monetization process in China, the variety of financial products also increased. In addition to cash and bank deposit, financial instruments such as bonds, stocks, funds, futures, and insurance products were emerging. The number of bonds in custody increased from 43 in 1997 to 4,857 in 2014 (112 times increase), and the value of the bond market rose from 478.08 billion RMB to 28.73 trillion RMB (59.1 times jump) during the same time. The stock market capitalization grew from 347.43 billion RMB in 1993 to 37.3 trillion RMB in 2014

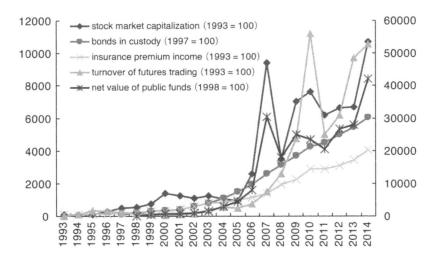

Figure 1-1 Rapid development of financial products

(106.2 times increase), the trading volume of the stock exchange jumped from 22.621 billion shares to 7375.461 billion (325 times surge), and the turnover went from 369.795 billion RMB to 74.4 trillion RMB (200.2 times increase). The net value of publicly offered funds rose from 10.76 billion RMB in 1998 to 4,535.36 billion RMB in 2014, a rise of 420.5 times. Trading of futures rose from 8.907 million lots in 1993 to 2.51 billion in 2014 (280.3 times increase), and the turnover went from 552.20 billion RMB to 292 trillion RMB (527.8 times surge). Insurance premium income rose from 49.96 billion RMB in 1993 to 2,023.48 billion RMB in 2014, increasing by 39.5 times. The balance of banks' wealth-management products rose from 530.00 billion RMB at the end of 2007 to 12.65 trillion RMB at the end of June 2014, a 22.9-time jump.

With the increase of financial products, a rigid regulatory system on interest rates can hardly provide reasonable pricing for financial products; instead, it could cause price distortion. In this regard, interest rate liberalization was an inevitable choice for China.

c   Market forces and government guidance both play their vital roles

Each step of interest rate liberalization was achieved with the concerted effort of the market and the government. At the initial stage when the reform of property rights for enterprises and financial institutions was advancing and the financial market was starting to take shape, it became inevitable to introduce market mechanisms into the allocation of capital. The CPC and the State Council took lessons from the past and set the agenda for reform. In 1993, *Decision on Some Issues Concerning the Establishment of Socialist Market Economy* and the *State Council*

Decision on Reform of the Financial System were passed during the 3rd Plenum of the 14th CPC Central Committee, which brought forward the ideas for interest rate liberalization. Under these two sets of guidelines, China's market-based interest rate reform was officially launched.

Ever since the 2000s, China's socialist market economy has been improving gradually. China's entry into the WTO further opened up the financial market to the outside world. Securities, funds, and insurance business have been developing fast, with new financial instruments emerging and foreign banks entering the domestic market. Under such circumstances, the report of the 16th Party Congress restated the need to steadily push forward market-based interest rate reform and optimize the allocation of financial resources. In 2003, *Decision on Some Issues Concerning the Improvement of Socialist Market Economic System* was announced at the 3rd Plenum of the 16th CPC Central Committee, which pointed out that interest rate liberalization should be pushed forward steadily, an interest rate formation mechanism based on market supply and demand should be established and promoted, and the central bank should provide guidance to interest rates through monetary policy instruments. A series of crucial decisions made by the CPC Central Committee and the State Council defined the direction and set the blueprint for the market-based interest rate reform. The reform took an important step in 2004 and achieved the goal of controlling the lower limit of lending rates and the upper limit of deposit rates.

In recent years, with the rapid development of wealth-management products, trust products, and Internet finance, China's economic growth and structural changes have undergone a transformation, and the landscape of the economy and financial market has changed fundamentally. It's an intrinsic demand of market players who started to take action to promote interest rate liberalization. To comply with market demand, the liberalization of deposit and lending rates were speeded up after 2012, with the complete liberalization of lending rates and the gradual relaxation of the upper limit on deposit rates. The 3rd Plenum of 18th CPC Central Committee made the decision to comprehensively deepen the reform, changing the wording from "steadily push forward interest rate liberalization" to "accelerate interest rate liberalization". China's reform of interest rates has since then entered a new stage. The upper limit on deposit rates was relaxed a few times from 2014 to 2015 and was completely removed in October 2015. Since then China has basically lifted all controls on interest rates.

d   The relations between reform, development, and stability

As international experience has shown, interest rate reform is a double-edged sword, which can enhance the efficiency of resource allocation and also create financial volatility, and therefore the trade-off between benefit and risk should be weighted carefully. As a transitional economy, China's institutional environment and market conditions are changing rapidly, which pose more risks than countries with a mature market economy. For China, reducing risks and maintaining stability during the process of interest rate reform is a priority. The relationship between reform, economic development, and financial stability must be handled well to make sure interest rate reform can progress smoothly. For China, reform, development, and stability are supportive of each other. The goal of reform is to achieve sustainable development and lasting stability; without steady development, people will lose faith in reform; and without stability, there will be no solid foundation for reform. However, it could be difficult to balance all three elements. When risks or development are the priority, reform measures would be delayed, but unsuccessful reform measures could also lead to chaos. For instance, when the regulation on interest rates was slightly loosened in the 1980s, the commercial banks in some regions started a war on interest rates. However, trial and error, correction mechanisms, and a coordinated reform approach helped manage the relations between development, reform, and stability. Most importantly, China emphasizes the effective coordination between reform and regulation. Whether it's the reform of lending and deposit rates in 2004 or the further promotion of this reform since 2012, the government has integrated reform into regulation and combined the need of monetary policy adjustment with market risks, achieving a good balance among reform, development, and stability.

2 Characteristics of China's interest rate system

The essence of market-based interest rate reform is to transfer the capital pricing power from the government to the market, and its core lies in deregulating interest rates to expand market players' pricing power and optimizing the allocation of resources. If developing and transitional economies want to successfully achieve the goals of reform, they need not only allow market players the pricing power but also foster many conditions for liberalization and establish a sound market-oriented interest rate formation mechanism. This will enable market players to form reasonable price equilibrium through competition.

In this regard, deregulating interest rates is an important step in market-based interest rate reform, but not the whole of it. Instead, whether reasonable equilibrium interest rates can be established under better market conditions is the core of the market-oriented reform. The *12th Five-year Plan of China's Financial Development and Reform* summed up the principles for China's interest rate liberalization as loosening rate controls, establishing market-based interest rates, and building an effective adjustment mechanism. On the one hand, the level, risk structure, and term structure of interest rates should be determined by capital supply and demand; on the other hand, it refers to an interest rate system with smooth rate transmission at different levels, in which the benchmark interest rate plays a dominant role. Therefore, China's market-based interest rate reform is not only a process of removing controls on interest rates but also a process of establishing a market-based interest rate formation mechanism. This chapter will study how market-based interest rates are formed and transmitted during the liberalization process.

I The dual-track feature of interest rates in the process of gradual reform

A Gradual reform and the dual-track price system

China's economic reform is a gradual transition from the planned economy to a socialist market economy. The price mechanism is the core of the market economy, and the liberalization of the price mechanism is the key in the transition to a market economy. The crucial aspect in the establishment and improvement of China's socialist market economy is to gradually remove price controls, ultimately set up a market price mechanism in which supply and demand play a decisive role, and realize the optimized allocation of social resources through price signals to microeconomic entities. China aims to introduce a market mechanism to the allocation of financial resources, improve capital allocation efficiency through price leverage, and change its regulation on financial resources from direct intervention to indirect market-oriented regulation. This is the key of the financial market reform and the purpose of interest rate liberalization.

In view of the complexity of price reform and its impact on the economy, China adopted a dual-track approach in the 1980s. This method had two pricing mechanisms: Price control was maintained in the planned system, while outside of the system the price was determined by supply and demand. Under normal circumstances, the planned prices were usually low. But when faced with competition from market prices, the manufacturing in the planned sector gradually contracted and the market sector expanded, and finally the market price system replaced the planned price system completely. Lau, Qian, and Roland (1997, 2000) demonstrated that the dual-track price reform was identical to a redistribution mechanism of goods and was a win–win strategy in terms of welfare as it increased the benefit of certain economic entities without harming others. Shrinking of the planned sector forced the economy to move toward resource allocation not based on plans, and therefore the dual-track price reform can be considered a Pareto improvement.

The effective implementation of the dual-track price system must fulfill one essential condition – the government must be able to control the planned sector's behavior and distinguish the planned sector from the market sector. Murphy, Shleifer, and Vishny (1992) studied the failure of former Soviet Union and Eastern European countries, and their analysis shows that those countries only implemented a partial price liberalization reform without strict control over the planning sector, which resulted in the massive transfer of resources, reduced the efficiency of resource allocation, and ultimately caused a net loss to social welfare. The practice of the dual-track price system in China also faced similar problems, and the price reform failure in 1988 fully exposed the disadvantages of the dual-track system. However, the interaction between the market price and the planned price greatly raised the efficiency of the planned sector. Even though the market prices were inevitably affected by the planned price, the movement of market prices pushed the government department in charge of planned prices to recognize the supply and demand relationship implied by market prices and therefore move planned prices closer to market prices. Although the price system went through a period of chaos in the late 1980s, the reform gradually moved forward. The supply and demand of goods and the institutional environment of the market economy improved greatly, and by the mid-1990s China had basically achieved price liberalization for general commodities and services. The successful experience of the dual-track pricing system provided a feasible path to financial liberalization, and the dual-track system of interest rates with interest rate liberalization as its goal has become an important part of China's financial reform (Yi, 2009).

B Characteristics of dual-track interest rate system: the narrowing of interest rate regulation and expansion of market interest rates

Given that financial markets at various levels exert varying degrees of influence on the allocation of financial resources, the liberalization of prices started from markets that have less effect on the economy. For example, since the exchange rate has a small effect on the allocation of domestic financial resources, China merged the dual-track exchange rates and reformed the exchange rate formation mechanism as early as 1994. In terms of interest rate liberalization,

> while maintaining interest rate regulation, the introduction of interest rate liberalization at the margin made the reform likely to be a Pareto improvement, which means it could improve the allocation efficiency of financial resources in the banking sector without harming the real economy.
>
> (Yi, 2009)

Therefore, along the process of liberalization, China's interest rate system shows dual-track features, i.e. the co-existence of controlled interest rates in the banking system and market-based interest rates outside the banking system.

"With the dominance of indirect financing, the liberalization of interest rates in the wholesale capital market would not affect corporate financing costs, but could help improve the efficiency of capital allocation" (Yi, 2009). China's interest rate liberalization therefore first achieved a breakthrough in the wholesale capital market. In 1996, China removed control on interbank offered rates and by 1999 had completed the liberalization of interest rates in the bond issuance and secondary markets. Meanwhile, by developing the interbank market, giving access to more market participants, and enriching the variety of products and payments, the interbank bond market had become China's main fixed-income market, providing favorable conditions for the yield curve improvement and indirect control of the monetary policy. The interest rates in the capital market, consisting of the money market and the bond market, were completely decided by supply and demand.

> The liberalization of interbank interest rates successfully established a capital allocation system beyond the controlled interest rate regime. The formation and improvement of interbank interest rates provided a benchmark yield curve for independent pricing by commercial banks, and paved the way for the liberalization of the controlled interest rates and banks' internal pricing mechanism.
>
> (Yi, 2009)

After the early exploration, the deposit and lending rates were gradually liberalized. Similarly, following the principle of risk minimization, China liberalized the interest rates of foreign currency first and then gradually expanded the floating range of RMB lending rates, and then achieved the goal of controlling only the upper limit of deposit rates and the lower limit of lending rates. Afterwards, China step by step expanded the floating range of lending rates for financial institutions and finally removed the lower limit of lending rates. China extended the reform from large fixed deposit rates to other deposit rates, allowed the deposit rates to go up, established the self-discipline mechanism in banks for interest rate pricing, carried out interbank certificate of deposit business, improved the capabilities of financial institutions in liabilities interest rate pricing and risk management, and ultimately lifted the ceiling on deposit interest rates.

The aim of RMB deposit and lending interest rates reform is Pareto improvement. China has been steadily promoting the reform by way of product innovation and expanding the scope of market pricing. Take deposit as an example. Since 1999, China had allowed commercial banks to employ market-based interest rates for long-term large deposits from institutions such as insurance companies, individual pension accounts, and the National Social Security Fund in the form of negotiated deposits. The interbank certificate of deposits business was first established to accumulate experience for large deposits business targeted at individuals and corporations. Meanwhile, the volumes of financial products substituting deposits whose prices are determined by the market, e.g. the wealth-management products (the WMPs) are gradually expanding. In recent years, the rapid development of financial innovation and financial disintermediation greatly enriched the variety of financial products and influenced the regulation on deposit rates. The source of bank funds showed clear features of the dual-track interest rates.

With the growth of general deposits slowing down, the weighted average yields of closed-end NAV and non-NAV wealth-management products and open-end non-NAV wealth-management products reached 5.07 percent, 5.06 percent, and 3.89 percent respectively in 2014. The balance of wealth-management products issued by banks rose from 10.2 trillion RMB at the end of 2013 to 15.02 trillion RMB in 2014, an increase of 46.68 percent; the average daily balance of wealth-management products issued by banks was 13.75 trillion RMB, increasing by 43.38 percent year on year,[1] while the balance of RMB deposits at the end of 2014 only rose by 9.1 percent compared to 2013, and the ratio between wealth-management products balance and RMB deposits balance surged from 9.8 percent at the end of 2013 to 13.2 percent at the end of 2014. Internet finance, led by products such as Yu'E Bao, was developing fast and the volume of money market funds had exceeded 2 trillion RMB. The liberalization of interest rates was not only a goal set by policymakers but also an intrinsic demand of market players. In particular, the rapid development of Internet finance fully illustrated the power of the market, and market participants' pursuit of high yields and the spontaneous adjustment of market supply had in fact broken the barriers for interest rate liberalization of large and small funds, disrupting the reform sequence of large capital first and small capital later and establishing a dual-track deposit interest rate landscape consisting of shadow banking rates and controlled deposit rates, which created favorable conditions for the ultimate deregulation of deposit rates.

C China's dual-track interest rate system and the progress of interest rate liberalization

a Interest rate liberalization from the perspective of social financing structure

Social financing mainly consists of RMB loans (housing loans and non-housing loans), foreign currency loans, entrusted loans, trust loans, non-discounted bank acceptance bills, corporate bond financing, and domestic equity financing by non-financial enterprises. As of June 7, 2012, only the lower limit of RMB lending rates was controlled. For instance, the lower limit of housing loans rates was 70 percent of the benchmark interest rate, and the lower limit of non-housing loans rates was 90 percent of the benchmark interest rate, while the pricing of other types of financing had largely been liberalized.

Regarding the share of financing, before 2011 when the lower limit of lending rates was adjusted, about 34.8 percent of total financing had been liberalized and about 58.2 percent of total financing (RMB loans) was still regulated with regard to the lower limit. The interest rates of 51.7 percent of the non-housing loans could float downward by 10 percent, and rates of 6.5 percent of the housing loans could float downward by 30 percent.

On June 8 and July 6, 2012, the lower limit on lending rates was adjusted to 80 percent of benchmark interest rates and then to 70 percent, respectively, but the lower limit on housing loan rates stayed the same. In the same year, around 43.1 percent of total social financing achieved interest rate liberalization, while 52.1 percent of RMB loans were still under regulation; of these, 31.4 percent were allowed to float up and down by 10 percent of the benchmark rates and 20.7 percent were allowed to float by 30 percent (about 14.6 percent were due to adjustment of the lower limit, and 6.1 percent were housing loans whose rates could fall by 30 percent originally).

On July 20, 2013, the lower limit on lending interest rates was removed except for housing loans, whose interest rates remained 70 percent of benchmark rates. In that year, about 58.2 percent of total social financing achieved interest rate liberalization (about 14.5 percent was due to the deregulation of the lower limit of lending rates, and about 43.7 percent was liberalized before 2013), and about 36.9 percent of social financing could float by 30 percent of benchmark interest rates.

In 2014, about 84.2 percent of social financing achieved interest rate liberalization, leaving only RMB housing loans with a lower limit of 70 percent of benchmark rates. The interest rate liberalization of social financing was basically accomplished by July 20, 2013.

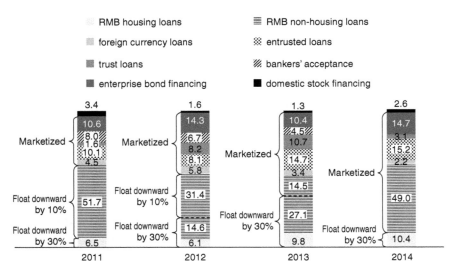

Figure 2-1 The progress of interest rate liberalization based on social financing structure

b   Interest rate liberalization from the perspective of banks' assets and liabilities

Banks have assets in four categories: Loans (housing loans and non-housing loans); marketable securities and equity investment; reserve deposits; and inter-bank transactions. As of June 7, 2012, the interest rates of non-housing loans could float by 10 percent of benchmark interest rates and that of housing loans could float downward by 30 percent. Marketable securities, equity investment, and interbank business had achieved market-oriented pricing. The interest rates on required reserves as policy interest rates were not targeted in the liberalization process.

The lower floating limit of RMB lending rates was adjusted from 10 percent below the benchmark to 20 percent on June 8, 2012, and then later to 30 percent on July 6, 2012, while the lower limit of housing loan interest rates remained the same at 70 percent of benchmark rates. At the end of Q1 2012, loans accounted for 56.1 percent of banks' assets, and the interest rates were regulated by a lower limit. For instance, the interest rates of non-housing loans (47.1 percent of assets) could float downward by 10 percent maximum and the interest rates of housing loans (9.0 percent of assets) could float downward by 30 percent maximum. Market-able securities and equity investment accounted for 20.5 percent of banks' assets, and interbank transactions accounted for 7.6 percent, and both had achieved market-oriented pricing. At the end of Q3 2012, loans accounted for 56.8 percent of banks' assets with a lower limit of 0.7 times benchmark interest rates; of these, non-housing loans (47.1 percent of assets) could float downward by 30 percent

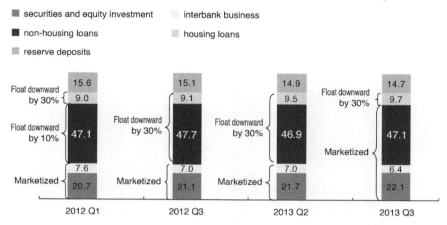

Figure 2-2 The progress of interest rate liberalization based on banks' assets

maximum due to the adjustment in July 2012 and that of housing loans (9.1 per-cent of assets) could float downward by 30 percent even before 2012. Marketable securities and equity investment (21.1 percent of assets) and interbank business (7 percent of assets) had achieved market-oriented pricing.

On July 20, 2013, the lower limit of RMB lending rates was removed, but the lower limit of housing loan rates, which was 70 percent of benchmark interest rates, was retained. At the end of Q2 2013, just before this adjustment, loans accounted for 56.4 percent of banks' assets (non-housing loans 46.9 percent and housing loans 9.5 percent), and loan rates were allowed to float downward to 70 percent of benchmark rates. Securities and equity investment accounted for 21.7 percent of banks' assets and interbank business accounted for 7.0 percent; both had achieved market-oriented pricing. At the end of Q3 2013, after the adjust-ment, non-housing loans, securities and equity investment, and interbank business accounted for 47.1 percent, 21.1 percent, and 6.4 percent of banks' assets respec-tively, and 74.6 percent in total. These three types of assets had achieved interest rate liberalization, of which non-housing loans (47.1 percent) were deregulated in this round of adjustment, while housing loans (9.7 percent) still retained the lower limit of 70 percent of the benchmark interest rate.

On the assets side at the end of Q3 2013, except for the less than 10 percent housing loans that still faced an interest rate lower limit of 70 percent of bench-mark rates, the pricing of other types of assets had been completely liberalized. The liberalization of the interest rates on the assets side of banks' balance sheets was basically accomplished by July 20, 2013.

On the liabilities side, there were four major categories, i.e. deposits, issuance of financial bonds, borrowing from the central bank, and interbank business. As of June 7, 2012, the lower limit of deposit rates was removed and the cap was the benchmark interest rate. The issuance of financial bonds and interbank business

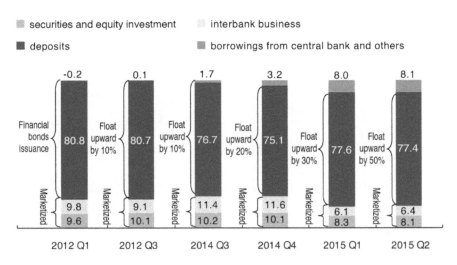

Figure 2-3 The progress of interest rate liberalization based on banks' liabilities

had already achieved market-oriented pricing. Borrowing from the central bank and others were not included in the scope of reform.

On June 8, 2012, the ceiling of RMB deposit rates was raised to 1.1 times the benchmark interest rates. Before this adjustment, at the end of Q1 2012, the deposits accounted for 80.8 percent of banks' liabilities, and a ceiling was imposed on deposit rates which were the benchmark rates. The issuance of bonds accounted for 9.6 percent, and the interbank business accounted for 9.8 percent; both types had accomplished marker-oriented pricing. After the adjustment, at the end of Q3 2012, the deposits accounted for 80.7 percent of banks' liabilities with a cap of 1.1 times the benchmark rates. The issuance of bonds (10.1 percent) and the interbank business (9.1 percent) had accomplished interest rate liberalization.

On November 22, 2014, the ceiling of RMB deposit rates was raised to 1.2 times the benchmark rates. At the end of Q3 2014, before this adjustment, the deposits accounted for 76.7 percent of banks' liabilities with an interest rate ceiling of 1.1 times the benchmark rates. The issuance of bonds accounted for 10.2 percent and the interbank business accounted for 11.4 percent; both types had achieved marker-oriented pricing. At the end of Q4 2014, after this adjustment, the deposits accounted for 75.1 percent of banks' liabilities, with an interest rate upper limit of 1.2 times benchmark interest rates. The issuance of bonds (10.1 percent) and the interbank business (11.6 percent) had both accomplished interest rate liberalization.

On March 1, 2015, the ceiling of RMB deposit rates was raised to 1.3 times the benchmark interest rates. At the end of Q1 2015, the deposits accounted for 77.6 percent of banks' liabilities, with an interest rate upper limit of 1.3 times the benchmark rates. The issuance of bonds (8.3 percent) and the interbank business (6.1 percent) had both accomplished interest rate liberalization.

On May 11, 2015, the ceiling of RMB deposit rates was raised to 1.5 times the benchmark rates. At the end of Q2 2015, the deposits accounted for 77.4 percent of banks' liabilities, with an interest rate upper limit of 1.5 times the benchmark interest rates. The issuance of bonds (8.1 percent) and the interbank business (6.4 percent) had both accomplished interest rate liberalization.

On October 24, 2015, the ceiling of RMB deposit rates was removed, and the liberalization of interest rates on banks' liabilities was successfully accomplished.

II   Status quo of China's interest rate system

China's interest rate regime has three levels: Central bank interest rates, financial market interest rates, and commercial banks' deposit and lending rates. Central bank interest rates refer to the interest rates of the central bank's monetary policy tools, such as the interest rates of open market operations, interest rates of required reserves and excess reserves, refinancing rates, rediscount rates, benchmark rates of financial institutions' deposits and loans, and interest rates of innovative liquidity management tools (e.g. SLF, MLF, and PSL). The interest rates in the financial market refer to the interest rates of various products in the financial market, including money market rates and medium- and long-term interest rates. Money market rates include interbank offered rates, interbank bond repo rates, short-term bill rates, and short-term commercial paper rates. The medium and long-term interest rates include bond yields and rates on medium-term notes. The interest rates of commercial banks' deposits and loans refer to the interest rates of savings from or loans to institutions or individuals.

A   Central bank interest rate system

The open market operation is a crucial monetary policy tool of the PBOC. China's open market bond operations include repos, spot trade, and issuance of central bank bills. Currently, the interest rate of the open market operations and that of the money market move in the same direction, and the lower limit is the central bank's excess reserve rate, while the upper limit is the rediscount rate.

The reserve rate refers to the interest rate that the central bank pays to the financial institutions for their reserve deposits. Required reserves and excess reserves had the same interest rate before 1996, but in August that year, the PBOC started to implement different interest rates for required reserves and excess reserves, and lowered the rates from 8.82 percent to 8.28 percent and 7.92 percent, respectively, and then to 7.56 percent and 7.02 percent, respectively, in 1997. Before 1998, the deposits from commercial banks were categorized as general deposits and provisions, and the two accounts were merged into one reserve account in March 1998; the interest rates of the two accounts were lowered from 7.56 percent to 7.02 percent, respectively (7.35 percent at weighted average level), to 5.22 percent. After four rounds of adjustment, the interest rate of the required reserves declined to 1.89 percent in February 2002. In December 2003, the PBOC again reformed the system, adopting an approach of one account and two interest rates for required

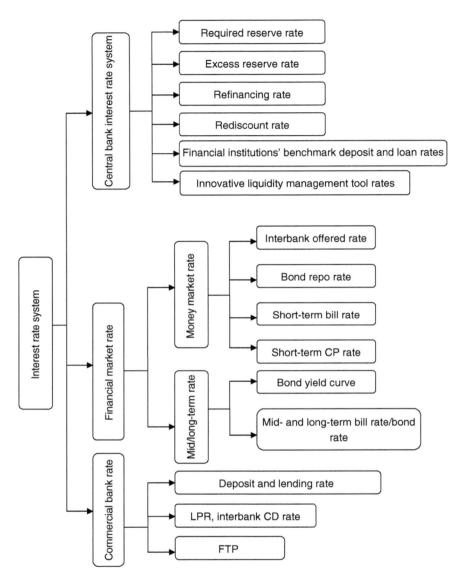

Figure 2-4 An illustration of China's interest rate system

reserves and excess reserves of financial institutions. Excess reserve rates actually served as the lower limit of money market interest rates.

Refinancing refers to credit that is provided by the central bank to commercial banks. The central bank could signal changes in its monetary policy stance to the public and commercial banks by adjusting the refinancing rates and in this way affect public expectations. To improve the central bank's interest rate formation mechanism, enhance its ability to guide market rates, streamline the relations between the central bank and borrowers, and establish a scientific, effective, and transparent refinancing management system, the PBOC started to implement a floating refinancing rate system in March 2004. Based on the benchmark refinancing (rediscount) interest rates, the central bank could timely set and declare the floating points, which enhanced the central bank's ability to adjust refinancing (rediscount) rates in line with the economic and financial situation. The interest rates of special-purpose refinancing loans beyond the central bank's approved limit and rates of refinancing loans for financial stability were 0.5 percentage points more than the weighted average rates of seven-year treasury bonds in the year before the issuance. The interest rates of refinancing loans for financial institutions' position adjustment and short-term liquidity support were 0.63 percentage points more than the weighted average rates, and the rediscount interest rates were 0.27 percentage points more than the weighted average rates. The central bank also aimed to further improve macro-regulation, standardize refinancing, and play a greater role in liquidity management and credit structure optimization. And for these purposes, the PBOC adjusted its categorization of refinancing loans, dividing the original liquidity refinancing into liquidity refinancing and credit policy support refinancing while keeping the classifications of financial stability refinancing and special-purpose policy refinancing in 2014. Liquidity refinancing and SLF established in 2013 were meant to provide liquidity support to financial institutions that could meet macro-prudential requirements; credit policy support refinancing included agricultural refinancing and small and medium institutions refinancing (refinancing for small and medium financial institutions).

Rediscount rates refer to the rates when commercial banks apply to the central bank for another discount of their holdings of discounted bills. In the infancy stage of the central bank's rediscount business, rediscount rates could float downward by 5 percent to 10 percent of banks' lending rates at corresponding categories over the same period. Since May 1996, the rediscount rate was allowed to float downward by 5 percent to 10 percent of the refinancing rates at corresponding categories over the same period. Since March 1998, the PBOC reformed the formation mechanism of rediscount rates and discount rates, and stipulated that rediscount rates be decided by the central bank and discount rates be based on rediscount rates. On March 25, 2004, upon approval by the State Council, the PBOC started to implement a floating rediscount rate system.

To improve the effect of the monetary policy, prevent liquidity risk in the banking system and enhance the effectiveness of controls over money market interest rates, the PBOC initiated open market Short-term Liquidity Operations (SLO) and Standing Lending Facility (SLF) at the beginning of 2013. As a necessary complement to regular open market operations, the SLO was mainly based on short-term repurchase operations within seven days and market-oriented interest rate bidding. The SLF aimed to meet the large long-term liquidity needs of financial institutions. The longest duration of SLF is three months, and its interest rate is determined in accordance with monetary policy and the method of issuance.

To maintain stable and moderate liquidity in the banking system and support the appropriate growth of credit, in September 2014 the PBOC created Medium-term Lending Facility (MLF) as a monetary policy tool to provide medium-term base money. In September and October 2014, the PBOC provided 500 billion RMB and 269.5 billion RMB to state-owned commercial banks, listed commercial banks, large urban commercial banks, and rural commercial banks through the MLF, with a three-month duration and 3.5 percent interest rate. This provided liquidity and a medium-term policy interest rate and guided commercial banks to reduce lending rates and social financing cost and support the growth of the real economy. In June 2014, the PBOC created Pledged Supplementary Lending (PSL) to guide medium-term interest rates based on the rates commercial banks received from the central bank with their pledged assets. To reduce high corporate financing cost, the PBOC modestly reduced the PSL interest rates in September 2014.

B   Money market and bond market interest rates

China's money market mainly consists of the interbank lending market, interbank bond market, and commercial bill market. The interbank lending market and bond market constitute the main body of money market transactions, of which pledged repo are the major part; the interbank lending rates and interbank pledged repo rates are the main money market rates.

Since 1986, when China allowed specialized banks to lend to each other, the interbank lending market based on financing centers established by local banks has been developing rapidly. In January 1996, the PBOC required that all interbank lending business must be processed via a national interbank network, thus officially establishing the interbank lending market and the interbank offered rates (Chibor). Financial institutions conducted short-term, credit-based lending business through this market, with four months as the longest maturity, which in 2007 was extended to one year.

On January 4, 2007, the National Interbank Funding Center officially launched a new money market benchmark interest rate – Shanghai Interbank Offered Rate (Shibor). Currently, the Shibor has eight maturities: Overnight, one week, two weeks, one month, three months, six months, nine months, and one year. In the beginning, Shibor was calculated from rates quoted by 16 banks, excluding the two lowest and the two highest. In December 2012, two more banks joined the quotation, and Shibor was calculated excluding the four lowest and the four highest.

Before 1997, China's bond market consisted mainly of the exchange market and bank counter certificate treasury bond market. Due to the lack of regulatory experience and high market risk at the initial stage,[2] the PBOC required commercial banks to exit the exchange bond market and established the interbank bond market in June 1997. Financial institutions were largely engaged in bond transactions and repurchase business in the interbank bond market. The repo transactions were divided into pledged repo and buyout repo: Pledged repo requires a freeze of pledge during transaction; buyout repo has the features of credit transaction. The

Table 2-1 China's money market

	2007	2008	2009	2010	2011	2012	2013	2014
Interbank Lending	10.70	15.00	19.40	27.90	33.40	46.70	35.50	37.70
Interbank Bond repo	44.8	58.1	70.3	87.6	99.5	141.7	158.2	224.4
o/w pledged	44.07	56.38	67.70	84.65	96.66	136.62	151.98	212.41
Interbank Bond spot	15.60	37.10	36.51	64.00	63.60	75.20	41.60	40.36
o/w less than one year	n.a.	n.a.	n.a.	14.4	19.3	22.5	10.58	n.a.
Exchange Spot	0.18	0.37	0.34	0.37	0.47	0.59	1.009	1.49
Exchange Repo	1.86	2.43	3.59	6.62	20.45	36.85	63.07	90.18
Issuance of bills of exchange	5.87	7.1	10.3	12.2	15.1	17.9	20.3	22.1
Discounting of bills of exchange	10.11	13.50	23.20	26.00	25.00	31.60	45.70	60.70
Quotations in the interbank bill market	20.45	53.37	66.56	11.00	10.88	15.79	20.87	18.76
o/w Rediscounting	19.75	40.59	62.07	4.93	3.78	7.80	12.16	10.61
Repo	0.69	12.77	4.49	6.07	7.10	7.99	8.71	8.09

Note: In trillions

pledged repo has 11 maturities: One day, seven days, 14 days, 21 days, one month, two months, three months, four months, six months, nine months, and one year. Buyout repo was initiated in May 2004 with seven maturities: One day, seven days, 14 days, 21 days, one month, two months, and three months.

Since June 1997, when the PBOC required commercial banks to exit the exchange bond market, the bond market has featured a landscape with the co-existence of the interbank market, the exchange market and the bank counter market, and the combination of the floor market and OTC market. In the past ten years, China's bond market has achieved rapid development with more market participants, more innovative products, more active transactions, more liquidity, and more reasonable pricing. In particular, the introduction of short-term commercial paper in 2005 and medium-term notes in 2008 greatly promoted the development of interbank bond market. At present, the interbank bond market has become the main channel of debt financing in China. The interbank market is also the main platform where the central bank carries out open market operations for indirect monetary control. According to BIS statistics, China's bond market has grown to be the third largest in the world, after the US and Japan. Since 1998, the interbank bond market has taken up a share of more than 90 percent of the total bond market, involving various participants such as securities firms, insurance companies, funds, and trusts. In terms of bond products, treasury bonds and bonds issued by policy banks are the main products in the market, accounting for 35.1 percent and 34.6 percent, respectively.[3] The medium- and long-term treasury bond yield curves and the Shibor formed a complete set of benchmark yield curves of the financial market.

China launched the commercial bill business officially in 1986, and this business was mainly conducted over the counter at specialized agencies in some major cities. In 2003, China Commercial Paper Network (chinacp.com.cn) was launched by China Foreign Exchange Trade System and National Interbank Funding Center, and in 2009 an electronic commercial paper system developed by the PBOC was put into use. The infrastructure for a national bill market achieved rapid progress. The market gradually extended to commercial banks, policy banks, urban and rural credit cooperatives, and other financial institutions and enterprises. The market has played a crucial role in serving the short-term financing needs of different enterprises. The interbank commercial paper market also started to grow, which greatly helped promote commercial paper financing and the negotiation of short-term notes of financial institutions.

On December 8, 2013, the People's Bank of China issued *Provisional Regulations on Management of Interbank Certificates of Deposit*, which took effect on December 9. Subsequently, about ten financial institutions, including the Bank of China, issued the first batch of interbank deposit products and initiated secondary market transactions one after another, establishing a bilateral offering market–maker system in the interbank certificate of deposit business. As the interbank certificate of deposit business is characterized by automation, standardization, high liquidity, and transparency, it can provide more transparent and market-oriented pricing reference to long and medium-term Shibor rates, broaden financing channels for deposit institutions in the banking sector, and effectively promote the development of interbank certificate of deposit business. The development of interbank certificate of deposit business can provide reference for the steady and orderly promotion of interest rate liberalization.

C   Lending and deposit rates of commercial banks

When interest rates were regulated, the lending and deposit rates were determined by the central bank. During the liberalization process, the lending and deposit rates could fluctuate around the lending and deposit benchmark interest rates released by the PBOC, and the floating range was decided by the central bank.

In order to enhance the independent pricing ability of commercial banks, the People's Bank of China urged financial institutions to strengthen their pricing mechanisms. The current pricing mechanisms of commercial banks include the internal funds transfer pricing system (FTP) and the risk pricing mechanism.

The FTP refers to an operation model in which commercial banks transfer funds between an internal fund center and business units based on rates set by an external benchmark price and their own business performance. The purpose of this system is to adjust business cost and profitability as well as regulate the balance sheets and capital structure. Currently, some banks have put the FTP model into practice. In terms of RMB interest rate products under the dual-track system, commercial banks usually adopt FTP with controlled interest rates and FTP with market-oriented interest rates to achieve internal transfer pricing. FTP with controlled interest rates refers to benchmark interest rates of various term structures published by the central bank, and FTP with market-oriented interest rates uses Shibor, central bank bill rates, and treasury rates as the benchmark. Foreign currency FTP is generally based on basic FTP rates and some adjusting factors. Basic FTP rates use market yield curves of various currencies, such as Libor and Hibor, while the adjusting factors reflect the difference between domestic and overseas markets and the management requirements of commercial banks.

Risk-based pricing is a price management model that measures both risks and returns. Under the risk-adjusted framework, the interest rate is determined by the credit risk in the asset portfolio of banks. Risk-based pricing can help enhance risk coverage, reduce overall credit risk, improve earnings, optimize the credit asset structure, and prevent moral hazard in asset pricing. The risk factors involved in the risk-adjusted loan pricing model include default rate, rate of loss from default, term structure, exposure to default risk, and capital requirements imposed by the regulatory authorities. At present, most commercial banks in China have taken risk-based pricing into consideration when setting loan rates; they also consider funding costs, operational cost, and risk compensation when setting the loan rate. The funding cost is regulated by the FTP pricing system and the operational cost is calculated by activity-based cost analysis. The core part is to calculate risk premium – estimating the probability of distribution and exposure of credit risk based on the internal and external ratings and calculating the probability of default and probable loss in case of default. Due to a lack of continuous historical data, Chinese banks need to improve their calculations on default probability and default loss.

In recent years, with the deepening of interest rate liberalization, domestic banks have started to improve their interest rate pricing mechanisms and management. In large banks, such as ICBC, ABC, BOC, and CBC, the interest rate pricing management is led by a number of management departments such as the asset and liability department or the accounting department; in national joint-equity commercial banks, the asset and liability management committee and financial department are established to develop pricing policies, and a hierarchical authorization system is set up to allow business units and branches to carry out pricing policies within their scope of authority delegated by the head office.

After July 2013, when the PBOC removed control on lending rates, the central bank established and enhanced the market-oriented interest rate pricing self-discipline mechanism to further improve the pricing mechanism of commercial banks, and introduced the LPR (loan prime rate) centralized quotation and release mechanism. The LPR is the lending rate offered by commercial banks to their best customers, and rates on other customers can be set above it. In this regard, the LPR serves as a benchmark rate for commercial banks' loan pricing.

After October 2015, when the ceiling on deposit rates was lifted, commercial banks are no longer restricted in their decisions on deposit and lending rates and can independently determine prices in accordance with market principles. However, an interest rate formation mechanism based on market supply and demand has yet to be set up. Under the current circumstances, the central bank will continue to publish benchmark deposit and lending rates to provide references for interest rate pricing to financial institutions.

III   The interest rate transmission mechanism in China

From the beginning of the reform to the removal of the cap on deposit rates, China's interest rate regime has shown a dual-track feature – the co-existence of both regulated and market-based rates. This section will elaborate on the interest rate transmission mechanism under the dual-track system.

A   *Transmission and interaction between regulated interest rates and market-oriented interest rates*

a   *The influence of regulated interest rates on market-oriented interest rates*

I   THE INTERACTION BETWEEN REGULATED INTEREST RATES AND MARKET-
   ORIENTED INTEREST RATES

The key of the dual-track system lies in the regulation on deposit rates, which is essential to the understanding of the transmission between regulated rates and market-oriented rates. A lower cap on deposit rates enables banks to acquire capital with lower cost and therefore provide loans to businesses with rates below the equilibrium level. The purpose of deposit rate regulation is to mobilize deposits at a relatively low cost, thereby stimulating investment and economic growth. It is for this reason that the adjustment of the upper limit of deposit rates has always been slow, which directly leads to a delay in the adjustment of lending rates. Low lending rates could push up demand and trigger excess liquidity and inflation. To restrain excessive credit expansion, the central bank had to take quantitative control rather than just price leverage. By regulating reserve requirements and the scale of credit, the central bank was able to control the number and size of loans and therefore achieve some sort of equilibrium between supply and demand of credit at relatively low interest rates.

Due to credit controls, banks acquired more low-cost deposits than the loans they disbursed, and the excess capital was invested in the money market and bond market. The money market was the main place for liquidity management, where large banks were major creditors while small and medium financial institutions, such as urban commercial banks, were borrowers. Though interest rates in the money and bond markets had been fully liberalized, the banks were still willing to provide funds to borrowers at a lower price than outside markets. Borrowers in the bond market were mostly enterprises with high credit ratings, and they would turn to the credit market if the bonds were issued with high rates. Therefore, the funding market interest rates were generally significantly lower than loan rates. In the case of excess liquidity, low interest rates in the money and bond markets would further push up the demand for liquidity and credit expansion, and the PBOC had to issue central bank bills and carry out repos to soak up liquidity and maintain relatively stable interest rates in order to constrain demand for funds.

The ceiling on deposit interest rates helped push down interest rates in the credit, money, and bond markets, whereas the central bank had to rely more on

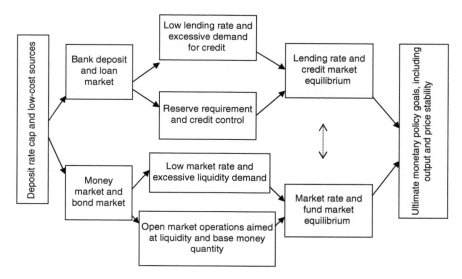

Figure 2-5 Interest rates transmission in the dual-track system

the quantitative monetary policy tools to achieve economic growth and stabilize consumer prices. Under the dual-track system, China's monetary policy transmission had been working both on the regulated track and the market track, and the two interacted with each other. When deposit and lending rates were under regulation, the adjustment of benchmark rates could directly affect the funding cost and further affect the supply of and demand for credit, and the central bank had to use quantitative tools such as the reserve requirement ratio and volume of credit to achieve an equilibrium level of credit. Meanwhile, the central bank aimed to regulate interest rates in the money and bond markets via open market operations so as to adjust supply and demand of capital. Studies (He and Wang, 2012, 2013) have shown that since the banking sector still prevailed in the dual-track system, there were arbitrage opportunities in the fund flow between the credit market and the money and bond markets. In this case, the control on deposit and lending rates and quantitative monetary policy tools had the biggest influence on the interest rates in the latter, while open market operations (including the issuance of central bank bills) had a relatively small effect.

II EMPIRICAL ANALYSIS OF THE RELATIONS BETWEEN BENCHMARK
    DEPOSIT RATES AND MONEY MARKET RATES

Analysis of the dual-track system shows that the ceiling on deposit rates had suppressed interest rates in the money market and had generated excessive liquidity. By studying the relations between regulated deposit rates and money market rates, we aim to examine the transmission mechanism between regulated and market interest rates under the dual-track condition. Here we use Granger causality analysis based on a VAR framework.

In terms of indicators, we choose a one-year deposit rate of financial institutions (Deposit1y) as the indicator of the regulated interest rate and a one-year Shanghai interbank offered rate (Shibor1y) as that of the market interest rate. We take the monthly data of the two rates from January 2007 to December 2014 as our sample. ADF stationary test shows that both Deposit1y and Shibor1y are I (1) series, and according to Sims, Stock, and Watson (1990), if the variables are both integrated of order one and have a co-integration relationship, the variables could be included into the VAR system without model misspecification. Hence, we put Deposit1y and Shibor1y series into VAR and ran a Granger causality test. The SC principles confirmed that the lag intervals for endogenous is 2, that the characteristic root falls inside the unit circle, and the result is robust. The result of the Granger causality test is as seen in Table 2-2.

It should be noted that the benchmark deposit rate is the Granger cause of Shibor 1y, and Shibor1y is not the Granger cause of one-year benchmark deposit rates, which indicates that the regulated deposit rate has an effect on the market rate, but not vice versa.

Based on the theoretical relations between the regulated interest rate and market interest rate, we could set up a structural VAR model; the relation between the structural residual u_t and the unconstrained residual ε_t in decomposition is shown as follows:

$$\begin{pmatrix} \varepsilon_t^{gap} \\ \varepsilon_t^{CPI} \end{pmatrix} = \begin{pmatrix} S_{11} & 0 \\ S_{21} & S_{22} \end{pmatrix} \begin{pmatrix} u_t^{gap} \\ u_t^{CPI} \end{pmatrix}$$

Based on the two variables' structural VAR models and impulse response functions, we find that the one-year Shibor rate responds positively to one unit structural shock of the deposit interest rate, and the maximum response appears after a five-month lag and gradually converges after 15 months; on the contrary, the regulated deposit rates respond very weakly to one unit structural shock of one-year Shibor, and the response hovers around zero and gradually converges

Table 2-2 Granger causality test of regulated and market interest rates

VAR Granger causality/block exogeneity wald tests							
Dependent variable: Deposit1y				*Dependent variable: Shibor1y*			
Excluded	Chi-sq	df	Prob.	Excluded	Chi-sq	df	Prob.
Shibor1y	0.637171	2	0.7272	Deposit1y	102.9722	2	0.0000
All	0.637171	2	0.7272	All	102.9722	2	0.0000

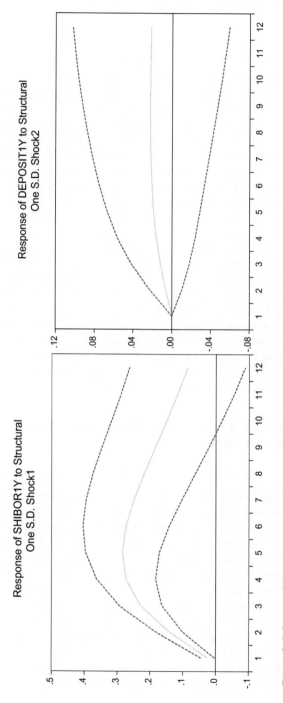

Figure 2-6 Structural impulse response functions of regulated and market interest rates

after 20 months, which further illustrates a definite causal relationship between the two rates.

b   *Effect of market-oriented interest rates on regulated interest rates*

As money market interest rates could be the opportunity cost of credit for some banks, it could have an impact on the loan rates in the banking system. With the expansion of the floating range of loan rates and the ensuing removal of regulation, the impact of money market rates on loan rates had been increasing. From Q4 2006 to Q2 2012, the correlation between overnight Shibor and the weighted average of general loan rates had reached 0.96 (Li, 2012). In 2013, due to high volatility in the money market and a surge of interest rates, many enterprises had to accept higher lending rates, and the proportion of loans with downward floating rates decreased significantly. At that time, the deposit rates could float upwards by 10 percent maximum, but due to hefty issuance of alternatives to bank deposits at market prices, there was an obvious linkage between their yields and money market rates. The expected yield of one month WMP issued in mid- and late June of 2013 increased from 4 percent at the beginning of June to 5.4 percent. Meanwhile, in terms of deposit rates alone, when deposit rates were allowed to float upwards by 10 percent maximum in mid-2012, only small- and medium-sized banks saw upward floating of their deposit rates. However, when money market rates went up in mid-2013, large banks also saw the gradual floating of their deposit rates, which further demonstrated the effect of money market rates on deposit rates. As deposits are an important source of funding for commercial banks, increase of deposit rates would inevitably lead to rising lending rates, strengthening the impact of money market rates on the lending rates of commercial banks.

B   **Transmission mechanism between the benchmark interest rate system and other interest rates**

a   *Market benchmark interest rates and interest rate liberalization*

The market benchmark interest rate system plays a fundamental role in a country's interest rates system as a reference for the pricing of other rates. It mainly consists of short-term money market benchmark rates (currently dominated by the offering rates such as the UK Libor and China's Shibor) and medium- and long-term yield curve of market funds (mainly the treasury yield curve). In the process of interest rate liberalization, in addition to the liberalization of deposit and lending rates, China should also gradually transit to price-based monetary controls, straighten out the interest rate transmission mechanism, establish a deposit insurance system, and develop interest rate risk management tools (Zhou, 2013a). All these financial infrastructure developments cannot be achieved without a benchmark interest rate system. Only a well-recognized market benchmark interest rate system could replace the deposit and lending rates set by the central bank, based on which commercial banks could price their deposits and loans and perform effective risk management. Only by establishing a sound and comprehensive market benchmark interest rate system can the central bank transmit short-term target rates to long-term interest rates to achieve the ultimate goals of monetary policy. As the basis for the pricing of financial products, a comprehensive benchmark interest rate system can help manage interest rate risks, mitigate shocks caused by interest rate liberalization, and prevent systemic financial risks. Meanwhile, with the increasing openness of China's economy and its integration into the global capital market, the benchmark interest rate system can play an important role in making full use of the interest rate parity mechanism, dealing with the impact of short-term international capital flows, promoting domestic economic coordination and the internationalization of RMB.

It should be noted that the development of the benchmark interest rate system is important in many ways: Deepening the market-oriented reform of interest rates, improving monetary policy transmission efficiency and the pricing mechanism of financial products, promoting the innovation of financial products, enhancing risk management of financial institutions, further refining the RMB exchange rate formation mechanism, pushing forward RMB internalization, and sustaining the healthy, stable, and orderly development of the financial system as a whole. China has long lacked a complete system of benchmark yield curves, especially due to the limited variety of short-term bond products, inadequate term structure, and slow development of a money market benchmark interest rate system, which to some extent restricted the progress of interest rate liberalization (Zhou, 2004).

A complete benchmark yield curve consists of money market rates and medium and long-term benchmark rates, among which money market benchmark rates of less than one year are more important. According to the expectation theory of interest rate term structure, there is a long-term equilibrium co-integration relationship (Campbell and Shiller, 1987) between the short-term interest rates and the long-term interest rates, and the shape of the yield curve can reflect the market expectation on inflation and economic growth (Fama, 1990; Estrella and Hardouvelis, 1991). As the basis for pricing of fixed-income products and other products and the reference for monetary policy operations, the development of a money market benchmark interest rate system is of greater significance.

b   The benchmark interest rate system in the financial market and benchmark loan rates

I   SHANGHAI INTERBANK OFFERED RATE (SHIBOR) AS THE MONEY MARKET
    BENCHMARK INTEREST RATE

According to the definition of the market benchmark interest rate, it is supposed to have the following attributes: Representative of the market and benchmarking, is stable and risk-free, has a complete term structure, and is relevant to the real economy. Market representativeness (or liquidness) means that the benchmark rate is formed by major market players actively engaged in market transactions, and there's a high level of correlation between the benchmark rate and other major market interest rates. Benchmark means that the rate plays a key and dominant role in the interest rate system, which could effectively influence other money market rates. Stability (or controllability, immunity to interference) means that the benchmark rate is sensitive to the market but can resist short-term disruptive factors so that the central bank can effectively affect the benchmark rate via monetary policy measures. Risk-free means that theoretically the benchmark rate should have the features of a risk-free rate, as the price of financial products is actually the present discounted value of future cash flows with various uncertainties considered, namely, the risk-free rate. Complete term structure means that the benchmark rate should be a yield curve of full term so that it can serve as the benchmark for the pricing of financial products of all terms. Correlation to the real economy means that the benchmark rate is able to affect macroeconomic variables and help achieve the goals of monetary policy.

Market representativeness and the benchmarking function are the core attributes of the money market benchmark rate. Only a rate determined and accepted by major market players could become a benchmark and used to determine financial flows arising from contractual agreements, price financial products, assess the performance of portfolios, and influence other major money market interest rates.[4] The importance of the other four attributions decreases successively in assessing money market benchmark rates, as they are the extension of the core attributions.

Drawing from international experience, China's money market benchmark rate – Shanghai Interbank Offered Rate (Shibor) – started a trial operation on October 8, 2006, and was officially launched in January 2007. In terms of market representativeness, Shibor was the arithmetic average of interbank interest rates offered independently by a group of banks with high credit rating, transparent disclosure system, and active trading. This group covers state-owned commercial

Table 2-3 Application of Shibor in financial product pricing

	2007	2008	2009	2010	2011	2012	2013	2014
Floating rate bonds	990 (18)	122 (4.6)	728 (19)	552 (13)	1303 (26.5)	n.a.	1793 (59)	n.a.
Short-term financing bonds	1376 (41)	1786 (42)	1272 (28)	2414 (37)	2418 (31)	3888 (46)	4453 (53)	10341 (98)
Corporate bonds	1657 (97)	2347 (100)	4252 (100)	3621 (100)	2499 (100)	6490 (100)	4715 (100)	6892 (100)
Interest rate swap	285 (13)	899.2 (22)	1292.6 (28)	6046.4 (40.3)	12175.6 (45.5)	14513.6 (50)	9056.3 (33.2)	7343.2 (18.2)
Forward rate agreement	11 (100)	114 (100)	60 (100)	34 (100)	3 (100)	2 (100)	0.5 (100)	n.a.

Notes: Unit: 100 million RMB, %
(Number) refers to the share in total transactions

Source: China Monetary Policy Implementation Report

banks, joint-equity commercial banks, urban commercial banks, and foreign banks, and are different in their asset size, business model, and competitiveness, which ensures their offers reflect market liquidity. Data show that these banks have engaged in about 80 percent of money market transactions since 2007,[5] which proves Shibor's strong market representativeness.

Due to common trading practices, currently the pricing of many financial products is based on the pledged repo rate, but Shibor is also widely used in the market-based pricing of financial products. In the first official year after Shibor was launched (2007), over 82 percent of interbank lending and repurchase transactions referenced Shibor, and interest rate swaps, forward rate agreements, and other innovative financial products based on Shibor were traded actively. Moreover, businesses such as discount of bills, transfer discount of bills, and interbank certificates of deposit all established a market-based pricing mechanism with Shibor as the benchmark, and the internal funds transfer pricing of offer banks was also linked to Shibor. Since 2008, the PBOC had signed a total of 1.67 trillion RMB currency swap agreements based on Shibor with central banks of Malaysia and South Korea. At present, pricing based on Shibor has been increasing in the financial market and the relations among various interest rates are becoming more reasonable and clearer. Shibor's status as a benchmark rate in the money market is well established.

Moreover, compared with the interbank rates and the repo rates, Shibor has proven its advantages in terms of risk and term structure. The interbank lending was a kind of credit transaction rather than a risk-free transaction. In 1996 when China Interbank Offered Rate (Chibor) was launched, China wanted it to function as a money market benchmark rate, but Chibor is the weighted average of interbank offered rates based on trading records. It mainly refers to short-term interbank loans less than seven days due to inactivity of transactions of longer terms. The same problem can be found in pledged repo transactions. Though pledged repo with bonds as guarantee carries less credit risk, its many varieties cover treasury bills, financial bonds, mid-term notes, and other bonds with different risk levels, and therefore pledged repo rate is not an entirely risk-free rate. Shibor is a simple interest rate and wholesale interest rate without guarantee and has eight maturities from overnight to one year, forming a complete interest rate curve with smooth features. The offer banks were usually high rating organizations with low credit risks. Though Shibor is based on offered rates and follows the practice of major benchmark rates such as Libor (for example, the banks offer prices at a fixed time of each day, and the final rate is the arithmetic average of all offers excluding the highest and lowest one), Shibor pays a lot of attention to supervision and risk prevention in terms of institutional arrangements, emphasizing the authenticity of offers and introducing third-party evaluation mechanism. Annual assessment is implemented to ensure the quality of offers, with the elimination of the least qualified offer. China's special conditions and institutional arrangements determine that Shibor has unparalleled advantages over Libor. In this regard, Shibor's low risk level and high-quality offers can support its role as a benchmark interest rate (Zhang, 2011).

II   THE MID- AND LONG-TERM BOND YIELD CURVE IS IMPROVING

According to the definition of the yield curve, the market benchmark rate should have a full-term structure. A yield curve covering interest rates of various maturities is needed for the purpose of asset pricing and valuation of derivatives. However, in reality, not all maturities are based on transactions, as most transactions in the money market are concentrated on overnight transactions and rarely on mid- and long-term (three months to one year) transactions. The launch of Libor in the 1980s was mainly to address the problem of pricing of derivatives (Zhang, 2011). Similarly, the market interest rates of mid- and long-term treasury bonds above one year also faced the problem of incomplete term structure. Especially in China, the banks as major players of the money market hold around 70 percent of total treasury bonds, and national banks hold about 80 percent of all banks; thus, the bank transactions have a very big impact on the bond market. Meanwhile, insurance companies and pension funds, which are also the main investors of treasury bonds, usually hold them until maturity rather than selling in the secondary market; they do this for the purpose of long-term financial asset allocation, but it can directly affect the formation of market-based bond prices. Moreover, the European and US markets have a much larger scale of OTC interest rate derivatives than underlying assets;[6] in comparison, China still has a long way to go. In other words, China's bond market (especially the treasury bond market) already has a certain width, but it still needs to go deeper. It is for this reason that the 3rd Plenum of the 18th CPC Central Committee marked the improvement of the treasury bond yield curve as an important agenda.

The treasury bond yield curve serves as the basis for a country's market-based financial system and as the benchmark for the pricing of other kinds of financial assets; it is also an important indicator of economic and financial situation and expectations. As an infrastructure provider to the bond market, the China Central Depository and Clearing Co., Ltd. (the CCDC) is the first to compile and release the RMB treasury bond yield curve, relying on its massive data and close links to the market.

Currently, almost all domestic studies on China's interest rate term structure adopt the NS or NSS polynomial fitting proposed by Nelson and Siegel (1987) and Svensson (1994) to estimate yield curves (Zhu and Chen, 2003; Kang and Wang, 2010). This method works better for relatively mature bond markets in developed countries and is adopted by the central banks of many developed countries.[7] The outliers would reduce the effect of spline fitting, and unusual transactions are largely not studied in domestic research. Practically, it's rather difficult to identify unusual transactions. Methods such as subjective judgment, relative position, and zero-volatility spread can be inaccurate. Though China has made great progress in the institutional development of the bond market in recent years, the market-oriented reform is still at an early stage with many specific transaction arrangements based on consideration of various interests, and thus a yield curve obtained from fitting method might not be ideal.

To ensure the accuracy of the yield curve, the CCDC decided to eliminate abnormal prices exercising subjective judgment. To identify abnormal prices, the CCDC compares the daily clearing prices of each type of bond to the yield curve of the last working day. Clearing prices that deviated from the yield curve and that couldn't be explained by policies of that day or by related financial factors might be deemed abnormal prices. The CCDC also eliminates abnormal prices caused by buyout repo or block trade. For possible defensive offers that might occur in bilateral quoting with higher credibility, the CCDC makes decisions on a case by case basis, taking into consideration factors such as whether the bilateral quoting is continuous and whether the bid–ask spread and yield spread is too large. The CCDC has an advantage in acquiring information and monitoring possible abnormal transactions. In terms of curve construction methods, the CCDC developed in 2006 a new model for constructing the bond yield curve based on Hermite interpolation.

Hermite interpolation is characterized by smoothness, flexibility, and stability. It can reflect all kinds of curves, and a change at certain point will not affect the whole yield curve. Therefore, the Hermite model could be applied to the bond market of less developed countries (which have more abnormal transactions, a big influence on liquidity, and higher volatility). Practically, the Hermite model is suitable for both Chinese and developed markets. For example, the US treasury yield curve is constructed by the Hermite model.[8] Related research show that China's treasury bond yield curve can effectively support the expectation theory and contains large amount of macroeconomic information (Li, 2012; Jiang and Li, 2013). In this regard, it can function as a medium and long-term market benchmark rate, providing necessary conditions for price-based monetary control.

III   SELF-DISCIPLINE MECHANISM FOR MARKET INTEREST RATE PRICING AND LOAN
      PRIME RATE (LPR)

After the control on interest rates is lifted, the pricing ability of financial institutions and a market self-discipline mechanism are crucial to the orderly competition and stability of the financial market. To maintain fair competition and promote healthy development, financial institutions should rely on self-discipline in the money and credit markets under the premise of rules and regulation. Based on the self-discipline mechanism, financial institutions are organized to offer lending rates to their best customers, which work as a reference for the pricing of credit products. It is of great importance to establish a self-discipline mechanism for market rate pricing and a centralized quotation and publishing mechanism for loan prime rates: First, it could effectively encourage financial institutions to strengthen financial constraints and achieve scientific and reasonable pricing; second, the establishment of credit market prime rates can provide a reference to the market-based pricing of credit products; third, it could help further develop the money market, regulate interbank business, and prevent financial risks; fourth, it could strengthen self-discipline on pricing and maintain fair and orderly market competition.

The first batch of financial institutions involved in this self-discipline mechanism included ten commercial banks such as the ICBC. Four special working groups were set up under this self-discipline framework: The due diligence and comprehensive evaluation group, the LPR group, the interbank certificate of deposit group, and the Shibor group. These four groups have played an active role in establishing an LPR quotation mechanism and issuing interbank deposits. In July 2014, another 93 banks joined the self-discipline mechanism, which contributed greatly to the further improvement of product pricing and rate quotation, including Shibor and LPR.

Combining international experience with China's practice, a centralized quote and publish mechanism of LPR was launched in October 2013. The LPR refers to lending rates offered by commercial banks to their best customers; it also serves as the basis for other lending rates. According to the centralized quote and publish mechanism, an authorized publisher will calculate the weighted average of LPRs offered by commercial banks and release it to the public. At the early stage, the published LPR is of one-year maturity.

The National Interbank Funding Center (NIFC) is the designated publisher for LPR, and the first quotation group consists of nine commercial banks. On each work day, the NIFC would exclude the highest and lowest quotations from commercial banks and calculate the weighted average of the valid quotations, and then publish the rate on the Shibor website. The weight is the ratio of each quotation bank's RMB loan balance to the overall balance of all banks at the end of last quarter. The self-discipline mechanism will evaluate the quality of quotations each year to enhance the credibility of LPR.

As an important component of the self-discipline mechanism, the centralized quotation and publish mechanism of LPR helps expand and supplement the Shibor mechanism in the credit market. Currently, the LPR system is operating steadily and its application in the pricing of credit products and derivatives is ever expanding. Statistics show that commercial banks had issued more than 30 billion loans based on LPR, and interest rate swaps based on LPR are also taking off.

c *Transmission mechanism between benchmark interest rate*
   and other interest rates

In a market-based system, the central bank chooses the short-term interest rate as the main policy target and aims to influence the pricing of financial products and the deposit and lending interest rates by adjusting the market benchmark interest rate. This will further change people's investment and consumption behavior and finally help achieve the ultimate policy goals of price stability and economic growth.

In terms of the transmission between the benchmark interest rates and other interest rates, it is achieved by movement in liquidity and valuation. Other interest rates are determined by adding certain term premiums and risk premiums to the benchmark rates based on expectations of future inflation and economic growth as well as risk judgment. The adjustment of benchmark rates can effectively affect liquidity in the financial market and then the prices of fixed-income products and stock products. The changing prices of financial assets can then influence the savings and consumption behavior of people and investment behavior of corporations through the wealth effect, and ultimately influence the real economy. In this way, a complete interest rate transmission chain from the market benchmark yield curve to financial market interest rate (bond and stock prices) and then to consumption and investment (real economy) is formed.

The US and other developed countries with a market-based interest rate system usually price their commercial loans by the prime rate model. The banks offer their prime rate to their best customers based on the risks of financial products and operation cost. The prime rate is linked to the central bank's benchmark interest rate and follows the movement of the policy interest rate target, while other interest rates are determined by adding certain risk and term premiums to the prime rate based on customer credit and product specification. For instance, the prime loan rate offered by the commercial banks in the US is about 300 basis points above the federal fund rate. Given market competition, the US commercial banks seldom adjust their prime rates before the central bank changes its interest rate policy. The determination of deposit rates is similar to that of loan rates, which is determined by the account balance and liquidity of different customers. In this way, a

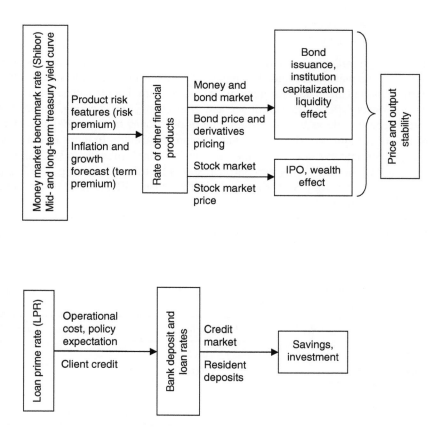

Figure 2-7 Transmission mechanism between the benchmark interest rate and other interest rates

complete monetary policy interest rate transmission chain from the prime rate to deposit and lending rates and then to the real economy and inflation is formed.

It should be noted that the base rates of banks in a market-based system is totally different from the deposit and lending benchmark rates of the central bank in China. Although in October 2014 China had removed the cap on the deposit rates, the benchmark lending rates set by the central bank actually draw up a "quasi loan prime rate curve" for financial institutions, which to some extent restricts the pricing capability of financial institutions on various term premiums. What's more, the rising interest rates may not be able to fully reflect the risks of loans, and thus credit rationing is likely to occur. When the interest rate is fully liberalized, the commercial banks can establish a sound pricing system and achieve the effective allocation of credit resources through the price leverage.

d   *Empirical analysis of the benchmark interest rate transmission mechanism in the financial market*

I   CORRELATION BETWEEN SHIBOR AND OTHER MAJOR TRADING RATES IN THE MONEY MARKET

The money market benchmark interest rate should represent the overall performance of the market. It should be composed of major market players with active participation in the market. In January 2007, China officially launched the Shanghai Interbank Offered Rate (Shibor), and after eight years' running, Shibor has established its role as the benchmark rate in the money market. The movement of Shibor is highly consistent with that of repo and Chibor. In terms of the most traded overnight and seven-day interest rates in China's money market,[9] Shibor, repo, and Chibor are highly correlated. It shows that there's a strong correlation between the seven-day Shibor and repo and interbank offered rates of the same period, and the coefficient is above 0.99.

In terms of institutional arrangements, the central bank has always emphasized regulation and risk prevention. A third-party evaluation mechanism was

Table 2-4 Correlation between overnight and seven-day Shibor and repo and interbank interest rates

Shibor1		*Repo1*	*Chibor1*	*Shibor7*		*Repo7*	*Chibor7*
Shibor1	1			Shibor7	1		
Repo1	0.9998 (494.8)***	1		Repo7	0.9998 (457.9)***	1	
Chibor1	0.9998 (526.8)***	0.9997 (393.0)***	1	Chibor7	0.9969 (123.1)***	0.9969 (122.6)***	1

Note: The sample period was from January 2007 to December 2012, the number in the brackets was t, and *** meant that the Pearson significance level was 1 percent

Table 2-5 Mean and variance equality test between overnight/7-day Shibor and repo/interbank offered rate

		Test method	Degree of freedom	Statistic	p value
Overnight rate	Test for the equality of means	Anova F-test	(2, 285)	0.006877	0.9931
		Welch F-test*	(2, 189.998)	0.006844	0.9932
	Test for the equality of variance	Bartlett	2	0.006258	0.9969
		Levene	(2, 285)	0.001934	0.9981
		Brown-Forsythe	(2, 285)	0.001882	0.9981
Seven-day rate	Test for the equality of means	Anova F-test	(2, 285)	0.1734	0.8409
		Welch F-test*	(2, 189.998)	0.1719	0.8422
	Test for the equality of variance	Bartlett	2	0.0243	0.9879
		Levene	(2, 285)	0.0100	0.9900
		Brown-Forsythe	(2, 285)	0.077	0.9923

Note: The sample period was from January 2007 to December 2014

introduced to ensure the quality of quotations and maximize the effect of money market benchmark interest rates (Zhang, 2011). Theoretically, if the Shibor quote is accurate, then the mean and variance should be the same for the quoted and actual rates. In addition to calculating the correlation of the two, we can also assess how representative the Shibor is of the market rate through the mean and variance analysis. Here, we mainly use variance analysis to construct the F-statistic to test the equality of the mean and variance of the two rates. Figure 2-5 shows that the value of p in the mean and variance test between overnight/seven-day Shibor and repo/interbank interest rate is quite large. Only the *p* value of seven-day Shibor average equality test is close to 0.85, while the rest are all above 0.98, which proves that Shibor can represent the market well.

II EFFECT OF TREASURY BOND YIELD ON CORPORATE BOND YIELD

When the interest rate is fully liberalized, financial institutions can price their products based on the benchmark interest rate, while also taking into consideration factors such as macroeconomic growth, inflation expectation, their own operation costs, and the risk features of the products (customer credit). Due to the lack of necessary data (China only removed regulation on loan rates in recent years), here we try to test the interest rate transmission mechanism by analyzing the correlation between the market benchmark rate and the interest rate of major financial products. We choose the 10-year treasury bond yield (Bond10y) and 10-year AAA level corporate debt yield (Debt10y) for the analysis. The sample period is from March 2006 to December 2014. Similar to the transmission analysis of dual-track interest rates, we use Ganger causality analysis under the VAR framework.

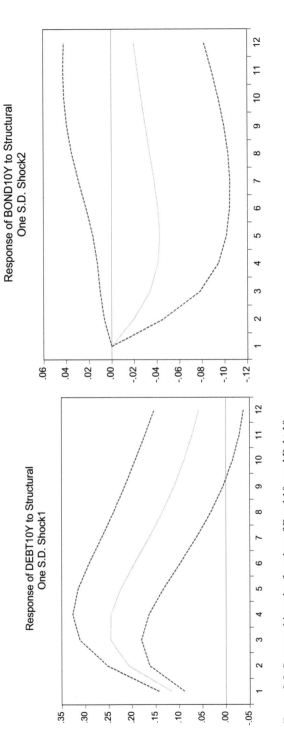

Figure 2-8 Structural impulse function of Bond 10y and Debt 10y

Table 2-6 Granger causality test on Bond 10y and Debt 10y

VAR Granger causality/block exogeneity wald tests							
Dependent variable: Bond10y				Dependent variable: Debt10y			
Excluded	Chi-sq	df	Prob.	Excluded	Chi-sq	df	Prob.
Debt10y	2.489425	2	0.2880	Bond10y	19.78855	2	0.0001
All	2.489425	2	0.2880	All	19.78855	2	0.0001

ADF stationary test shows that the 10-year treasury bond yield and corporate debt yield are both I (1) sequences, and the SC principles confirm that the lag order of VAR is 2, with the characteristic root of VAR falling within the unit circle. After establishing the VAR system, we conduct a Granger causality test on the variables, and the result is as seen in Table 2-6.

It can be noted that the 10-year treasury bond yield is always the Granger cause of 10-year corporate debt yield, but not vice versa, which indicates that the movement of treasury interest rates would significantly influence the movement of corporate bond rates, and that the treasury rate is working as the medium- and long-term benchmark rates in the financial market. Similarly, we construct a VAR model for the treasury interest rate and the corporate bond rate and find that the corporate bond yield always responds positively to one unit structural shock of the treasury yield, and the maximum response appears after a three-month lag and then gradually converges after 20 months. On the contrary, the treasury yield responds weakly and negatively to one unit structural shock of the corporate debt yield, and the effect is around zero and gradually converges after 18 months, which further confirms the causality between the two.

IV   A summary of the characteristics of China's interest rate system

According to the guidelines of gradual reform, the liberalization of the price of financial factors should start from markets with the least impact on resource allocation, based on the principle of minimum risk. In this case, China's reform first started in the foreign exchange market. In terms of RMB interest rate liberalization,

> interest rate regulation and the introduction of interest rate liberalization at the margin made the reform a Pareto improvement, which means it could improve allocation efficiency of financial resources in the banking sector without compromising the interests of the real economy.
>
> (Yi, 2009)

Therefore, during the process of interest rate liberalization, China's interest rate system shows features of a dual-track system: The co-existence of controlled interest rates in the banking system and market-based interest rates outside the banking system. One characteristic of China's dual-track interest rate system is that liberalization is ever expanding while regulation is steadily narrowing its scope.

In terms of interest rate transmission, controlled interest rates and market-based interest rates can influence each other. Past empirical analysis shows that controlled interest rates have a significant impact on market-based interest rates, while the latter only has a weak effect on the former. With the progress of liberalization, market-based interest rates would have an even bigger impact on banks' deposit and loan rates.

With the advancement of financial reform and development, China has currently established an interest rate system with three levels: Central bank interest rates, financial market interest rates, and banks' deposit and loan interest rates. Specifically, central bank interest rates refer to those of monetary policy tools, including open market operation interest rate, rate on required reserve, rate on excess reserve, refinancing interest rate, rediscount rate, and the rate of innovative liquidity management tools (such as the SLF, MLF, and PSL). Financial market interest rates refer to the rates of various financial products in the financial market, including money market interest rates and the medium and long-term interest rates, and money market interest rates include interbank offered rates, interbank bond repo rates, short-term bill market rates, and short-term financing bill rates; the medium and long-term interest rates include bond yield curve and medium-term bill rates. Generally speaking, China has a relatively complete interest rate system with a complicated structure. For example, China's central bank interest rate system is very diversified and complex, and Chinese banks' deposit and loan rates include benchmark rates, loan prime rates, and deposit and loan rates. As China deepens its market-based reform, the interest rate system will take on a clear structure.

In the meantime, the central bank should pave the way for reform and establish a market-based interest rate formation mechanism. On the one hand, the central bank should strengthen the pricing mechanism of financial institutions; on the other hand, it should promote the benchmark interest rate system in the financial market. Currently, the pricing mechanisms of commercial banks include internal fund transfer pricing (FTP) and risk pricing mechanism. With the deepening of interest rate liberalization, domestic banks could strengthen interest rate pricing management, develop interest rate pricing models, set up pricing support systems, and improve pricing management mechanisms.

In terms of benchmark interest rate systems, China has established a system of short-term benchmark interest rates (represented by Shibor) and a system of medium and long-term benchmark interest rates (represented by the treasury bond yield curve). After the deregulation of loan rates, China has established a centralized quotation and publishing mechanism on loan prime rates. So far, the LPR system has been operating steadily and its application in the pricing of credit products and derivatives is expanding. Empirical results show that the movement of market interest rates is consistent with that of benchmark interest rates, and that the spread structure fully reflects the risk structure. However, Shibor's status as the benchmark interest rate has yet to be consolidated, and China has to further improve its financial market to draw up a complete and reasonable yield curve.

On the whole, before the ceiling of deposit rates was removed, China's interest rate level as well as its risk structure and term structure had already been determined largely by market supply and demand. However, interest rates in China are not completely determined by the market, as regulation still prevails and the financial market is underdeveloped. The risk structure and term structure are not as appropriate as expected, and the transmission mechanism is not strong. In this regard, China should aim to enhance the role of the market in interest rate formation and improve the transmission mechanism in the interest rate system.

Notes

1 Annual Report on Banks' Wealth-Management Products in China (2014), China Central Depository & Clearing Co., Ltd. (CCDC), "Information Registry System for Banks' Wealth-Management Products", May 2015.
2 Affected by the "327 Accident" on government bond futures, the exchange market was nearly suspended in the mid-1990s.
3 Based on the classification criteria of the CCDC.
4 The Wheatley Report of Libor: Final Report, www.hm-treasury.gov.uk, September 28, 2012.
5 See "China Monetary Policy Report" and Shibor work conference documents over the years: www.pbc.gov.cn.
6 According to BIS statistics, the turnover of OTC interest rate derivatives at end 2013 was US$584.4 trillion (of which interest rate swaps account for 78.9 percent). Meanwhile, the global bond market was only US$90.9 trillion. At the end of 2013, China's bond market trading reached a historical high of 30.6 trillion RMB, while the maximum turnover of interest rate derivative was only 2.92 trillion RMB in 2012, and most of the trading was interest rate swaps.
7 Except for the US and Japan, most central banks and treasury departments in developed countries use NS or NSS to compile yield curve; see BIS (2005).
8 "Treasury Yield Curve Methodology", Office of Debt Management, Department of the Treasury, www.treasury.gov/resource-center/data-chart-center/interest-rates/Pages/yieldmethod.aspx, February 26, 2009.
9 From 2007 to 2014, overnight and seven-day pledged repo accounts for 52.2 percent, 63.9 percent, 77.8 percent, 80.0 percent, 75.4 percent, 81.2 percent, 79.1 percent, 78.6 percent and 35.9 percent, 26.7 percent, 15.4 percent, 14.3 percent, 16.2 percent, 12.6 percent, 12.9 percent, 14.1 percent, respectively, of the total transactions. Overnight and seven-day borrowing accounts for 75.4 percent, 70.8 percent, 83.5 percent, 87.9 percent, 81.7 percent, 86.2 percent, 81.5 percent, 78.2 percent and 20.5 percent, 23.3 percent, 11.0 percent, 8.7 percent, 12.7 percent, 8.9 percent, 12.4 percent, 16.2 percent. Overnight and seven-day are the two most-traded maturities in China's money market.

3 Central bank interest rate adjustment over the course of market-based interest rate reform

It is generally believed that interest rate liberalization means the market determines interest rates. However, interest rates are not the price of ordinary commodities, but the price of money. Under the modern credit and central banking system, the central banks are, in theory, able to directly determine interest rates. In practice, whether under a controlled or a market-based interest rate system, central banks may influence or even directly determine the formation and level of real interest rates. In this sense, market-based interest rates should be more properly defined as jointly decided by central bank policies and market forces (He and Wang, 2013). Accordingly, interest rate reform in China has two dimensions. First, to establish a market-based interest rate formation mechanism. The types, terms, and levels of interest rates are no longer stipulated by monetary authorities; instead, they are decided by the demand and supply of financial assets based on market conditions. Second, to establish a market-based interest rate adjustment and control mechanism. Instead of resorting to administrative controls, the central bank adjusts its own balance sheet and benchmark interest rates to influence market rates. China's interest rate reform sets its theme on relaxing control, forming prices, and adjusting rates. The first two emphasize liberalizing the rate formation mechanism and the last emphasizes liberalizing controls by the central bank. Compared with the reforms in relaxing control and forming prices, the liberalizing of central bank controls has lagged behind and still has a long way to go. While liberalizing deposit and lending rates, if the PBOC can set sound and credible policy rates as the prime reference for market pricing, it can then adjust interest rates in the money market and bond yields, and influence deposit and lending rates and the prices of other financial products. Currently, with the deepening of reforms, interest rates are increasingly determined by market forces, which require the central bank to set up policy rates as benchmarks for market pricing. Financial innovation also requires that the central bank improve its interest rate adjustment mechanism. Therefore, how to set up an effective interest rate adjustment mechanism is a pressing issue for the current round of reform.

I Overview of the history of interest rate adjustment and control

From the establishment of the PRC in 1949 to the introduction of reform and opening-up, China adopted a highly centralized planned economy. Economic operation was decided by national plans and budget management. Bank credit took a subordinate position. Administrative measures, including general credit plan, cash planning, and cash control, were used to cap cash and credit volume so as to boost the economy and ensure market supply. As a result, the interest rate was not used as a financial leverage. Some people even regarded high rates as means to acquire surplus product and encourage income without work. Therefore, strict interest rate control was adopted. The interest rates had fewer classifications and were set at low levels with small spreads, and the management was highly centralized. While turning to a market economy and establishing a system of modern macroeconomic policies, China has also standardized its financial management and improved its financial operation. The interest rate plays an increasingly important role in macro-level regulation and monetary policy. The PBOC also pays closer attention to the interest rate adjustment mechanism.

Since 1949, China has developed its economy, started interest rate liberalization, and adopted different interest rate policies. Seen from these three aspects, China's interest rate adjustment includes four distinctive periods: The planned economy period, the period of direct credit control after the reform and opening-up, the period of indirect control mainly of money supply, and the period of transitioning to a price-based monetary policy.

A   The planned economy period

From the establishment of the PRC to the introduction of reform and opening-up, China adopted a highly centralized planned economy. Interest rate control was an integral part of the plans for social production, circulation, and distribution. The interest rate was determined by the State Council and administered by the PBOC. The interest rate system featured few classifications, low rate level, small spread, and highly centralized management. Changes of interest rate policies at this stage are as seen in Table 3-1.

The influence of interest rate policies was limited by the highly centralized planned economy. The leveraging effect of interest rates was weakened or even denied. Meanwhile, interest rate management was rigid, lacking flexible adjustment. As microeconomic activities were not sensitive to interest rate changes, interest rate elasticity was extremely low.

B   The period of direct credit control after the reform and opening-up (1978–1998)

In the first few years of the reform and opening-up, interest rate adjustment mainly aimed at stabilizing bank deposits and limiting enterprises' needs for funds. The goal, to a large extent, was to stabilize deposit volumes against inflation. Also, interest rate adjustment was an important measure for the PBOC to control inflation and was often used to complement direct control measures. Therefore, interest rate adjustment became the PBOC's only tool of indirect control. At this stage, the PBOC controlled interest rates mainly through direct adjustment of the deposit and lending rates. The PBOC emphasized the distribution of interest rates among

Table 3-1 Changes in interest rate policy (1949 to 1978)

Time	Interest rate policies	Description/influence
1949–1952 Recovery of national economy	1 April 1949: The PBOC issued the *Tentative Regulation on Current and Term Deposits* 2 March 1950: The PBOC issued the *Instruction on Adjusting Market Price and the Interest Rate of April*, requiring its branches to give due play to interest rate without violating general economic principles 3 1951: Interest rate policy should aim at raising fund, adjusting credit, curbing speculation, and boosting production 4 June 1952: The PBOC issued the *Instruction on Lowering within a Time Limit the Deposit and Lending Rates for Both the Public and Private Sector*, cutting overall interest rates and unifying all rates for Inner China	Adopting interest rate policies for standardized management
1953–1957 The first five-year plan	1 Significantly lowered deposit and lending rates 2 Simplified interest rate classification	1 Promoting socialist transformation of private businesses 2 Promoting the integration of agricultural and individual, handicraft production; improving enterprises' fund use
1958–1966 The "Great Leap Forward" and subsequent adjustment of the economy	1 During the "Great Leap Forward", the law of value was neglected, the interest rate was adjusted downward and the leveraging effect was weakened 2 During the economic adjustment, interest rate policies were rarely resorted to	Neglected and weakened the financial leveraging role of interest rate
1966–1977 The Cultural Revolution	1 Interest rates were considered bourgeois rights 2 Interest rate level was even lower 3 Spread between deposit and lending rates further narrowed 4 Classifications diminished 5 The leveraging effect was denied	

depositors, banks, enterprises, and state authorities and did not aim at adjusting the money supply, prices, and output. Interest rate policies lagged behind economic development.

As the reform and opening-up deepens, China has made much progress with interest rate policy and management. For example, China has determined principles for interest rate regulation, expanded accruable deposits, added interest rate classifications, introduced a floating rate system, and offered a reference for the commercial bank rate, financial institutional rate, and interbank offered rate. At this stage, interest rate policies still faced difficulties including lagging adjustment, overreaching management, little independence of commercial banks, deviation of the interest rate from the value of funds, and stagnant liberalization.

C   The period of indirect control mainly with quantitative measures (1998–2002)

In 1996, China set appropriate money supply as the intermediate target of its monetary policy. In 1998, China lifted the cap on the total credit of commercial banks solely funded by the state. Therefore, the status of appropriate money supply as the intermediate target was further enhanced. At the same time, China restructured and improved its monetary policy toolkit: Instead of relying on direct control, China mainly relied on indirect measures. At that time, the financial market was at its preliminary stage and the liberalization of financial pricing remained stagnant; the credit mechanism played an essential role in the transmission of monetary policy and the interest rate transmission was blocked. Against this backdrop, China mainly took quantitative measures in undertaking its monetary policy. It focused on the intermediate target of appropriate money supply and undertook open market operations and other measures for liquidity adjustment. Meanwhile, policymakers attached great importance to the leveraging effect of the interest rates. Quantitative and price adjustments interact with each other: Price pass-through may be blocked if money supply is beyond a reasonable range; likewise, quantitative tools may be less effective without consideration of the price. Therefore, at the preliminary stage of indirect monetary policy, the PBOC gave full play to interest rate adjustment while relying heavily on quantitative tools (Zhou, 2006). On one hand, interest rate policy played a more important role in macro-control; on the

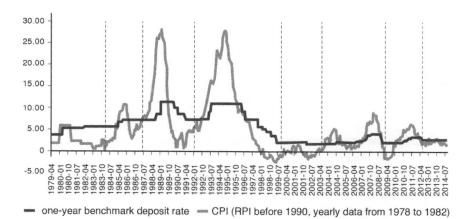

— one-year benchmark deposit rate   — CPI (RPI before 1990, yearly data from 1978 to 1982)

Figure 3-1 One-year benchmark deposit rate and inflation (%)

Source: CEIC

other hand, interest rate liberalization was steadily pushed forward. Interest rate control was further relaxed and the financial market became more sophisticated. With the improved management system, interest rates were given full play in the process of macro-control.

Since then, the PBOC has turned to a dual-track approach in interest rate adjustment. On one hand, PBOC adjusts interest rates directly by changing benchmark rates and their floating ranges for deposit and lending; on the other hand, it uses open market operations (repo, reverse repo, central bank bills) and monetary policy instruments (i.e. reserve requirement) to adjust liquidity and influence interest rate indirectly.

Overall, indirect adjustment by monetary policy instruments aims mainly to stabilize money market rates, while the adjustment of deposit and lending rates have counter-cyclical targets and should be kept in line with monetary policies. As the market economy becomes more sophisticated, the mechanism of deposit and lending rate adjustment keeps improving. Take the one-year benchmark deposit rate as an example. Since the reform and opening-up, this rate has gone through eight cycles of adjustment. The adjustment was undertaken against rises and falls in inflation and in line with the PBOC's responsibility of stabilizing market prices and boosting growth. The adjustment has become more frequent, fine-tuned, and flexible than before the transition to indirect adjustment in 1998.

Table 3-2 covers the duration of each cycle and the margin and frequency of rate changes. Seen from these aspects, influenced by the deflation after the Asian financial crisis, China's interest rate policies after June 1999 focused on stimulating consumption and investment. Therefore, the interest rate was adjusted to the lowest level since the reform and opening-up period. Between June 1996 and February 2002, the interest rate has been cut every 16 months, with an average margin of decrease of 0.9 percentage points. After that, as the economy showed an upward trend, the interest rate was raised 8 times, with an average margin of increase of only 0.3 percentage points. Since 2010, the average increase/decrease margin of the benchmark deposit rate has been further lowered to 0.25 percentage points. As a result, the margin of interest rate adjustment in China has become more in line with international convention. As shown in Table 3-2, after 1998, interest rate adjustment featured decreased margins and increased frequency. Therefore, after the transition to indirect adjustment, the PBOC paid more attention to the expectation of market players and fully used the price signal to guide the market.

D The period of transitioning to a price-based monetary policy (2013 till now)

In July 2013, China completely lifted the lending rate control and accordingly changed the mechanism of interest rate adjustment. The PBOC still determines and releases benchmark deposit and lending rates. However, as lending rates have been liberalized, the PBOC's direct control has been weakened. Under these circumstances, the PBOC tried to establish a self-discipline mechanism of market pricing and introduced a unified quotation and release mechanism for loan prime rates (LPR).

Table 3-2 Changes in interest rate policy after the reform and opening-up

Cycle	Duration	Active interest rate adjustment	One-year benchmark deposit rate (%)	Margin of increase (percentage point)	Margin of decrease (percentage point)	Times of increase	Times of decrease	Average margin of increase/decrease (percentage point)
1	1979–1982	1979.4–1982.4	3.24–5.76	2.52		3		0.84
2	1983–1986	1985.4–1985.8	5.76–7.2	1.44		2		0.72
3	1987–1991	1988.9–1989.2/ 1990.3–1991.4	7.2–11.34–7.56	4.14	3.78	2	3	1.58
4	1992–1998	1993.5–1993.7/ 1996.4–1998.12	7.56–10.98–3.78	3.42	7.2	2	6	1.33
5	1999–2002	1999.6–2002.2	3.78–1.98		1.8		2	0.90
6	2003–2007	2004.10–2007.12	1.98–4.41	2.43		8		0.30
7	2008–2011	2008.10–2008.12/ 2010.12–2011.7	4.14–2.25–3.5	1.25	2.16	5	4	0.38
8	2012–now	2012.6–2015.5	3.5–2.25		1.25		5	0.25

Based on market conditions, the PBOC now keeps reforming relevant mechanisms while undertaking effective control. Faced with mounting downward pressure on economic growth and subdued inflation pressure, the PBOC cut the interest rate six consecutive times between November 2014 and October 2015. It expanded the floating range of deposit rates three times and eventually lifted the cap on deposit rates. The PBOC aims to improve the market-oriented formation mechanism of interest rates, give full play to interest rates in leveraging resources, and release market vitality. Therefore, PBOC's interest rate policies can help with economic stability, structural adjustment, and people's well-being.

The removal of a deposit rate cap in October 2015 further weakened the PBOC's direct control on deposit and loan rates. China's interest rate adjustment now enters a new stage in which market-oriented monetary policy instruments and transmission mechanisms play a larger role. The PBOC will establish a policy framework to guide and adjust market rates. In this way, the PBOC can guide all market rates, including prime rates and yield curves, to achieve monetary policy objectives. Specifically, for short-term interest rates, the PBOC will use short-term repo rates and Standing Lending Facility (SLF) rates to nurture and guide market rates; for medium- to long-term rates, the PBOC will use central bank lending, Medium-term Lending Facility (MLF), and Pledged Supplementary Lending (PSL) to adjust medium- to long-term liquidity. It will also use the medium-term policy rate to guide the market and stabilize medium- and long-term rates.

II   The urgency of improving the central bank's interest rate adjustment mechanism

A   *Deepening the market-based reform requires transforming monetary policies*

If the economic and financial structure remains stable, the relationship between monetary policy indicators and major macroeconomic variables is stable. In this case, taking quantitative measures based on economic and financial conditions can be effective in realizing the objectives of macro-control. In a planned economy, quantitative measures are emphasized and supply and demand are balanced with quantitative targets. For the financial sector, plan and control of total credit is necessary. Therefore, quantitative monetary policy instruments show the mindset of a planned economy. Meanwhile, if incentive and self-discipline mechanisms for market players are not yet established, price-oriented measures are usually less effective than quantitative adjustment. After the cap on total credit was lifted in 1998, China mainly resorted to quantitative and indirect measures to undertake monetary policies. This was consistent with the specific stage of economic and financial development and economic transition. In the initial years after the transition to the indirect approach, quantitative monetary adjustments produced satisfying results.

Quantitative adjustments require that the relationship between economic variables remain stable or, in other words, the situation described in the "Lucas

Critique" be avoided. However, quantitative adjustments inevitably affect price levels and may lead to price distortions. As a result, monetary policy adjustment inevitably faces the time inconsistency of policies, which hampers economic stability. Over-emphasizing quantitative measures while overlooking price mechanisms would only harm the effectiveness of monetary policy. In China, economic imbalance has existed for a long time, and since 2003 both balance of payments surplus and foreign exchange reserve have increased rapidly. As a result, sterilization has become less effective. With low consumption and high investment, credit demand remains high. Quantitative adjustments become less effective and may easily lead to administrative interventions at specific junctures. Administrative interventions may result in macroeconomic volatilities as they usually overlook individual conditions and cause sudden changes.

Under price guidance, unlike under quantitative control, market players adjust their own behavior according to macroeconomic signals, which is conducive to minimizing the adverse effects of macro-control. Market rates include a risk premium that reflect structural factors, which is conducive to establishing a mechanism for competition, optimizing resource allocation, promoting structural adjustment, and maintaining balanced growth. As interest rates are a core variable of financial factor pricing, only with an effective interest rate system can effective resource allocation be realized. Paying more attention to the price factor is also essential to the market-oriented reform of monetary policy. Only when the interest rate system is fully liberalized can the market-oriented financial reform be considered complete. While the market plays a decisive role in allocating financial resources, monetary authorities use the policy interest rate as a price instrument to make adjustment in the financial system. In this way, the government can play a better role in financial adjustment.

B Financial innovation requires improving the PBOC's interest rate adjustment

As interest rate liberalization progresses, in recent years, financial innovations such as the wealth-management products of banks have grown rapidly. Financial disintermediation aimed at circumventing interest rate control has become very common (Song, 2009). The limits of traditional quantitative measures have become more evident. Just like in developed countries, with the increase of new financial instruments and products, the products become highly substitutable and the boundary is further blurred between trading and investment accounts and between broad money and narrow money. Therefore, traditional quantitative measures become less effective. On one hand, financial innovation and disintermediation aimed at circumventing interest rate control make the financial sector a more inter-dependent system and liability management a more common practice. The products and structure of the financial market become more sophisticated and the money demand function becomes increasingly unstable. Even when money supply is kept at a specific level, the correlation between money aggregates and output prices still remains volatile (Goodhart, 1986). On the other hand, because of financial innovation and disintermediation, massive capital leaves traditional depository institutions (i.e. banks) and enters directly into the financial market through direct fundraising (i.e. money market funds). As a result, the credit creation mechanism, which was previously intermediated by bank deposits, becomes more complicated than ever. The marginal effects of money multipliers are further magnified. Even if central banks can effectively control base money, they face mounting difficulties in controlling broad money aggregates (Li and Su, 2017).

Against the background of financial innovation and disintermediation, relying on quantitative measures (i.e. reserve requirement) has more evident negative effects. Unstable demand for money and liquidity may easily magnify the impact of quantitative measures on market positions and short-term interest rates. Banks and other financial institutions try harder to innovate in order to evade high reserve requirements, which in turn weakens the effectiveness of quantitative monetary policy. Therefore, while adjusting monetary supply targets, many developed countries have to revise the method of gathering and releasing money statistics. For example, from 1971 to 1986, the Federal Reserve changed the measures of money supply six times; from 1970 to 1984, the Bank of England changed the measures of money supply nine times. Similarly, in October 2011, the PBOC incorporated savings of non-depository institutions and the provident fund into the M2 classification when gathering financial statistics, aiming to boost the performance of quantitative adjustments. However, changing the measures of money statistics is similar to evaluating the economy with an ever-changing standard. Such changes do not help with the effort to understand economic conditions and adopt appropriate policies; they also damage the credibility of central bank policies. At the same time, broadening the coverage of money measures faces difficulties. Statistics are not easily available as the information held by securities firms, insurance companies, and other financial institutions is limited and fragmented. For example, securities investment funds do not have the information on the classification and the holders' structure, while capital for insurance companies does not have the information on their investors' structure. In practice, these institutions can only rely on estimation based on different algorithms. In addition, many statistics are not gathered in a timely manner or released frequently. As a result, relevant indicators become less valuable in understanding economic trends, adding to the difficulties of understanding the relationship between microeconomic indicators and macroeconomic ones like growth and inflation rate.

C   Interest rate liberalization requires that relevant mechanisms of interest rate adjustment further improve

Market-based interest rate liberalization requires changes of both the interest rate formation mechanism and the adjustment mechanism, The former means varieties of interest rates, term, and level shall be determined by the supply and demand sides according to the financial market; the latter means that the central bank's adjustment in the interest rate system shall be through the adjustment of its own balance sheet and the benchmark interest rate instead of through issuing administrative provisions. With the relaxation of interest rate control and the improvement of financial market infrastructure, the interest rate formation mechanism has largely been liberalized. This development poses challenges to the previous dual-track approach and calls for the central bank to improve adjustment mechanisms and turn to a more indirect approach.

The PBOC is exerting an ever-increasing influence on market rates through monetary policy tools. In recent years, while paying attention to liquidity in the quantitative dimension, the PBOC has been strengthening its guidance on market interest rates. In monetary policy reports and announcements of PBOC's monetary policy committee such language as "adjusting liquidity in a timely manner based on economic and financial developments so as to maintain the stability of market interest rates" often appears. Both liquidity adjustment facilities and policy rates of central bank bills and repos are exerting an increasing influence on market rates. Xiang Weixing and Li Hongjin (2014) analyzed the PBOC's open market operations and conducted the Granger causality test. They pointed out that the stated rate of central bank bills has some features of a benchmark rate. Liang, Zhang, and Guo (2010) performed a Granger test based on a Vector Error Correction Model (VECM) and argued that the stated rate of central bank bills play a critical role in influencing market rates and that the position of Shibor as the prime rate still needs to be enhanced. Yao Yudong and Tan Haiming (2011) reached similar conclusions using theoretical model analysis, Granger test, and variance decomposition of forecast errors. He Dong and Wang Honglin (2011) affirmed the influence of both the stated rate of central bank bills and the reserve requirement ratios on money market rates.

In China, interest rates of banks and in the financial market are on two different tracks, and the wholesale funding market has little influence on the prices in the retail funding market. As a result, the transmission of money market rates to deposit and lending rates is not obvious. For example, in the past two years, faced with mounting downward pressure in the overall economy and market price and high financing cost of small and medium-sized enterprises, the PBOC has maintained an appropriate level of liquidity in the banking system. Although interbank rates dropped considerably, bank deposit and lending rates only dropped slightly.

Meanwhile, although changes in benchmark deposit and lending rates directly influence the fundraising entities, the impacts have also been diminishing in recent years. On one hand, commercial banks enjoy more autonomy as the cap on lending rates is lifted and the floating range of deposit and lending rates has widened. On the other hand, the influence of direct control has been narrowed. Changing the deposit and loan benchmark rates can only cover banks' deposits and loans. Relevant measures have little influence on off-balance-sheet financing and fundraising in the bond or stock markets. However, off-balance-sheet financing and the bond market have been developing rapidly in recent years and the proportion of bank loans in total social financing has been diminishing. Therefore, the influence of direct interest rate adjustments has been squeezed. Meanwhile, rate adjustments cannot be transmitted to the whole economy as the interest rate system is not effective or sufficiently integrated. Banks and other financial intermediaries can evade central bank adjustment by developing off-balance-sheet financing. Such practices counter-balance macro-control measures and weaken their effect. Therefore, for the interest rate reform, improving the PBOC's adjustment mechanism is the key priority.

D   Adopting price-based adjustment can help the PBOC communicate with the public, guide market expectation, and improve the transparency and effectiveness of monetary policies

Triggered by the rational expectations theory in the 1970s, central banks around the world became aware that communicating with the public and improving policy transparency are important for more effective implementation of monetary policies (Woodford, 2005; Blinder et al., 2008). Only with communication and transparency can central banks effectively guide market expectation and maximize the effects of their policies. Starting from the mid-1980s, major economies entered into an era of Great Moderation (Bernanke, 2004) that features high growth and low inflation. This era emerged for many reasons. However, an essential factor was that central banks, while adopting rational and principled monetary policies, heeded market players' expectations, communicated effectively with the public, and improved policy transparency (Gali and Gambetti, 2009). On the contrary, central banks such as the Federal Reserve were distracted by incidents like 9–11 and the Iraq War and had to align to complex rules and regulations. Since 2001, these central banks have turned to discretionary decision-making, which hampered policy transparency, consistency, and credibility. As a result, the global financial crisis occurred (Taylor, 2012).

While streamlining decision-making, improving disclosure, and strengthening expectation guidance, central banks are paying more attention to interest rate adjustment, an important monetary policy instrument. People generally are more concerned with current and future prices than with money aggregates (Barro, 1986). Information on prices is more transparent and easily measurable, while information on money aggregates usually has a time lag. Quantitative variables are also less controllable. Empirical studies also demonstrate that in the US money aggregates play an unsatisfying role when considered as an economic variable and monetary policy reference and instrument. Similar results have been obtained from M3 data of Germany. Moreover, comprehensive interest rate policies play an important role in smoothing income fluctuations, while policies emphasizing only money aggregates do not have similar effects (Estrella and Mishkin, 1997).

III   Interest rate adjustment of central banks around the world

A   A common practice is establishing policy rates and corresponding adjustment mechanisms

As traditional Keynesian demand management triggered stagnation, central banks started to use the interest rate as a policy instrument to adjust money supply and base money. In recent years, the financial market has developed rapidly and progress in payment and trading technologies has driven forward financial innovations. Against this background, the correlation between quantitative indicators and economic growth has weakened and traditional money multipliers have become increasingly unstable. Consequently, quantitative adjustments of reserve requirements and money supply faded as monetarism failed to produce expected results. Central banks in major developed countries gained wide success in stabilizing inflation and output by announcing policy interest rates and adjusting market rates according to policy targets through certain mechanisms (Laurens, 2005). For example, when the US turned from the quantitative control over base money to policy rate adjustment in the mid-1980s, it had just liberalized its deposit rates and witnessed a rapid growth of financial innovations, including money market funds. Shocks to monetary policy came more from interest rate fluctuations in the financial market than from the changes in aggregate demand in the traditional sense. On one hand, rapid growth of money market funds has rendered demand for base money and funds unstable; on the other hand, the substitution of money market funds for deposits and the relaxation of deposit rate control have made money creation channels more complicated and the money multiplier and money supply less stable. Moreover, long-term financing in the bond market and through mortgages has increased dramatically. Interest rate changes become more frequent and easily transmitted among rates of different terms. It is natural for central banks to prioritize interest rate adjustment over other traditional monetary policy instruments.

Table 3-3 Central bank policy interest rates in major countries

Type of central bank policy rate	Central bank	Central bank policy rate
Central bank target rate	Federal Reserve	Federal funds rate
	Bank of Japan	Uncollateralized overnight call rate
	Reserve Bank of Australia	Cash rate target
	Bank of Canada	Overnight rate target
	Bank of Korea	Uncollateralized overnight call rate
	Central Bank of Brazil	Overnight interbank rate on mortgage-backed government bonds
Central bank operation rate	European Central Bank	Main refinancing rate
	Bank of England	Official bank rate
	Swedish National Bank	Repo rate
	Bank of Russia	Refinancing rate
	Reserve Bank of India	Repo and reverse repo rate
	South Africa Reserve Bank	Repo rate
Market prime rate	Swiss National Bank	Target range for 3-month LIBOR CHF

Source: Public information

Specifically, central banks consider two things when deciding the policy rate: The conditions on the financial market and how they react to short-term economic volatilities. The policy rate could be a central bank target rate (corresponding to monetary policy targets) or a central bank operational rate (corresponding to monetary policy instruments). The policy rate can also be a market prime rate. For example, the federal funds rate of the Federal Reserve and the overnight interbank rate (Selic) of the Central Bank of Brazil are target rates; the refinancing rate of the European Central Bank and the repo rate or reverse repo rate of the Reserve Bank of India are operational rates. In countries where interest rate liberalization has yet to be completed, the policy rate could even be the long-term deposit and lending rates of commercial banks (which are in fact the intermediate targets of these countries' monetary policies). For example, one-year deposit and lending rates are viewed as China's policy rates. In addition, central banks set different benchmark rates at different times. For example, after gaining autonomy in formulating interest rate policy in 1997, the Bank of England made the short-term repo rate the benchmark rate; but after 2006, Britain's official rate changed to the rate on the voluntary reserve of financial institutions at the central bank.

B   Approaches of developed countries to interest rate adjustment

Since the 1990s, many central banks refocused their approaches to adjusting short-term interest rates. However, instead of taking the Keynesian approach, central banks started to prioritize market expectation and policies' predictability, transparency, and credibility. Taylor's Rule (Taylor, 1993) is a well-known description of the principles of interest rate adjustment. With the development of theories like rational expectations and dynamic inconsistency, central banks started to realize that principled monetary policies are essential. Since the 1990s, central banks have set short-term interest rate targets based on the ultimate objectives of their monetary policy (inflation and output). In pursuing the ultimate objectives of their monetary policy, central banks closely observe market expectation and improve decision-making; they disclose information on monetary policy in a timely manner to enhance communication with the market; they issue open statements to help the public better understand their policies and to guide market expectation. Central banks close the gap between market rates and the target rates mainly through open market operations or the interest rate corridor. We will take the Federal Reserve and the European Central Bank as examples.

a   Federal Reserve's approach: open market operations

In the mid-1980s, after giving up money supply targets, the Federal Reserve started to focus on market interest rates. In 1994, the Federal Reserve officially established a monetary policy framework with the federal funds rate as its target. In this policy framework, the Federal Open Market Committee (FOMC) is the decision-making body, responsible for formulating monetary policies and guiding and supervising open market operations. The committee consists of 12 members –

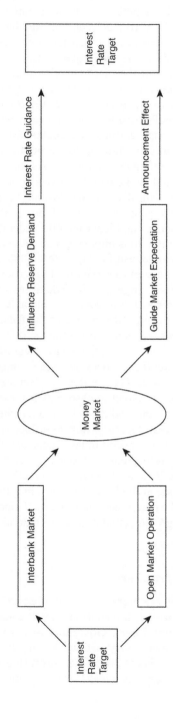

Figure 3-2 The Federal Reserve's open market operations

the seven members of the Board of Governors of the Federal Reserve System and the five Federal Reserve Bank presidents. Board members and the president of the Federal Reserve Bank of New York are standing members; four of the remaining 11 Reserve Bank presidents serve one-year terms on a rotating basis. FOMC members meet about every six weeks and make decisions on whether to change the federal funds rate. They will then issue a brief statement. On these meetings, the Federal Reserve announces their preference for future rate changes and reveals economic conditions to the market in advance. Such announcements are considered the forecast of the Federal Reserve monetary policies. The Chairperson appears before Congressional hearings on a regular basis and relevant officials speak on various occasions to communicate to the public the Federal Reserve's understanding of economic conditions and the reasons for its policies. Therefore, the market can fully understand the Federal Reserve's policy intentions.

Specifically, since the 1980s, the discount window has been less effective and is now only an instrument of emergency assistance of the central banks. In 2003, the Federal Reserve set the discount rate higher than the federal overnight interbank repo rate (the federal funds rate), thus imposing a *de facto* cap on money market rates. But there was no formal deposit facility before 2008. As the largest player in the interbank market, the Federal Reserve mainly focuses on the federal funds rate in realizing monetary policy targets. If the federal repo rate is lower than the market rates, banks would borrow funds from the Federal Reserve and the market repo rate would drop. If the Federal Reserve raises the federal repo rate, the scenarios under different market conditions are as follows: If the market faces money shortage, the federal funds rate itself faces upward pressure and will rise along with the repo rate; if the market faces money surplus, commercial banks will borrow from other banks instead of the Federal Reserve. But the Federal Reserve can sell treasury bonds on the open market to absorb banks' excessive reserve. As a result, banks face strained positions and the federal funds rate and the federal repo rate rise in lockstep. The Federal Reserve is able to influence market rates and has undertaken similar operations for several times. Therefore, the market now has a rational expectation. As long as the Federal Reserve raises the repo rate, the whole market will respond and the Federal Reserve can directly announce changes of the federal funds rate. The federal funds rate thus becomes the bridge between the Fed's monetary policy and the macro-economy. Through open market operations, the Federal Reserve can align the actual and target federal fund rates to realize monetary policy objectives.

b   ECB's approach: interest rate corridor

The Governing Council is ECB's highest decision-making body and is responsible for determining the eurozone's monetary policy. It consists of six Executive Board members and the central bank Governors of euro area countries. The Governing Council used to meet every two weeks and discuss the interest rate issue at every other meeting. Since 2015, the Governing Council has held its monetary policy meeting every six weeks. Each member of the Governing

Council had one vote and a simple majority was required for decision-making. When the vote was tied, the ECB president had the final say. Since Lithuania joined the euro area in 2015, a rotation of voting rights has been adopted within the Governing Council: Six Executive Board members enjoy permanent voting rights, while the central bank Governors take turns using the rights on a monthly rotation. Countries in the eurozone are divided into groups according to the size of their economies and their financial sectors. The Governors from countries ranked first to fifth – currently, Germany, France, Italy, Spain, and the Netherlands – share four voting rights. All others (14 since Lithuania joined on January 1, 2015) share 11 voting rights. After monetary policy meetings, the President of the Governing Council will hold a press conference and explain the Council's decisions. The Economic Bulletin (formerly Monthly Bulletin) presents the economic and monetary information which forms the basis for the Governing Council's policy decisions; it also includes analytical papers on monetary policy. The President, Vice-Presidents, and other officials of the ECB communicate with the public on various occasions to explain ECB's monetary policy strategy and analytical framework.

Unlike the US Federal Reserve, the ECB does not have an official interest rate target. The ECB sends policy signals through refinancing operations and its Governing Council meets on a regular basis to discuss refinancing rate levels. Therefore, the refinancing rate acts like the ECB's benchmark rate. In open market operations, the ECB's main focus is on short-term refinancing. However, the ECB's marginal lending facility and deposit facility and the subsequent interest rate corridor play a more important part in guiding money market rates. The ECB requires credit institutions established in the eurozone to hold "minimum" or "required" reserves. The Euro system offers credit institutions standing facilities. Under the margin lending facility, a credit institution can obtain funds at a higher rate from the central bank should it fail to meet the minimum reserve requirement by the end of the day, the higher rate being the cap for overnight rates; under the deposit facility, a credit institution can deposit its surplus position with the central bank and get corresponding interest at a rate lower than market overnight rates, this lower rate being the floor of overnight rates. An interest rate corridor is thus established and overnight rates are kept within the range of this corridor. A commercial bank is required to keep its account balanced by end-of-day clearance; in the case of a deficit, it has to avail itself of central bank loans, and in the case of a surplus, it automatically deposits the surplus in the central bank and gets interest accordingly. Under this arrangement, central banks can achieve interest rate targets by influencing commercial banks' liquidity. Commercial banks will not borrow money from the market at a higher overnight rate if they can get central bank loans at a given rate (the cap for overnight rates). Likewise, commercial banks will not lend money at a lower rate if they can deposit their surplus reserve at a given deposit rate (the floor for overnight rate) with the central bank. The possibility for interbank arbitrage is nearly zero. Therefore, overnight rates are kept within the rate corridor set by the central bank and the upper and lower limits are effective for market interest rates.

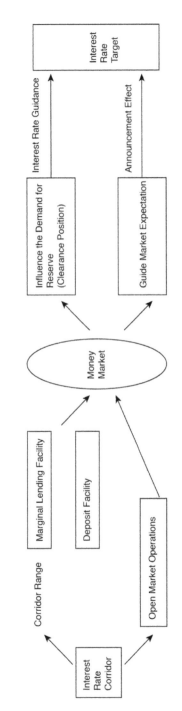

Figure 3-3 The ECB's interest rate corridor

c Comparison of different approaches

It is necessary to point out that the approaches focusing on open market operations and the interest rate corridor are complementary and interconnected. Refinancing (rediscount) is common among almost all central banks. Only some central banks do not pay interest on financial institutions' deposits (one-side interest rate corridor). After the 2008 global financial crisis, both the US and Japan started to pay interest on (surplus) reserve, leading to the emergence of interest rate corridors and deposit and lending facilities. Adjustment through the interest rate corridor has become a trend (Hu, 2014). At the end of 2008, the Federal Reserve started to pay interest on depository institutions' required and surplus reserves. Currently, the Federal Reserve pays an interest of 1.25 percent (the upper limit of federal funds rate target) on surplus reserve, which actually imposes a lower limit on money market rates. Regarded as the lending facility rate, the federal discount rate is 1.75 percent at the moment. The target range of the federal funds rate is 1–1.25 percent and it seems unlikely for the rate to be zero. Therefore, the Federal Reserve's interest rate corridor covers a range of 50 basis points. However, institutions outside the Federal Reserve System cannot get interest on their reserves and are thus willing to lend money at a rate lower than the lower limit of deposit rates. Therefore, the effective federal funds rate remains 10 to 15 basis points below the target (Bech and Klee, 2011). As discount business decreases, the Federal Reserve manages liquidity mainly through open market operations. Deposit and lending facilities are less frequently used and less effective in interest rate guidance. The Federal Reserve achieves its monetary policy objectives mainly through open market operations. Japan's situation is similar to that in the US. In Japan, however, the target rate is at a lower level (near zero).

The ECB will remunerate minimum reserve holdings at a level corresponding to the rate of its main refinancing operations (MRO). In July 2012, the MRO rate dropped to 0.75 percent and the rate under the deposit facility dropped to zero. Faced with a weak economy and potential deflation, on June 11, 2016, the ECB lowered the MRO rate by 10 basis points to 0.15 percent, overnight deposit rate (0 percent originally) by 10 basis points to −0.1 percent, and overnight lending rate by 35 basis points to 0.4 percent. These measures were applied to eurozone countries, thus initiating an age of negative rates. On September 10, 2014, the ECB further cut the MRO rate to 0.05 percent (a near zero level), deposit facility rate to −0.2 percent, and marginal lending facility rate to 0.3 percent. Therefore, as policy rates are near zero bound, ECB takes a similar approach as the US before the financial crisis. The market rates face an upper limit (the rate under marginal lending facility) but no effective lower limit. Market rates fluctuate around the target level and move closer to zero bound.

Nevertheless, differences exist among different countries' approaches. For approaches focusing on the interest rate corridor, under normal economic conditions, marginal lending and deposit facility provide an expectable upper/lower limit for market rates. Central banks can effectively manage market expectation and liquidity without frequently resorting to open market operations. Similar effectiveness can be achieved compared to the Federal Reserve's operations. For

Table 3-4 Benchmark rate, interest rate operational target, and open market operations in major developed countries

Country	Central bank policy rate	Operational target for interest rate	Deposit and lending facilities	Reserve Requirement	Main open market operations	Term	Frequency of open market operations
Australia	Cash rate target	Interbank cash rate	Yes, ±25BP	No	Repo and reverse repo	Overnight to about one year	Daily
Canada	Overnight rate target (collateralized overnight rate)	Collateralized overnight rate	Yes, ±25BP	No	Intra-day lending facility targeting overnight rate; end-of-day position management for Large Value Transfer System (LVTS) settlements	One business day	Occasionally; distribution of government deposits and commercial bank's settlement position through a daily auction
Euro area	Main refinancing rate	No official operational target	Yes, ±25BP	Yes	Repo or collateralized lending	One week or three months	Weekly or monthly
Japan	Uncollateralized overnight call rate	Uncollateralized overnight call rate	Yes, +20BP – 0BP	Yes	Repo or securities lending, direct purchase of government securities (long-term financing)	Overnight to one year (direct purchase of government securities excluded)	Daily for short-term operations; four times a month for long-term financing

Korea	Bank of Korea base rate	Interbank overnight call rate	Yes, ±100BP	Yes	Repo and reverse repo; issuance and buy-back of Monetary Stabilization Bonds (MSBs)	7-day repo or reverse repo, maximum term of two years	Weekly
Sweden	Repo rate	Interbank overnight rate	Yes, ±75BP	No	Repo	One week	Weekly
Switzerland	3-month LIBOR CHF	Target range for 3-month LIBOR CHF	No, only loan arrangement	Yes	Repo, fixed term auction, FX swap	Normally one week	Daily
UK	Official bank rate	Overnight rate	Yes, ±25BP	No	Repo	Overnight to one year	Daily
US	Uncollateralized federal funds rate target	Uncollateralized federal funds rate	No formal deposit facility before October 2008	Yes	Repo with major dealers	Normally overnight to 14 days, as long as 65 trading days in exceptional cases	Daily for short-term operations, weekly for long-term operations

Note: Only recent situations reflected and subject to policy changes

Source: BIS market committee, www.bis.org/about/factmktc.htm; central bank websites

example, the scale of open market operations carried out by the Reserve Bank of New Zealand in 2002 was only one-tenth of that in 1999 when the Bank first adopted an interest rate corridor. Currently the Bank rarely intervenes in the market. Moreover, studies (e.g. Bindseil and Jablecki, 2011) show that institutional arrangements such as interest remuneration on deposit reserves, assessment of the compliance with reserve requirement factoring in a time lag, better policy communication and policy transparency, frequent open market operations, adoption of the interest rate corridor and narrow interest rate corridor, etc. can reduce the deviation of money market rates from the central bank target rate and help monetary authorities to guide interest rate movements.

In addition, the width of the interest rate corridor is essential to the effectiveness of interest rate guidance and monetary policy. Normally, the wider the interest rate corridor, the larger the fluctuations in money market rates and transactions. However, this doesn't mean the corridor should be zero, in which case transaction cost will not be compensated and the central bank will be the only provider of liquidity. Therefore, a corridor at zero is evidently not an optimal choice. Australia's experience is a good example. When introducing the interest rate corridor, the Reserve Bank of Australia set the width at only 10 basis points. It turned out that banks were even more unwilling to borrow in the market. Finally, the corridor was widened to 25 basis points (Woodford, 2005). Certainly, under systemic crises such as the 2008 global financial meltdown, a narrower corridor is beneficial for central banks to provide liquidity and stabilize the financial market and overall economy (Bindseil and Jablecki, 2011). The ECB narrowed the interest rate corridor from 200 to 150 basis points in May 2009 and further to 50 basis points in 2014. Such choices were made to cope with the financial crisis.

d   Changes after the global financial crisis

The ECB's policy rates are extremely low and even negative for deposits. All these show the ECB's resolution to stimulate economic growth through low rates and the limit of conventional approaches to interest rate adjustment. If central banks want to guide market rates with the benchmark rate and thus realize monetary policy targets including price stability and economic growth, the prerequisite is that the policy rate target should be above zero, negative nominal rates being unacceptable. Otherwise, there is little room for further rate cut. Against economic depression and deflationary pressure, the primary objective of monetary policy is to stabilize the financial market and stimulate economic recovery. During the Great Depression of the 1930s (Friedman and Schwartz, 1963), although nominal rates were very low, real interest rates were still at a very high level. The Federal Reserve had to resort to quantitative easing, an unconventional approach. The Federal Reserve expanded its balance sheet through bond and asset purchase to inject liquidity into the economy and realize economic stability and recovery. Under a low rate circumstance, central banks provide massive liquidity through open market operations and the unconventional measure of quantitative easing. As a result, central banks effectively boost recovery. This is the main reason why after 2008, almost all major central banks took a zero-interest rate policy.

Meanwhile, to effectively undertake unconventional policies and guide market expectation, central banks have enhanced their policy transparency and communication with the market. Central bank communication is even regarded as a new monetary policy pass-through (Blinder et al., 2008). Against the global financial crisis, major central banks adopted forward guidance to improve public communication and strengthen the effectiveness of the zero-interest rate policy and unconventional monetary policies. Through disclosure in advance, central banks can better guide market expectation and execute their policies. The information disclosed includes economic forecast and analysis and the possible future course of monetary policies. The information is forward-looking (anticipative), subjective, and subject to change. In the broad sense, forward guidance includes releasing the forecast on the overall economy (Saborowski and Weber, 2013); in the narrow sense, it means monetary authorities' communication with the public of their stance and policy pathway (mainly the interest rate channel) (Plosser, 2013; Woodford, 2012). Before the 2008 financial crisis, New Zealand (1997), Norway (2005), Sweden (2007), Iceland (2007), and Czech Republic (2007) all explored possible interest rate channels. These countries adopted inflation targeting, established transparent policy frameworks, and issued forecasts on key economic indicators and policy rates. Monetary authorities stressed that the policy pathway released was only a projection rather than a promise. After the 2008 financial crisis, in addition to regular communication and economic forecast, the Federal Reserve, Bank of Japan, and Bank of England all made certain promises in their interest rate guidance to reduce long-term interest rates and uncertainties.

In October 2010, the Bank of Japan adopted a package of monetary easing policies (including direct provision of liquidity). The central bank also announced that it would not change the zero-interest rate policy until it considered price stability was achieved and evident risk for financial imbalance eliminated. In April 2013, the Bank of Japan announced the "qualitative and quantitative monetary easing policies". To realize the 2 percent inflation target within two years, the central bank would spare no effort to undertake qualitative and quantitative easing. The announcement included both a specific timeframe (two years) and a clear target (2 percent of inflation).

In August 2011, the Federal Reserve incorporated a timeframe in its guidance. The Federal Reserve expected the low rate policy to remain unchanged till at least mid-2013. In January and September 2012, the Federal Reserve extended the timeframe to the end of 2014 and mid-2015 respectively. In December 2012, the Federal Reserve identified certain conditions in its policy guidance:

> the Committee . . . anticipates that this exceptionally low range for the federal funds rate will be appropriate at least as long as the unemployment rate remains above 6–1/2 percent, inflation between one and two years ahead is projected to be no more than a half percentage point above the Committee's 2 percent longer-run goal, and longer-term inflation expectations continue to be well anchored.
>
> (The Federal Reserve System, 2012)

In March 2014, with the improvement of the labor market (unemployment rate at 6.6 percent), the Federal Reserve declared that when determining how long the low rate policy would last, it would consider multiple factors, including labor market conditions, inflation pressure, and expectation and financial developments. The current target range for the federal funds rate may continue for a considerable time after quantitative easing ends, especially if projected inflation continues to run below the Committee's 2 percent long-term goal and provided that long-term inflation expectations remain well anchored. In September, the Federal Reserve did not change the language "a considerable time" and projected the federal funds rate at the end of 2015 to be at 1.25–1.5 percent.

In August 2013, the Bank of England formally adopted forward guidance with two specific conditions. While reemphasizing the inflation target, the central bank pointed out a specific policy pathway: The exceptionally low benchmark interest rate (0.5 percent) and asset purchase plans would remain unchanged until unemployment fell below 7 percent. This policy was subject to three "knock-outs": If CPI inflation was likely to be at or above 2.5 percent for over an 18–24 month period; if inflation looked like it might not be properly controlled during the medium-term; if the Financial Policy Committee believed this could be a threat to financial stability and the Financial Policy Committee and authorities of financial regulation and prudent supervision had no corresponding policies.

In July 2013, the ECB also adopted similar practice of open-ended guidance. President Draghi stated that the ECB expected its key interest rates to remain at or below the current level for a considerable time. He reiterated this stance in 2014.

Certainly, it is necessary to note that quantitative easing and forward guidance can only be used during crises as unconventional measures. After all, in Japan, the expansion of the central bank's balance sheet has not effectively stimulated aggregate demand (Posen and Kuttner, 2004). Once economic conditions are better, monetary authorities should return to normal approaches in adjusting the interest rate (Taylor, 2012). With a stronger recovery and reduced unemployment, since 2014, the Federal Reserve has accelerated its effort to exit quantitative easing. At the monetary policy meeting on October 28–29, 2014, the Federal Reserve announced the end of QE3. Although the Federal Reserve kept the wording "a considerable time" in its forward guidance, the market widely anticipated that the Federal Reserve would raise the interest rate in 2015 and return to conventional approaches to interest rate adjustment.

III   Communication with the market is essential

Liquidity effect and expectation effect together determine the effectiveness of central banks' interest rate guidance. In theory, between liquidity and the interest rate exists an obviously negative correlation, the so-called liquidity effect. Central banks used to achieve policy goals through adjusting liquidity. Since the emergence of Rational Expectation theory in the 1970s, central banks attached greater importance to market expectation and prospective, transparent, and reliable monetary policies. Theoretical and empirical studies have shown that optimal policy design depends on the expectation of the public, enterprises, and the financial market. In an optimization model, the private sector's behavior is forward-looking: The expectation of future market conditions is an important factor in their current decision-making. Evidence shows that as central banks increasingly get involved with market operations, the private sector considers monetary policy commitments when making forecasts. Since the 1990s, as central banks became increasingly aware that public communication is essential to the effectiveness of monetary policies, the liquidity effect in interest rate transmission has diminished (Hamilton, 1997; Christiano, Eichenbaum and Evans, 1999; Friedman and Kuttner, 2010), while the expectation effect has strengthened.

In terms of managing market expectation, central banks have gone through a transition from secrecy and surprise to active communication and public announcement. Before the 1990s, affected by the Policy Ineffectiveness Proposition, central banks believed that only unexpected policies could affect people's behavior and obscurity would lead to effectiveness of monetary policies. Therefore, policymakers should keep silent to influence the market by surprise. The Federal Reserve and other major central banks all kept their monetary policies in the dark. They refrained from public communication and information disclosure and gave no explanation of the necessity and effect of monetary policies. This practice of zero communication did not lead to satisfying results. For example, faced with the inflation of the 1960s, the Federal Reserve failed to take effective measures to tackle inflation and was considered uncommitted to inflation control. Market expectation for inflation was highly unstable until the 1973 oil crisis. The oil price hike led to intensified overall inflation and the prospect of higher inflation affected the public's expectation and behavior. Workers expected price hikes and demanded higher wages while enterprises expected higher cost and increased selling prices. All this further aggravated inflation. Although the Federal Reserve took measures to curb inflation, these policies were largely ineffective as the public believed that these policies were not enough. In the 1980s, the Federal Reserve had to dramatically raise the target rate of federal funds several times and thus finally gained the trust of the public. Although the inflation was under control, economic recession ensued due to insufficient public communication and late adoption of policy measures.

Theoretical studies changed central banks' attitude toward public communication. Increasing policy transparency became an irreversible trend. Brunner (1981) politely criticized that central banks refused to communicate, which showed that central bank communication hardly existed. In 1996, in a speech at the LSE, Robbins first proposed that "central bank communication is beneficial to the effectiveness of monetary policy" (Blinder, 1998). Woodford (2005) maintained that the core of monetary policy is the art of expectation management, the key to which is central bank communication. Central banks soon took up these new thoughts and gave up their previous secrecy. Central banks became happy to pursue monetary policies through public communication. Guidance of market expectation by monetary policies has become more explicit (see Table 3-5).

Table 3-5 Central bank communications in different countries

Central bank	Central bank communication						
	Monetary policy meeting	Press conference	Monetary policy report	Inflation report	Financial stability report	Annual report	Others
Federal Reserve	Eight times a year Policy statement on the day of the meeting Minutes available three weeks after each meeting For every four meetings, the addendum to the minutes discloses the Committee's projection of key interest rates and the projection is incorporated in the Summaries of Economic Projection (SEP) issued every January, April, June, and October Historical minutes with "slight" editing are available after a five-year lag	Quarterly	Semiannually	–	–	Annually	Monthly reports on Credit and Liquidity Programs and the Balance Sheet Written reports to the Congress Congressional testimony Beige Books (8 time annually) Speeches and interviews
European Central Bank	Twice a month The first assesses recent monetary and economic situations and determines corresponding policies; the second decides on issues concerning the payment system, financial stability, and statistical, monetary, and legal affairs No minutes disclosed	After each month's first Governing Council meeting	Economic Bulletin published one week after each monetary policy meeting of the Governing Council Economic projections in the Economic Bulletin for March, June, September, and December	–	Every six months	Annually	Speeches and interviews

Bank of England	Every month. Statement on the day of the meeting. Minutes released at 9:30 on the second Wednesday after the meeting	–	Quarterly. Quarterly projections on economic and inflation conditions by the Monetary Policy Committee. Pie charts used to illustrate relevant risks and uncertainties	Every six months	Annually. Restraints on Monetary Policy Committee members' public talks. Policy communication with educational purposes (Target Two Point Zero). Survey on inflation expectation. Speeches and interviews
Bank of Japan	Monthly. Statement on policy decisions on the day of the meeting. Minutes available four weeks after the meeting	Monthly Report on the next day of the monetary policy meeting. Reports to the Diet in June and December.	After each monetary policy committee meeting. –	Financial System Report issued every six months	Annually. Outlook Report (the Banks View) available at 3:00 p.m. on the day of monetary policy meeting in April and October and the full context available at 2:00 p.m. the next day. Speeches and interviews
Reserve Bank of New Zealand	Eight times a year. Monetary policy statement and interest rate decision after the meeting. Minutes available a few weeks after	–	Quarterly. –	Every six months	Annually. Disclosure of the economic model used in the evaluation of economic situation and policy-making. Speeches and interviews

In February 1994, for the first time the FOMC issued a statement and disclosed monetary policy changes to the public after its regular meeting. The US thus entered an era of central bank communication. Before December 1998, the FOMC only communicated with the public when there were policy changes. Since then, the FOMC has been issuing policy statements whether or not there are interest rate adjustments or policy changes. In 2000, the FOMC started to release its outlook on the economy after each regular meeting. The committee provided overall assessments of economic risks and disclosed possible changes of the federal funds rate. In August 2003, the Federal Reserve started to use forward guidance to better manage public expectation. This was the first time public communication was regarded as a prime monetary policy instrument. Since then, the Federal Reserve started to consider communication itself as monetary policy instead of using communication to facilitate federal funds rate adjustment.

The Federal Reserve has gained public trust through continuously enhancing public communication. All this has played a positive role in managing market expectation. In the second half of 2008, faced with the most severe situation after the Great Depression, the Federal Reserve cut the federal funds rate to near zero and has maintained this historically low level until today. There was no room for further rate cut. And as the financial market was gravely damaged and the transmission of policy rates was blocked, the Federal Reserve turned to unconventional measures and more diversified communication to stabilize the market. For example, to drive down long-term rates through large-scale asset purchases, the Federal Reserve has explained to the public the intentions of holding these securities many times. In addition, the Federal Reserve has given more detailed explanations of the possible duration of the near zero rate. From the simple wording of "for a considerable time" to the timetable for key interest rate rises, from the identified trigger and threshold of policy actions to the FOMC's forecasts of key policy rates with bar graphs and scatter grams, all these have clearly informed the public of the Federal Reserve's perception of future financial developments and its reasons for policy changes. Likewise, although the Federal Reserve had not officially decided to cut its asset purchase programs until the meeting at the end of 2013, QE exit had already been discussed in mid-2013. Even at the very beginning of QE, the Federal Reserve explained to the public how to exit and how to avoid relevant negative effects. With these measures, the Federal Reserve wanted the public to be confident and believe that monetary policies would stabilize the financial market without leading to future inflation.

IV   The path to policy rate adjustment by the PBOC

A   *Environment and conditions*

From the analysis above, we can see that the factors influencing the effectiveness of central banks' interest rate regulation include micro-level factors such as individual behavior and interest rate elasticity and macro-level factors such as financial market conditions, financing structure, central banks' authority and credibility, and the institutional environment. Meanwhile, we should note that although interest rate elasticity and market conditions do influence policy effectiveness, central banks enjoy a special status and natural authority in using policy rates to guide market rates. Central bank communication can substantially make up for the weakness of an underdeveloped financial market. It promotes the development of the financial market and enhances the effect of the interest rate on microeconomic entities.

*a   Basic conditions for interest rate adjustment through policy
     rate changes*

In theory, monetary policy instruments used by central banks are determined by relevant transmission mechanisms (Zhou, 2004). The differences in the choice of the adjustment approach results from the different understanding of the transmission mechanism of monetary policies. Chinese experts traditionally hold that the credit channel should take up a critical position in monetary policy transmission as the interest rate formation mechanism needs improvement, the financial market is still not mature, microeconomic players are not sensitive enough to interest rate changes, indirect financing takes up a leading role, and substantial financial control still exists. This line of reasoning is only a revision of the traditional adjustment mechanism through the interest rate channel. Credit channel is not a distinct, freestanding alternative to the traditional transmission mechanism; it just enhances and amplifies the interest rate channel (Bernanke and Gertler, 1995). In this sense, it is hard to totally separate the effect of interest channel, credit channel, and money supply adjustment; it is also inappropriate to conclude that China's monetary policy transmission mainly relies on quantitative measures simply because China has yet to establish multi-tier market rates and transmission mechanisms or microeconomic players are not sufficiently interest rate sensitive. Moreover, judging from the market environment and PBOC's influence on interest rates, China has already established a market-based interest rate system and transmission mechanism that is sensitive and effective (Zhou, 2013b).

First, the environment has been greatly improved for the interest rate transmission mechanism. Although disagreements still exist, more and more studies hold that China's environment has been greatly improved for interest rate transmission. Three major driving forces are the increased proportion of financial disintermediation and direct financing; deepened interest rate liberalization; and strengthened interest rate elasticity at the micro-level.

Second, the PBOC's influence on the money market rate has been enhancing. Although the PBOC has not declared a specific target or floating range of policy interest rate, it can still effectively guide money market rates. In implementing monetary policies, while focusing on liquidity management, the PBOC has been strengthening its guidance on money market rates. In monetary policy reports and announcements of the monetary policy committee, we can often find expressions like "adjusting liquidity in a timely and appropriate manner based on economic and financial conditions and maintaining the stability of money market rates". In terms of the effects of regulation, various instruments such as central bank bills, repos, and open market operations all show increasing influence over the capital market interest rates. Also, the correlation between Shibor and capital market interest rates has seen remarkable rise. All this shows that the ability of the PBOC in guiding market interest rates has been improving.

Third, the PBOC has gained experience in communicating with the public and guiding market expectation. In addition to liquidity management through open market operations, the PBOC is now more experienced in communicating with the market. According to the PBOC Financial Survey and Statistics Department (2012), the PBOC communicates with the public mainly through reports (i.e. Monetary Policy Report, Financial Stability Report), PBOC website, speeches, and interviews. PBOC communication mainly covers monetary policy targets, operations, and decisions for specific targets, financial statistics, analysis of the current situation and expected policies, and other things that the public needs to know. Empirical studies have shown that now the PBOC can influence market expectation at the micro and individual level. Especially, the PBOC releases the survey on banks, depositors, and entrepreneurs on a regular basis. These surveys cover a huge sample and have great influence on market expectation. When results of the PBOC survey on depositors are incorporated into the projected inflation rate analysis, the model's goodness of fit is greatly enhanced (Zhang, 2011).

b   Hindrances to interest rates regulation

Generally, the prerequisite for price-based adjustment is that the market plays a decisive role in resource allocation and the financial market is highly developed. Price signals, especially interest rate changes, can guide resource allocation. If the price mechanism fails, the central bank can hardly regulate the macro-economy through interest rates. The failure of price signals is due to the unsophisticated financial market and some institutional constraints outside the financial market.

First, the financial market is still underdeveloped. China lags behind developed countries in terms of money market development. The types and terms of financial trading are not diversified enough; financial trading is concentrated and homogenous; the derivative market lags behind financial development. All these hinder price discovery and transmission. Also, neither investors nor fundraisers have abundant choices of competitive products, and the financial market cannot offer sufficient information for pricing. The financial market and infrastructure are underdeveloped, and problems like market segmentation, unclear regulation responsibility, and opaque disclosure still exist. As a result, financial transmission, especially interest rate transmission, is not effective and the interest rates of various products are not closely linked. All the above-mentioned issues hamper the PBOC's effort to adjust interest rates through operations in the financial market.

Second, institutional factors also caused passive issuance of currency and the soft budget constraint. On the one hand, local governments preferred large-scale of investment and tend to monetize fiscal deficit. Local governments have stopped direct overdrafts from the central government. However, through institutional arrangements and implicit government guarantee, local governments can still run up massive hidden overdrafts to the banking system and the PBOC. China thus faces a potential danger of fiscal risks turning into financial risks, which hinders the transmission of policy rates in the market. On the other hand, certain market players are still under soft budget constraints. The soft budget constraint reflects the shortcomings of a transition economy. Since the reform and opening-up, huge progress has been made in mitigating soft budget constraints. However, the problem still exists due to institutional and policy reasons. On some local financing platforms where the credit of government and credit of enterprises are hardly separated, the interest rate cost may still be ignored in the pursuit of fund availability. Meanwhile, the operations of financial institutions are highly homogenous. Financial institutions need to be more willing and able to set prices independently. All this will impede the transmission of interest rate policies.

Third, if the exchange rate is not elastic enough, the interest rate transmission will be hindered. The impossible trinity shows the relationship between independent monetary policy, exchange rate flexibility, and capital account convertibility. As most developing countries exert capital controls, whether central banks can decide independently on interest rate policies and whether such decisions are effectively transmitted largely depend on the flexibility of the exchange rate. Cas, Carrión-Menéndez, and Frantischek (2011) compared the interest rate transmission in some Central American countries and six Latin American countries (Brazil, Chili, Columbia, Mexico, Peru, and Uruguay). The results show that in the six Latin American countries with higher exchange rate elasticity, the financial sector is more vibrant and interest rate transmission is more effective. Gigineishvili (2011) analyzed a sample of over 70 countries, covering developed, developing, and low-income countries, and found that compared with countries with fixed exchange rates, countries with floating exchange rates enjoy more effective transmission of interest rates, especially long-term rates. According to the IMF, a floating exchange rate can be a freely floating, floating, or managed floating system. A cross-national study that covers more than 120 countries, including China (Saborowski and Weber, 2013), shows that higher exchange rate elasticity can enhance the interest rate transmission. When a country transforms from a pegged rate system to a floating rate system, the efficiency of interest rates transmission is supposed to increase by 25–50 percent. Meanwhile, exchange rate elasticity has greater influence in developed countries. In China, exchange rate elasticity has greatly increased over the past few years, and the proportion of current account surplus in GDP has dropped from 10 percent to around 2.5 percent. However, further reforms are still needed in the exchange rate formation mechanism and current account convertibility to give the central bank more autonomy in making monetary policies and increase the effectiveness of interest rate transmission.

Fourth, expanded micro-regulation makes macro-regulation and interest rate adjustment more difficult. In macro financial management and supervision, the relationship between the PBOC and regulatory authorities, their respective organizational structures, and their policy instruments all need to be clearly defined. Right now, the responsibilities and authorities of these institutions are still mismatched to some extent, and institutional arrangements are imperfect. In practice, micro-regulation can be blurred with macro-control. The coordination between the PBOC, CSRC, CBRC, and CIRC does not have clear-cut responsibilities or sufficient policy tools. Money market rates are influenced by multiple factors and the interest rate adjustment thus becomes harder. For example, constrained by the loan to deposit (LTD) ratio, financial institutions are more dependent on deposits and pay less attention to the money market. The transmission from the money market to the bond and credit markets becomes more difficult. In the second half of 2011, regulatory authorities checked more strictly on financial institutions' bill businesses undertaken to avoid credit control. As a result, bill rates first went up rapidly and then plummeted when the inspection became less intensified in early 2012. The volatility was more severe for bill rates than for money market rates. In recent years, regulatory authorities adjusted their compliance requirements for wealth-management and interbank businesses. Such changes also greatly influenced money market rates.

Under current market conditions and institutional arrangements, relying fully on policy rate adjustment still faces many challenges. However, China has proper conditions in the financial market, central bank operations, and public communication for policy rate adjustment. Meanwhile, we do not have to wait until all conditions are ripe to advance the interest rate reform. As the basic conditions for interest rate adjustment are met, establishing the framework of PBOC's interest rate adjustment would be conducive to improving market conditions and institutional arrangements. We do not need all the conditions to be optimal to start our reform.

B   *Choice of approaches of policy rate adjustment*

Internationally, central banks' policy rates often refer to overnight (short-term) rates. As the expectation hypothesis of the term structure of interest rates suggest, the short-term and long-term rates reach a co-integration of long-term equilibrium (Engle and Granger, 1987; Campbell and Shiller, 1987), and the term structure of interest rates mainly depends on the market expectation for future inflation and growth (Fama, 1990; Mishkin, 2009; Estrella and Hardouvelis, 1991). Central banks can adjust short-term rates to influence long-term rates and thus the real economy, realizing the monetary policy objectives. Empirical studies of China's term structure of interest rates show that the expectation hypothesis also applies in China (Li, 2012). In fact, if the central bank decides (pegs) the long-term interest rates, it will be determining the term structure of market rates and imposing rate control. This both violates market economy principles and may go beyond the central bank's capability. Judging from the market environment and the macroeconomy, China has met the basic requirement for policy rate adjustment. The market environment for interest rate transmission has been improving and the PBOC's guidance on money market rates has been increasing. Shibor becomes increasingly correlated with money market rates. The PBOC has also gained experience in public communication and expectation management. Therefore, the

PBOC can choose a short-term rate and declare it as the policy rate. The short-term rate chosen should be controllable, representative, and able to serve as a prime reference.

In terms of adjustment approaches, an interest rate corridor has been formed to some extent, with the surplus reserve rates being the lower limit of money market rates and the rediscount rate being the upper limit of money market rates (Zhou, 2012). Some researchers suggest that China adopt the approach focusing on the interest rate corridor. According to the research group of PBOC Operation Office (2013), China's approach to interest rate adjustment should be establishing an interest rate corridor through deposit and marginal lending facilities and managing liquidity and expectation through open market operations. He Dong, Wang Honglin, and Yu Xiangrong (2013) also hold that with the liberalization of deposit rates and the rapid growth of debt products, China can draw upon foreign experience to establish an interest rate corridor that centers on an equilibrium rate. The authors believe that the specific approach can be evaluated and improved along the process of interest rate liberalization.

C Supporting reforms

While the interest rate corridor and policy rate are deemed issues at the technical level, institutional arrangements and market conditions are deemed essential to whether the policy rate is effective and whether negative results can be avoided. The supporting reforms for interest rate regulations are and will be the key to speeding up interest rate liberalization, improving policy rates and macro financial regulation, and maintaining financial stability.

First, China needs to further reduce the surplus and adjust the economic structure, creating conditions for increasing RMB exchange rate elasticity. As early as 2007, the Central Economic Work Conference set the target of structural adjustment, surplus cut, and balanced development. This target is an expediency against a huge inflow of foreign currency but represents a fundamental decision to transform the development mode for China's open economy. Correspondingly, China needs to accommodate the open economy in setting its monetary policies and to establish a policy framework centering on interest rate adjustment. The significance of strengthening policy adjustment is not only to cope with the issue that money supply becomes less manageable due to external impacts such as financial innovations. More importantly, China needs to transform its mindset from the traditional emphasis on exchange rate stability of minor countries to the emphasis on proactive interest rate adjustment and domestic demand of major countries. This transformation is where the interest rate liberalization and policy rate control start and where the strategic importance of these reforms lies. Therefore, China needs to follow the requirement set by the 3rd Plenum of the 18th CPC Central Committee and speed up the factor price reform and structural adjustment. At the same time, China needs to further improve the exchange rate formation mechanism so as to create a favorable environment for policy interest rate adjustment.

Second, a multi-level financial market, or a multi-level money market to be specific, needs to be established. This effort is important for interest rate regulation and effective pricing of the financial market; it is also essential to independent business operation and independent consumer choice under the modern market economy as set forth in the 3rd Plenum.

Third, China needs to transform the government function in order to eliminate soft budget constraint. As is pointed out in the 3rd Plenum, to let the market play a decisive role, both an integrated and open market system for orderly competition and improved government function are required. Problems appear, including the weak interest rate constraint on local government financing platforms and the passive issuance of liquidity due to fiscal pressure. These problems are, in essence, due to the failure in the transformation of the government's role and in the separation of the credit of government and enterprises. The problems will inevitably damage the credit rating, pricing, and filtering mechanisms of the financial market. They will also impede the central bank's policy regulation. It is necessary to improve the performance evaluation system, taxation scheme, and administrative system in order to transform the government's function and create a favorable condition for the central bank's interest rate regulation.

Fourth, China needs to reform the supervisory system and coordinate micro- and macro-regulation.

4 Interest rate liberalization and economic and financial development

A large number of papers have examined the effects of interest rate liberalization on economic and financial development, but there have been few systematic studies about the impacts of the latter on interest rate liberalization. Some researchers have said that macroeconomic and financial stability was the prerequisite for the success of interest rate liberalization reform. Many studies have claimed that financial innovation and disintermediation can promote interest rate liberalization and that economic and financial development also has an effect on the reform. After observing the process and results of interest rate liberalization in many countries, it can be concluded that interest rate liberalization is in fact greatly affected by the stages of economic development and the structural changes. Based on the global experiences, this chapter analyzes the advantages and limitations of the different stages of economic and financial development on interest rate liberalization in order to comprehensively understand the reform process in China.

I Impact of different stages of economic development on the interest rate system

A The gradual change of interest rate system: from theory to empirical study

The financial structure and financial deepening theory have analyzed the reasons and necessity of interest rate liberalization, and some countries and regions liberalized their interest rate based on the above theory in the 1970s and 1980s. However, the consequences of those reforms in some regions, such as Africa and Latin America, were far from the situation predicted by the theory. The Asian financial crisis, which erupted in 1997, especially prompted a rethinking of the policies by the countries that experienced the turmoil. After reflecting on the practical problems of the financial deepening theory, known as the financial liberalization trap, McKinnon (1991) said:

> The general case favoring financial liberalization has been called into question by a series of bank panics and collapses in the Southern Cone of Latin America.

The financial restraint theory proposed by Hellmann, Murdock, and Stiglitz in 1997 can be regarded as the refinement and development of the financial deepening theory, in which the issues about the environment for realizing interest rate liberalization and the appropriate approach to the reform were discussed in depth. For developing countries with a relatively weak market base, a certain degree of policy interventions is more helpful for economic growth than the fully market-oriented policies. Selective intervention – *financial restraint* – may help rather than hinder financial deepening. Two key policies are necessary to implement financial restraint – interest rate controls and asset substitution, of which the former is the vital one. Maintaining positive but lower deposit interest rates (lower than the equilibrium rate) through the government's financial restraint policies can achieve the following results: First, lower rates can force down the financing costs of the financial institutions and may also mitigate the borrower's default risk through lending rate controls; second, higher spreads may help to create profits for financial institutions and thus encourage them to provide the market with a more comprehensive financial services, which can promote financial deepening and economic growth; third, interest rate controls could be removed when the market develops to a higher-level, and reach full interest rate liberalization.

A considerable number of empirical studies have also indicated that the impacts of different stages of economic development on the interest rate system and on the degree of interest rate liberalization were significant. At different levels of income and risk, the influence of raising real interest rates on consumption growth and output is uncertain, because the changes in interest rates have two opposite effects – substitution effect and income effect (Levhari and Srinivasan, 1969; Jappell and Pagano, 1994). Reinhart and Tokatlidis (2005) compared and analyzed the economic performance before and after interest rate liberalization, then found that interest rate liberalization was often accompanied by a rise in real interest rates, which did not lower the economic growth rate but brought more FDI and capital flows. However, the effect of financial liberalization and deepening on output and capital flow was only significant in countries with higher income levels and not so obvious in many low-income countries, because the latter mainly faced the problem of survival. In fact, the real interest rate was not the only factor that determined the consumption growth and economic growth for most developing countries. Factors such as the low-income level, the imperfect capital market, the lack of financial products, the incomplete rule of law, and so on can all have an effect on the consumption level and growth rate.

The stage and the level of economic development will also affect the probability of financial crisis after interest rate liberalization reform. International experiences show that financial crisis has occurred in some countries but not in others after the reform. We can investigate this issue from the perspective of the level of economic development. Using GDP per capita representing the level of economic development as the vertical axis and the predicted probability of a crisis after interest rate liberalization reform as the horizontal axis, we can draw the following scatter plot seen in Figure 4-1.

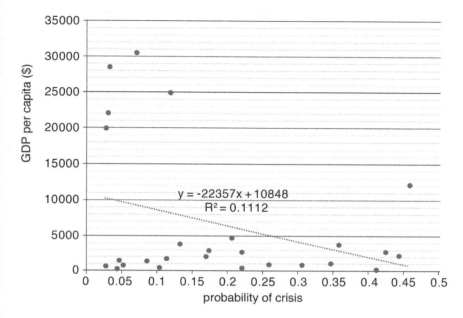

Figure 4-1 Relationship between GDP per capita and the probability of crisis after interest
rate liberalization

Source: The World Bank

The scatter plot can be divided into two parts: One is the countries whose GDP
per capita is below US$5,000, and their probabilities of a crisis distribute quite
evenly in the range of zero to 0.5; the other part is the countries whose GDP per
capita is higher than US$15,000, and their probabilities of a crisis distribute in
the range of zero to 0.15. It can be noted that when the GDP per capita is lower
than US$5,000, interest rate liberalization may or may not lead to crisis and the
probability distribution is relatively average. But when the GDP per capita is high,
probability of a crisis after interest rate liberalization can be greatly decreased.

B Selecting interest rate system according to the stage of economic development, and gradually moving toward interest rate liberalization: the common experiences of most countries

Global experiences have revealed that interest rate systems of most countries generally underwent the stages of laissez-faire–control–liberalization. In the early
stage of economic development, interest rate control was especially a popular
choice for most nations.

After the industrial revolution, the banking industry began to play an important
role in the western economy. However, from then to the beginning of the twentieth

century, there had been no interest rate control. Except for a few regional short-term agreements, there is little literature describing the interest rate control in western countries. Even when the central banks, represented by the Bank of England and the Bank of France, emerged, their functions at that time were mainly to offer rediscount financing for commercial banks, support national finance, promote the circulation of the national unified currency, and ensure the exchange of bank notes for gold and silver. Moreover, few central banks directly placed limits on the level of interest rates.

The banking system had been largely undermined by the two world wars and a global economic crisis in the first half of the twentieth century. Countries implemented financial controls to protect the banking system and rebuild the financial system. In terms of macroeconomic school of thought, Keynes's intervention theory had overturned the free market ideals, and the modern central banking system emerged, which further promoted the prevalence of ideological trends of state intervention and regulation.

In the United States, the Roosevelt administration abandoned traditional principles of laissez-faire when dealing with the 1929 crisis. The government intervened in the economy and society with state power, which also promoted the Keynesian state intervention theory to be more systematic and completed. During the Second World War, the United States had maintained interest rates at a low level for a long time in order to raise funds for the war. In 1951, the Federal Reserve reached an agreement with the US Treasury and gained the right to determine the level of interest rates, with a promise to prevent the sharp rise of interest rates. From 1933 to 1935, the United States passed a series of financial regulatory bills, such as *Banking Law, Securities Law, Securities Exchange Act, Federal Reserve Act, National Bank Act*, etc., which limited banks to pay interest on deposits, prohibited banks from investing in securities, established the deposit insurance system, strengthened the power of the Federal Reserve, and regulated and supervised the financial markets and banking institutions. Under this background, the well-known Regulation Q was promulgated. In addition to imposing interest rate ceilings on various types of bank deposits, including savings and time deposits, it was also used to prohibit the payment of interest on demand deposits. Therefore, Regulation Q became a synonym for deposit rates control. After two years of interest rate control, the supervision of the Federal Reserve System extended from only member banks to insured non-member banks. In 1935, the Federal Deposit Insurance Company (FDIC) was granted the same regulatory function according to the *Banking Law*. Since then, both of the above two federal agencies had the rights to stipulate the highest level of interest rates on time and savings deposits that banks should pay. In September 1966, the provisional *Interest Rate Control Act* was enacted to extend the supervision of the *Regulation Q* to depository financial institutions such as mutual savings banks and savings and loan associations. As far as the policy goals were concerned, the financial authorities of the United States aimed to use interest rate control as an auxiliary tool of their monetary policy to affect the credit expansion of the banks, as well as ensuring the safety and stability of the banking sector through the restrictions on interest rate competition. With regard to the policy effect, the implementation of the interest rate control policies such as *Regulation Q* played a positive role in the restoration of the financial order in the 1930s, the low-cost financing for the war from the 1940s to the beginning of the 1950s, and in the quick recovery of the US economy after the war.

Japan took an unbalanced economic approach after the Second World War – big industrial cities experienced rapid development, while remote areas fell into poverty and backwardness. Even in the same industrial sector, there were both advanced large enterprises and backward small and medium-sized enterprises (SMEs). In addition, as a defeated country, the Japanese economy had nearly collapsed and capital was extremely scarce after the war, so Japan had no choice but to devote capital to push economic recovery and growth. From the end of the Second World War to the end of the 1970s, Japan had exerted financial control and imposed strict limits on the business scope of financial institutions and the interest rates. It introduced the *Temporary Interest Rate Adjustment Act* in 1947, using *Regulation Q* of the United States as reference. The control policies imposed by the Bank of Japan (BOJ) could be divided into two categories: Direct and directive restrictions, and the government-controlled rates, including deposit rates, short-term lending rates, long-term concessional loans rates, and bond issuance rates. More specifically, the BOJ placed ceilings on deposit rates and short-term lending rates, and limited the level of interest rates through guidance. There was no direct restriction on the upper limit of long-term lending rates, but the rates should be linked to long-term financial bonds rates which were decided together by the BOJ, the Ministry of Finance, and the bond issuer, thus actually bringing long-term lending rates under control to some extent. Demand deposit rates and interbank offered rates were not restricted, but the valuation method for them had to be determined by the Norinchukin Bank (the main supplier of the capital) and the city banks (the parties who needed the capital) through consultations, and hence the rates were not subject to change at any time. As far as the policy effect was concerned, the long-term interest rates remained at a low level, which was helpful to devote domestic capital to restoring production and promoting economic recovery. The growth rate of Japanese economy remained at a high level from the end of the Second World War to the beginning of the 1970s, turning it from the ruins of the war into a global economic power.

In Europe, the United Kingdom limited interest rates through interest rates agreement just after the First World War. The French government strengthened credit management after the Second World War, and the National Credit Council capped the deposit rates at a low level in order to meet the needs of large amount of capital for economic development. In France, the real interest rate had been negative for a long period of time, which had played an important role in stimulating investments and accelerating economic growth. Germany started implementing interest rate control since 1932, and the policies lasted for a long time after the end of the Second World War. Interest rate control was first presented in the form of interbank interest rates agreement, and later became an administrative fiat. The scope of interest rate control was very extensive, including the deposit rate as well as the discount rate of bills and various fees. Generally speaking, the lending rates fluctuated around the discount rate of the central bank. The Bundesbank affected the level and structure of the interest rates by adjusting the rediscount rate, thereby influencing the credit scale and effectively controlling the whole economy. The above policies achieved good economic effects and drove Germany to become one of the countries whose economy returned to growth very quickly after the war.

The experiences of the main developed countries show that interest rate control can provide more impetus to economic development when the country's economic development is still relatively low level, or the country is in the economic recovery or takeoff phase. While there were some welfare losses, maintaining lower deposit rates (than the equilibrium rate) was helpful for reducing the cost of absorbing deposits for the banks, which created franchise value allowing banks to earn rents and provide an effective incentive mechanism for banks' operation. Government implemented lending rates control to keep the rates lower than the equilibrium rate, which helped to cut the financing costs of the enterprises, created rent opportunities for the corporate sector, and stimulated the growth in demand for loans and the growth in investments, thus promoting economic growth.

Of course, interest rate control was only a special phenomenon in the specific stage of economic development. After the 1970s, the world economy and financial situation changed greatly, and many of the monetary and credit controls implemented by the governments were weakened by the changes in all levels of economic development, the inflation situation, and the financial markets. The main developed countries enacted a series of wide-ranging financial reforms such as interest rate liberalization to adapt to the changes. At this stage, the primary purpose of interest rate policy and the interest rate system was no longer to pool financial resources to stimulate investment demand, but to reflect the relationship between supply and demand of the capital and the rate of return of financial assets correctly, flexibly, and in a timely manner, regulate the allocation of financial resources in the whole society effectively, and then guide the efficient allocation of economic resources in the whole society. At the same time, such an interest rate system should be able to facilitate the monetary policy operation of the central bank, enabling it to affect the level and structure of interest rates to regulate the operation of the national economy. Since then, the major developed countries gradually entered the stage of market-oriented interest rate system.

II   The stage of economic development and interest rate liberalization reform in China

China's market-based interest rate reform was carried out under the background of economic and financial reforms, opening-up, and development. During that period, China not only experienced changes in the economic and financial system and the rapid growth of economic grosses, but also underwent many structural changes. According to the theoretical analysis and international experiences mentioned in the previous section, the above changes will have an impact on interest rate liberalization reform.

A   Interest rate liberalization during the period of strong economic growth

After the reform and opening-up in 1978, China's economic development can be roughly divided into two major periods: The period of rapid growth before the global financial crisis and the period of structural adjustment after it. Of course, each period contains different stages and cycles.

China's rapid growth period included three stages: The shortage economy stage after the mid-1990s, the adjustment stage after the Asian financial crisis, and the rapid growth stage driven by a high investment rate and swelling exports from 2003 to 2008. Let us observe the market-oriented interest rate reforms of different stages one by one.

From the reform and opening-up to the mid-1990s, China was in the early stage of economic and financial development. The reform and opening-up removed the shackles on economic and financial development, people's pent-up demand that had been depressed for a long time was released, and the shortage characteristics of the planned economy were further highlighted. At this stage, the economic growth rate often fluctuated extraordinarily despite the rapid pace, because the economic and financial aggregates were relatively small. During the planned economy period, the concept and policies of only paying attention to material production and the development of heavy industry led to deformity in the economic structure and financial repression. Therefore, the market-oriented interest rate reform faced not only institutional constraints but also economic and financial hurdles. As the shortage problem was serious and the demand for capital was strong, fully liberalizing rates may have led to high level of interest rates while not necessarily subduing funding needs. Moreover, China still faced the challenge of soft budget constraint at that time. In addition, China's economy had the features of high volatility and high inflation, so interest rate liberalization would inevitably exacerbate economic fluctuations further. More importantly, because China's financial system was still in the early stage of development and the financial market had not yet formed, interest rate deregulation was far from interest rate liberalization. In fact, China had explored floating rate many times to invigorate the economy, but the above attempts often resulted in financial chaos, making the interest rate management swing between control and release repeatedly. Of course, the main reason behind the problem was institutional constraints, but the low level of economic and financial development contributed as well.

After a period of development, China's economic and financial output had reached a certain scale, the economic and financial structure had improved, there was more economic stability, and the inflation rate had gradually come down. In 1997, a phenomenon of oversupply of many commodities appeared in China, and the Asian financial crisis erupted at the same time. In the following years, China's economic growth was greatly impacted and the problem of non-performing assets of the banks also came to light, which prompted the government to make great efforts to carry out economic reform and adjustment. At this stage, the interest rate liberalization reform had been substantially advanced. China abolished the ceiling on interbank offered rates in 1996 and basically liberalized the interbank rates in 1999. In order to encourage lending to SMEs and solve serious problems faced by them in securing loans during the economic downturn, the floating range of financial institutions' lending rates targeted for small enterprises expanded from 10 percent to 20 percent, and that of rural credit cooperatives increased from 40 percent to 50 percent after October 31, 1998.

Benefiting from the adjustments, reforms, and positive effect of becoming a member of the WTO, China in 2003 entered a new round of rapid growth defined as a traditional model of economic growth. This kind of extensive growth was characterized by high input, high consumption, and high export and led by government under a catch-up strategy of economic development. So-called government-led means that the government takes the dominant position and plays a guiding role in economic development, and the government also controls the allocation of critical and fundamental resources (Wei, 2011). The so-called catch-up model means that the government places the rapid growth of the economy in an important and significant position. In terms of the inputs, this kind of development model features high resource consumption, high capital investment, and the use of a large amount of low-cost labor; in terms of the production structure, it shows the characteristics of an excessively high proportion of secondary industry and the insufficient development of tertiary industry; in terms of the demand structure, it features a high ratio of investment and export and a low proportion of consumption. To adapt to the growth model, China introduced a series of supporting policies, including the interest rate policies.

Under the traditional model of economic growth, financial resources should meet capital requirements at a low-cost, whether giving priority to economic growth rate, to economic scale, or to investment. Furthermore, China had an abundant supply of capital for a long time due to the high savings rate and large trade surplus, and the banks and enterprises were in an environment of excess liquidity, making it possible to achieve extensive expansion of economic scale driven by a low level of interest rate. Therefore, the incremental reforms of interest rate liberalization and a certain degree of interest rate control were endogenous choices of the traditional model of economic growth and suitable for it, which satisfied the needs of rapid economic growth to a great extent.

It is worth noting that exports had made a great contribution to economic growth under the traditional model. The exchange rate policy should also be supportive to maintain the steady growth of exports, which will affect the interest rate reform and policy. In addition, the impact of foreign factors cannot be ignored with the deepening of globalization. Some researchers estimated equilibrium interest rate using Fisher hypothesis, Taylor rule, interest rate parity, and dynamic stochastic general equilibrium model (DSGE). The result showed that China's interest rates level reflected the complex internal and external conditions. Equilibrium interest rate of a country is determined by the global forces under the background of financial globalization. When the government designs the interest rate policies, it should not only consider the domestic inflation and output gap, but also consider the interest rate level of international market as well as the impact of exchange rate and even the balance of payments (BOP). The interest rate policies especially will face a dilemma when domestic inflation is caused by the flood of liquidity from global markets and the resulting external imbalances while the exchange rate struggles to respond fully and in a timely manner to external imbalances. On the one hand, the interest rates need to rise in order to deal with domestic inflation and overheating pressures of economic growth; on the other hand, interest rates need to be reduced in order to avoid the expansion of spread between domestic and foreign interest rates and alleviate pressure on the exchange rate appreciation and capital inflows (Jin and Hao, 2015). The dilemma of the interest rate policy will also influence the time choice for launching the deposit and lending rates reform. Consequently, the market-oriented interest rate reform at this stage was promoted mostly from the aspects of improving the basic environment and conditions.

B   Adjustment of economic structure and interest rate liberalization reform

Global experiences show that the economic growth model of a country is largely influenced by its factor endowment, and is also related to its development strategy and development stage. Generally speaking, a country adopts an extensive growth pattern in the early stage of development, and then moves to intensive growth pattern when the economy reaches a certain stage. In East Asian countries, the governments played a leading role in the economic growth, so most countries faced the problem of upgrading the industrial structure and turning to a more balanced economic structure after rapid economic growth under the export-oriented model of development.

Currently, China is at a crucial stage of accelerating the economic transformation. In terms of international environment, the world economy is still struggling to shake off the effects of the global financial crisis, and it is very hard for the world economy to free itself from the low growth rate in a short time; in terms of domestic environment, the original growth model is facing big challenges, including the problem of overcapacity, rising labor costs, and enhanced resource and environmental constraints. The development opportunity China has today is a new one that will force it to increase domestic consumption and enhance capacity for innovation to promote the transformation of economic development model, instead of the traditional one under which it just merged into the international economic division system, expanded exports, and accelerated investments.

International experiences show that it is of great significance for economic development whether the financial innovation can support the economic transformation and technological innovation at the stage of economic transformation and industrial structure upgrading. The organic integration of financial innovation and economic and technological innovation is a powerful driving force to push forward economic development to a new level. Conversely, if the financial industry cannot keep up with the economic development and the financial innovation fails to promote the development of technological innovation, not only will the economy stagnate, but also the financial system could go off track of serving the real economy, which will do harm to the development of the real economy. Given that financial innovation could break through the interest rate control and also requires the environment of market-oriented interest rates, the government should promote interest rate liberalization reform.

There is not only an urgent need for China to push forward interest rate liberalization reform but also an opportunity to accelerate the transformation of the financial services industry with the deepening of the new round of economic transition and structural adjustment.

a   Accelerating interest rate liberalization is the requirement for giving play to the decisive role of the market in resource allocation

An important part of the transformation of China's economic growth is to shift from a government-led growth model to the model under which the market plays a decisive role, which requires the improvement of pricing mechanisms that should be determined mainly by the market, meaning that any price that can be formed by the market must be left to the market and the government does not intervene unnecessarily. It is helpful to establish the virtuous circle of the financial system and economic development by promoting interest rate liberalization and coordinating reforms such as exchange rate regime reform and RMB capital account liberalization to enable the price of money to fully reflect the actual supply and demand situation. This issue concerns the overall situation of the transformation of development patterns and structural adjustment.

It should be stressed that China should pay attention to the systematicness and coordination of the reforms during the process of advancing interest rate liberalization in the future. First, it should focus on financial institutions and financial markets, such as accelerating the development of the market pricing benchmark and building the pricing capability of financial institutions. Second, it should improve the external environment, such as supporting fair access and promoting full competition in the market. Third, China should speed up the transformation of government functions, make efforts to solve the problem of excessive government intervention in resource allocation and lack of distinction between government and enterprise credit, and encourage the benign interaction of market-based reform of capital factors and other reforms.

b   Accelerating interest rate liberalization is a requirement for the transformation of growth momentum from external demand to domestic demand

As the second largest economy in the world, China is a big country with an open economy. It can learn lessons from international experiences that the typical characteristics of the large economies are the dominance and stability of domestic demand (Chenery and Syrquin, 1988). China has achieved remarkable progress with an export-oriented economy in the past and should continue to make use of the overseas market in the future. Nevertheless, the same export share of the large economies and the corresponding economic growth driven by the exports brings less economic welfare compared with the small economies. On the one hand, over-reliance on exports may lead to supply imbalance of production factors between domestic demand and external demand; on the other hand, a country may force down the cost of its exports through price controls, tax reductions, and excessive tolerance of environmental damages in order to raise the export share, which will aggravate the welfare losses of export-oriented growth.

To realize the transformation of growth momentum from external demand to domestic demand, one of the solutions is to correct the distortion of resources allocation caused by price controls and accelerate the prices reform of the production factors. As the price of capital elements, interest rates can play a critical role in promoting the economic transformation of a big country. The rate of return on investment (ROI) is the fundamental factor for market participants to determine their investment allocation. To evaluate whether the formation mechanisms of ROI is perfect or not, we should analyze two key elements. The first one is whether the pricing of the products and services is liberalized. At present, this problem has been basically solved except for a small number of energy resources and public goods, but China still needs to accelerate the reform as the pricing of some fundamental products and services is still under control. Another important element is the price of capital – the interest rate. If interest rates cannot reflect the changes in the supply and demand of capital fully and in a timely manner, it may encourage excessive investment, and it is also then difficult to advance industrial transformation and upgrading by optimizing the investment structure. As far as the financial market is concerned, the base rates control will inevitably affect the pricing of almost all financial products, which will weaken their basic function of optimizing the resources allocation and lead to either overcapacity or asset bubbles. As far as macro-regulation is concerned, interest rates are also very important. Big countries whose economies are open and led by domestic demand (the United States, the eurozone, and even emerging economies such as India) often use interest rates as their main instrument of monetary policy; for those economies, the exchange rate is mostly a natural result of the foreign exchange market, which is affected by many variables, including interest rates, and the exchange rate will fluctuate automatically with the changes in the supply and demand of BOP. The developed economies adopted a lot of unconventional monetary policies, particularly quantitative easing policies, after the global financial crisis. The transmission mechanism of those policies is to lower the interest rates to stimulate economic recovery, and the exchange rate volatility is also closely related to the low interest rates.

As a main instrument of macro-regulation, interest rates should play a greater role in boosting the domestic demand of China, which is a big country with an open economy; the amount of imports and exports accounted for 50 percent of GDP in China, and the cross-border capital flows such as FDI, ODI, and RMB assets will increase in the future with the further liberalization of capital account and the growing cross-border use of RMB. China's economy now is gradually changing from the assumptions of a small country with an open economy that was passively affected by the international economy in the past, to the open economy of a big country that can interact with the global economy. Thus, as a big country with an open economy, it is necessary for China to give full play to the important role of interest rates in macroeconomic regulation for the purpose of expanding the domestic demand and improving terms of trade and investment. Therefore, it is essential to promote interest rate liberalization, and especially accelerate the development of market-oriented interest rate environment, make great efforts to enhance the corporate governance of financial institutions and strengthen financial constraints, unify the regulatory standards of financial markets and build a sound financial market system, promote the establishment of market structure that can correctly determine interest rates, and create the conditions to give play to the basic role of interest rates in the resources allocation.

c Accelerating interest rate liberalization is the requirement for the change from investment-driven to consumption-driven

Many studies reveal that there is an imbalance between investment and consumption in terms of China's economic structure. More than 50 percent of GDP comes from capital formation in China. The data from the *World Economic Outlook* released by the IMF shows that China's investment rate is much higher than other countries at the moment, and the result is the same when compared with that of the same development stage of other countries. China's investment rate was close to 50 percent in 2013, 20 percentage points higher than the average level of emerging economies, and 13.9 and 29.7 percentage points higher than the BRICS countries India and Brazil. The investment rates in developed countries are generally less than 25 percent. In "Asian tigers", the investment rates were only about 35 percent when their economies grew very rapidly in the 1980s.

The investment rate is too high and the consumption rate of the household sector is too low in China, which has brought serious challenges to economy and society: On the one hand, the high investment rate increased the risk of economic overheating, asset bubbles, and overcapacity and reduced the sustainability of economic growth (Huang and Wang, 2010); on the other hand, high investment rate also badly influenced household consumption, and the welfare of the residents was not improved simultaneously with economic growth.

The imbalance between investment and consumption had many causes, and comprehensive policies should be applied to improve the structure of investment and consumption; however, interest rate liberalization is also a very important part of those policies. The experiences of Japan, South Korea, and Chinese Taiwan suggest that interest rate liberalization usually was realized or promoted in the background of the adjustment of the economic structure, and contributed to the structural improvement of investment and consumption.

Table 4-1 Investment ratio of selected counties

	1980	1985	1990	1995	2000	2005	2010	2013
Developed economies								
US	23.3	24.1	21.5	21.1	23.6	23.2	18.4	19.4
Italy	27.6	23.8	22.6	20.6	20.8	20.9	20.1	17.4
Canada	23.9	21.7	21.7	19.5	20.8	22.8	23.3	24.3
Germany	28.2	23.5	25.6	22.3	22.3	17.3	17.3	17.6
UK	17.6	18.2	20.1	17.2	17.9	17.1	15.0	14.0
Japan	32.1	28.2	32.5	28.1	25.1	22.5	19.8	20.7
France	23.4	18.4	21.6	17.9	19.9	20.0	19.3	19.6
Australia	27.0	27.1	26.3	25.2	24.7	28.0	27.0	28.5
Four Asian tigers								
Singapore	45.0	40.9	35.1	33.3	33.2	20.0	21.4	26.4
Hong Kong	35.0	21.6	27.2	34.2	27.6	21.1	23.9	26.3
South Korea	32.9	30.9	38.1	36.9	30.6	29.7	29.5	26.8
Taiwan	33.3	19.4	24.4	26.7	25.7	22.7	22.4	19.9
Emerging economies								
China	35.0	38.3	36.1	41.9	35.1	42.1	48.2	48.9
India	18.8	24.6	26.6	27.1	24.8	34.7	36.8	35.0
Indonesia	32.2	37.7	45.0	31.9	22.2	25.1	32.3	34.6
Thailand	26.4	28.2	41.1	42.1	22.8	31.4	25.9	30.0
Malaysia	32.4	27.5	32.8	43.6	26.9	22.4	23.3	27.1
Chile		18.8	26.5	27.7	22.0	22.0	22.4	25.7
Mexico	26.6	21.9	20.4	26.1	24.8	23.9	23.6	24.2
Brazil	21.1	17.4	18.4	18.0	18.3	16.2	20.2	19.2
Less developed economies								
Syria	27.9	24.1	16.5	27.2	16.5	18.4	26.7	
Mongolia	54.5	63.8	15.7	27.4	25.7	36.5	40.8	56.5
Algeria	32.6	27.7	24.1	30.2	25.0	31.3	41.7	43.3
Tanzania	35.1	26.2	24.5	18.5	16.8	25.1	32.0	36.7
Nepal	6.6	21.0	16.9	23.5	22.6	26.7	37.0	31.8

Source: IMF World Economic Outlook Database

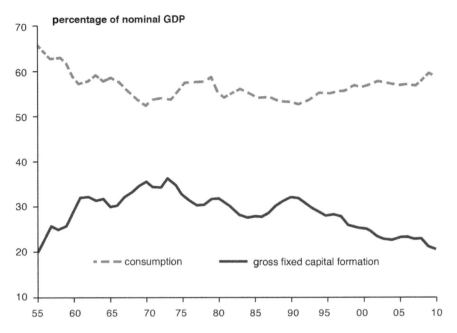

Figure 4-2 Consumption and investment in Japan

III   Financial innovation, transformation of financial structure, and interest rate liberalization

A   *The impetus for interest rate liberalization: financial innovation and financial disintermediation theory*

Interest rate control restrains market competition and reduces market efficiency, while financial institutions seek various opportunities to break through the control and carry out financial innovation to make a profit. In practice, financial innovation and financial regulation are contradictory in nature. The purpose of financial control measures is to ensure the security and stability of the financial system and prevent market failure, but they also affect the efficiency of market and the profitability of financial institutions. Kane proposed the famous Circumventive Innovation Theory in the 1980s. He believes that financial innovation results from financial institutions' behaviors of obtaining profits and avoiding various financial controls imposed by governments. Although the main target of government regulation is to maintain the stability and equilibrium of the economy for the public interest, a lot of control measures actually impose taxes on banks, thus hindering the improvement of their operation and profitability. Hence, financial institutions must improve their capacity for sustainable development and business efficiency through the interaction of control and innovation. Silber further puts forward the Constraint-induced Innovation Theory, based on Kane. He believes that the primary reason for financial innovation is that the financial industry needs to avoid or get rid of internal and external financial repression. Government regulation is the external reason for financial innovation, and the internal rules and regulations are the internal repression for financial organizations. In order to get the opportunities to maximize their profits, financial institutions will strive to innovate and explore new products, services, and management methods to compensate for the loss caused by internal and external repression.

The above financial innovation theories give a strong explanation for the various innovation behaviors during the period of financial control in the 1970s.

Financial disintermediation develops rapidly with accelerated financial innovation. Financial disintermediation first appeared in the United States in the 1960s, referring to the phenomenon in which the deposit funding of deposit-taking institutions flowed to the securities with higher yields when the level of market interest rates was higher than the deposit rates that depository institutions could afford under the deposit rates ceilings, which reduced the funds of the banks that can be loaned out. Japan, France, Italy, Germany, Britain, and other western developed countries had also followed a phenomenon of financial disintermediation. Hester (1969) first proposed the concept of financial disintermediation. He argued that "financial disintermediation was the phenomenon where assets bypassed banks and were allocated directly by other financial institutions and capital markets". Here the intermediation actually refers to the narrow sense of the intermediary – banks. In the 1970s, Hendershott, Vernon, and Solvin discussed the reasons for financial disintermediation theoretically and empirically. Their research shows that financial disintermediation became one of the most important characteristics in the development of financial industry in many countries because of financial innovation caused by the breakthrough of the interest rate control. Therefore, many countries had to speed up interest rate liberalization reform to deal with various problems raised by financial disintermediation.

International experience shows that interest rate liberalization and financial innovation are always of mutual promotion and reciprocal causation. On the one hand, interest rate liberalization provides a broader space for financial innovation, and market-based pricing is helpful to promote the diversification of financial innovation. On the other hand, new financial products are required to manage the new risks in the process of financial deregulation which may create further price volatility. Practically, interest rate liberalization has brought both opportunities and challenges to the commercial banks. In terms of opportunities, it can promote financial innovation, develop intermediary business, enhance the ability of independent pricing, raise revenue on deposits and loans, prompt banks to actively manage their assets and liabilities, optimize the structure of bank customers, and promote the strategic transition of the banking business. In terms of challenges, it will reduce bank profits and lead to the risk of interest rates fluctuations as well as business transformation and systemic financial risks.

Financial disintermediation is a natural phenomenon when the economy develops to a certain stage, and it is also an inevitable result of interest rate liberalization. From the perspective of the real economy, financial disintermediation means the diversification and enrichment of financial products, making it possible for enterprises to broaden their sources of financing and improve their balance sheet. From the perspective of the financial sector, interest rate liberalization enables the risk to be released, so the financial sectors need to provide different kinds of contracts to manage the risks. Specifically, on the one hand, financial disintermediation promotes the transition from interest rate control to interest rate liberalization, from indirect financing to direct financing, and from the separated-business to mixed-business. Therefore, financial disintermediation is a powerful driving force of interest rate liberalization. On the other hand, interest rate liberalization will enhance fierce market competition between banks and other financial institutions. The financial intermediaries and financial organizations with low efficiency will be disintermediated from the market and replaced by more competitive financial institutions through competition, thus creating a cycle between disintermediation and anti-disintermediation. Therefore, in this sense, interest rate liberalization will promote financial disintermediation to some extent.

B   The international experiences of financial innovation and interest rate liberalization reform

In the US, interest rate liberalization reform was always accompanied by financial innovation and can be regarded as a reference.

After the 1960s, the interest rate control represented by *Regulation Q* and financial control could not catch up with the economic and financial development, and its drawbacks have become increasingly prominent. First, money did not flow to the good-quality banks due to the rigid price of funds; thus, the banks with strong operational capability found it difficult to expand, and it was hard to achieve the goal of choosing the fittest one in the banking system through the normal market competition. Second, rigid interest rate control can't adapt to the severe problem of inflation. The banks ran into difficulties and were unable to deal with the challenges that came from the securities market, which led to the instability of the financial system. In the 1960s, the inflation rate of the US once reached 20 percent; the market interest rates began to rise significantly, sometimes above the upper limit of deposit rates, which made bank deposits unattractive for the investors. At the same time, a flood of bank deposits flew to the security market or the currency market with the rapid development of financial markets, the deepening of financial internationalization, and the diversification of investments. The traditional banking business declined sharply, and some deposit-taking financial institutions were trapped in a survival crisis. For instance, when the monetary policy was tightened and interest rates in the money market rose in 1966 and 1969, the adjustment on the deposit rates ceiling was lagging and inadequate because of *Regulation Q*; a large amount of capital moved from banks to the money market, resulting in the instability of the financial system and the crisis of American

Table 4-2 Financial innovations brought about by interest rate regulation in 1960–1980

Year	Financial innovations
1961	Negotiable CDs
1963	Subordinated debentures
1965	Short-term promissory note
1966	Eurodollars
1969	Bank-related commercial paper
1969	Loan RPs
1969	Working capital acceptances
1974	Floating rate notes
1972–1982	MMMFs
	Money market certificates
	Stripped bonds
	Deep discount (zero coupon) bonds
	Bonds with put options or warrants
	Euro currency bonds

Source: *Financial Innovation*, Philip Molyneux and Nidal Shamroukh, John Wiley & Sons, 1999

Savings and Loan Association. Third, the distortion of the financial system had an adverse effect on the monetary regulation mechanism. And the deposit rates ceiling limited the ability of banks to absorb deposits. The supply of credit was insufficient when the demand for funds was strong, leading to a series of bank credit crises after 1966.

In order to get through the difficulty, banks in the United States created a lot of new financial instruments to avoid regulation and expand the sources of funds. One famous example was the negotiable certificates of deposit (CDs) created by the First National City Bank (now Citibank) in 1961. It is actually a kind of money market instrument and is beyond the control of the deposit rate ceiling. The CDs can provide cash liquidity and offer higher interest rates for the depositors, and also can provide a stable source of funding. The commercial banks also actively secured funding by issuing commercial paper, absorbing the Eurodollar deposits, and so on. For the next two decades, interest rate control led to a large number of innovative financial instruments.

Now let's analyze the relationship between financial disintermediation and interest rate liberalization. The competitiveness of the commercial banks was constantly declining because of separated-business and interest rate control in the environment of high inflation in the 1960s. A large amount of money flew from bank deposits into the securities market, and the problem of bank disintermediation became increasingly serious. In order to evade the controls and achieve anti-disintermediation, the commercial banks vigorously developed off-balance-sheet business and increased overseas branches, which contributed to the transformation of commercial banks' strategy and business and kick-started interest rate liberalization in the United States. Since the 1970s, the direct financing function of the securities market had become increasingly prominent with the development of new financial products and the increases in demand, while the indirect financing function of the lending market had been shrinking, and the proportion of financial assets controlled by commercial banks to all financial assets fell from more than 60 percent to less than 25 percent. The non-bank financial institutions led by investment banks had replaced the commercial banks gradually and dominated the financial sector, and a financial system centered on the capital market emerged in the United States.

Similar to the United States, the banks of Britain, Germany, and other countries founded a mixed account to break through the interest rate controls in the late 1960s. From the end of the war to 1975, Japan had followed the example of the United States for a long time in imposing strict control on the deposit and loan interest rates. The spreads of all the banks were roughly the same, so the more money they pooled, the more profit they earned. Different that American financial innovation, which mainly focused on the capital market, the banks in Japan drove financial innovation by making every attempt to attract deposits through non-interest rate competition, because indirect financing played a more important role in Japan's financial system. For instance, under the circumstances of the low level of financial information at that time, banks provided payroll service for the enterprises free of charge (1969), transferred money automatically for public accounts and tax accounts (1965), generalized credit card and ATM facilities (1969), and introduced CDs (1979) and other financial products (Kang, 1989).

C Financial innovation calls for China's interest rate liberalization reform

The Bank of International Settlements (1986) summarized the historical experiences of financial innovation and pointed out that "financial innovation was a process of changing the characteristics of financial assets (such as the income, risk, duration and liquidity) in a certain direction". As a result, financial innovation refers to the usage of a variety of financial instruments, the development of new financial markets, and new ways to provide financial services (Llewellyn, 1985). In terms of the current development trend of China's financial system, the financial markets, or ways to provide financial services, are undergoing rapid changes and are becoming powerful driving forces to further promote interest rate liberalization reform.

a The financial market and direct financing are developing steadily and financial disintermediation is emerging

With the deepening of financial reform, China's financial market is developing steadily. The multi-level capital market has been taking shape, and the stock market, bond market, futures and derivatives markets, and wealth-management markets are thriving; securities companies, fund companies, futures companies, and other intermediaries in the capital market are growing. At the end of October 2014, there were 2,584 listed companies in Shanghai and Shenzhen stock market, with a market capitalization of 30.05 trillion RMB and effective stock trading accounts of about 135 million; at the end of September, there were already 1,153 listed companies in the New OTC Market, raising RMB 9285 million in total. Currently, there are 32 regional equity transfer markets and more than 7,400 listed companies in China, and the scope of the services is expanding. In addition, the pilot of the OTC market has been carried out in 15 securities companies and achieved remarkable results. China's bond market is comprised of the interbank market, exchange market, and OTC market of commercial banks, and the market structure with floor trading market and OTC market is coming into being gradually, which is similar to the mature markets overseas. Measured by the total amount of bond custodianship, the interbank market is the major component, and the exchange bond market is an important part of China's bond market. At the end of September 2014, the face value of the bond custodian stood at 34.14 trillion RMB, among which the interbank bond market accounted for about 90.82 percent, the exchange bond market comprised about 6.97 percent, the bank counter market made up 1.70 percent, and other markets accounted for 0.51 percent. At the same time, product innovation in the bond market and asset securitization has been steadily promoted, with the range of products constantly widened, covering government bonds, local government bonds, central bank bills, government-backed agencies' bonds, financial bonds, enterprise bonds, medium-term notes, collection of notes for SMEs, short-term commercial paper, non-public directional debt financing instruments, corporate bonds, convertible bonds, equity warrant bonds (WBs) and SMEs private placement bonds, and so on.

As far as financing structure is concerned, the proportion of RMB loans in social financing has declined year by year. New RMB loans reached 91.9 percent of the social financing in 2002, but the proportion slid to 51.4 percent in 2013. The financial market and direct financing are growing steadily, which is gradually changing the situation that the banking industry has unipolar strength in China, and a multi-level and diversified financial system and financing structure is emerging. But according to the factor endowments of this stage and the requirements for promoting economic transformation, direct financing is yet to be developed, which is not favorable for implementing innovation-driven development strategy. We should adhere to market orientation, accelerate fundamental financial reforms such as interest rate liberalization, and effectively stimulate the innovation power of market participants in an environment where the pricing mechanism is reasonable and competition is fair.

*b   The innovative financial products symbolized by the
      wealth-management products are flourishing*

One of the characteristics of China's monetary policy framework is the dual-track interest rate system: The benchmark deposit interest rates are regulated by the central bank while money and bond rates are market-determined. This system is considered to be part of the process of transition from planned economy to market economy and is consistent with China's gradualist approach to economic reform (He and Wang, 2011). In recent years, dual-track interest rates have also been appearing in the credit market: The bank deposit rates and rate of return on wealth-management products. Statistics show that nearly 8,169 kinds of wealth-management products came out in 2009 (almost 25 new products every day), increasing by about 20 percent compared with 2008. A total of 43,000 financial products were issued by 211 commercial banks in 2013, raising about 28.6 trillion RMB, up by 40.3 percent and 29.5 percent, respectively, compared with 2012. From 2011 to 2013, the one-year benchmark deposit rates varied from 2.75 percent to 3.5 percent, while the expected annual rates of return of one-year wealth-management products ranged from 5.14 percent to 5.34 percent, which were far higher than the deposit rates. In addition to the wealth-management products, other products are also increasingly improving and developing, including foreign exchange wealth-management products, loan products, bank card products, fund products, QDII products, debt products, insurance products, trust products, sunshine private equity products, and brokerage collections of wealth-management products.

The emergence of the wealth-management products is the innovation of the financial institutions and investors for solving the problem of insufficient financial products and is in response to financial control. The arrival of many new financial products represented by wealth-management products not only means that the interest rate is already under the process of liberalization, but also shows that commercial banks have the ability to set a price and innovate independently, benefiting from financial products innovation, which gives them the motivation to find the true interest rates and push the unification of the dual-track interest rates. Moreover, the commercial banks are becoming strong drivers in promoting interest rate liberalization reform.

c   *New forms of financial institutions and financial industry are developing rapidly*

After a period of time, China's small and medium-sized financial institutions began to grow substantially, and private capital started to enter the financial sector. For example, 1,134 new types of rural financial institutions (including the ones at planning stage and already operating) had been established all over the country as of the end of 2013, including 1,071 village banks, 14 loan companies, and 49 rural mutual funds cooperatives. The private capital invested into village banks directly and indirectly accounted for 71 percent, and the proportion of outstanding loans to farmers and small and micro enterprises was above 90 percent. Private capital entering the banking sector and financial institutions laid the foundation for the establishment of modern banks which have clear property rights, defined restrictions on the power of the large shareholders, and good corporate governance, and provided a new opportunity for breaking the monopolistic positions of the banks, promoting the innovation of the financial services, and expanding the coverage of inclusive financial services. Recently, various models of Internet financial innovation, including P2P, e-commerce micro-credit, third-party online payment platforms, and Internet financial services, have become more and more popular. Internet financial products, such as Yu'E Bao, have especially created a great impact on the traditional financial market. Yu'E Bao has been in the grip of a wave of investor enthusiasm since its launch in June 2013, and more than 100 million people have invested more than 600 billion RMB in it at the end of June 2014. Benefiting from Yu'E Bao, Tianhong Asset Management Company became China's largest and the world's fourth-largest monetary fund in January 2014. From the history of financial innovation, we can conclude that online financial products such as Yu'E Bao are the Chinese version of the Negotiable Order of Withdrawal Account (NOWS) and Money Market Mutual Funds (MMMFs) of the United States in the 1970s and 1980s, and those two instruments were the most important innovations to promote the deregulation of interest rates in the United States.

On the one hand, new forms of financial institutions and the financial industry are supplements to the traditional financial system, and they can provide more investment channels for the customers and new capital raising windows for enterprises, especially the small and micro enterprises; on the other hand, they will break the original financial order and compete with the traditional banks and other financial institutions, which will encourage reform and upgrading of traditional financial institutions and improve the efficiency of the whole financial market. This is the impetus behind the interest rate liberalization reform.

D   Accelerating interest rate liberalization is the requirement for the transformation of financial structure

Using scale indicators such as financial interrelation ratio to measure the degree of financial deepening, the total assets of China's financial institutions grew fairly fast and reached three times the scale nominal GDP. But the level of financial development needs improvement, as reflected by the indicators of quality such as structure and efficiency. To be more specific, the financial structure ratio (bank credit to private sector /market value of the stock market + market value of the private bond) is still above that of the developed countries, and even much higher than that of other BRICS countries, although direct financing has seen rapid growth in recent years. In terms of the structure of financial institutions, the market concentration of China's banking industry has gradually decreased in recent years, but some studies indicate that the lower level of market concentration is unable to encourage diversified competition of market participants and enhance the efficiency of supply if the mechanism of the market-access is unfair (Yang and Zhong, 2013). In terms of the behaviors of market participants, the trend of homogeneous competition among banks becomes more and more obvious, and the financial institutions prefer to focus on businesses related to mortgage guarantees, state sectors, financing platform, large-scale lending, long-term loans, and loans to monopolistic industries, which essentially reflects the lack of core competitiveness such as credit screening, pricing, and risk management.

According to the theory of endogenous financial development, when economic development enters into a mature stage from extensive competition, technological

Table 4-3 Evolution of financial structure

Bank-oriented financial system				Market-oriented financial system			
Country	Financial structure ratio (fs)			Country	Financial structure ratio (fs)		
	1990– 2009 (20-year) annual average (a)	2000– 2009 (10-year) annual average (b)	Trend		1990– 2009 (20-year) annual average (a)	2000– 2009 (10-year) annual average (b)	Trend
Middle-income and emerging economies							
China	4.927	2.997	Decrease	Argentina	0.932	0.315	Decrease
Greece	1.480	1.108	→1	Brazil	0.891	0.544	Decrease
Hungary	3.410	1.539	Decrease	India	0.794	0.647	Decrease
Indonesia	1.753	0.727	<1	Mexico	0.583	0.424	Decrease
South Korea	1.242	0.928	<1	Russia	0.729	0.436	Decrease
Poland	2.643	1.236	Decrease	South Africa	0.625	0.636	Stable
Turkey	1.242	0.743	<1				
High income economies							
Austria	1.886	1.550	Decrease	Australia	0.730	0.603	Decrease
Canada	1.142	1.028	→1	Belgium	0.714	0.716	Stable
Germany	1.223	1.175	→1	Denmark	0.538	0.800	Increase
Ireland	1.638	1.762	Increase	Finland	0.752	0.438	Decrease
Italy	1.031	0.907	<1	France	0.862	0.683	Decrease
Japan	1.225	0.913	<1	Luxembourg	0.827	0.725	Decrease
Netherland	1.154	0.907	<1	Sweden	0.823	0.635	Decrease
Portugal	2.119	1.882	Decrease	UK	0.928	0.994	Increase
Saudi Arabia	1.175	0.792	<1	US	0.757	0.736	Decrease
Spain	1.318	0.993	→1				

Notes: (1) Financial structure ratio converges to 1, representing a financial structure with equal importance of bank and market; the bigger the ratio, the greater importance of banks; the small the ratio, the greater importance of the market

(2) Because of the different data availability, the calculations of column (a) start with different years from 1990 for some countries, including China (1992), Hungary (1992), India (1980), Indonesia (1991), Korea (1976), Germany (1992), Luxemburg (1989), and Russia (1995)

(3) With private debt data missing for counties, including Luxemburg, Poland, Russia, and Saudi Arabia, their financial structure ratios are calculated as the ratio of private credit financing and stock market capitalization

Source: Calculation based on the World Bank Financial Development and Structure Database

progress will play a more important role in economic development, market competition will be more intensive, and direct financing that is good at diversifying risks and managing the transaction costs will increase (Allen and Gale, 1999).

In the past, especially since the 11th Five-Year Plan, China's financial sector has been showing some positive changes in many aspects, including institution, market, and product structure, with the transformation of the real economy and the deepening of financial reform, and the multi-level and diversified financial system and financing structure are emerging. However, after observing the characteristics of the present stage of China's economic development and the need for transformation, we can see that the small and medium-sized financial institutions and private financial institutions still need to be developed, and financial support for "rural areas, agriculture and farmers", private economy, small enterprises, fields of energy saving and environmental protection, and Chinese enterprises' going global also need to be strengthened; the role of the bond market should be further enhanced compared with the credit financing, and the multi-leveled stock market needs to be deepened. The advantages of the insurance market in risk management are far from fully realized due to the low level of its depth and density, which in part increases the responsibility of the government to maintain social stability.

It is crucial to accelerate interest rate liberalization and other basic financial reforms to promote the establishment of a financial structure that adapts to the economic transformation. The incentives to innovate by microeconomic entities can be effectively inspired in a market environment with reasonable pricing mechanisms and fair competition mechanisms, and the financial structure will naturally be optimized if the financial institutions can adapt themselves to the transformation of economic structure actively. Instead, if the pricing mechanism is not scientific, the competition is unfair, and the regulatory regime is unreasonable, then it is impossible to optimize the financial structure even with perfect industrial policy and government planning. There are a lot of lessons to be learned in the field of industrial structure adjustment. In this sense, the key of optimizing financial structure is to correctly price money and achieve the optimal allocation of capital.

IV   Challenges of interest rate liberalization under the background of "three superimposed periods"[1]

At present, China's interest rate liberalization reform is facing a more complex environment. In terms of the trend of domestic economic development, China has to simultaneously deal with the slowdown in economic growth, make difficult structural adjustments, and absorb the effects of previous economic stimulus policies. Long-term structural contradictions and short-term cyclical contradictions coexist, and there are risks to the real economy paralleling the financial risks. In particular, the existing growth momentum for external demand and real estate has weakened, but a new engine for economic growth remains to be enhanced. Since the new century, China's investment rate has been showing an upward trend for more than ten years. In recent years especially, the investment rate has been significantly higher than the previous level, so it will become more difficult to keep high-speed growth in the future. Nowadays, the investments in manufacturing industry and real estate are on a downward trend with fluctuation, and economic growth is largely fueled by infrastructure investments. In addition, low-efficient enterprises have taken up a large number of resources, which is leading to inefficient usage of resources. The debt levels of the whole society have risen rapidly, and risks are spreading fast from the real economy to the financial sector. Under such circumstances, China should give a comprehensive consideration of breakthrough points, steps, and the intensity of promoting market-based interest rate reform. In terms of the external environment, global trade, investment, and the financial environment have been undergoing important changes since the crisis, and the rebalancing of the global economy is on the ascendant as a result of profound restructuring. With the deeper integration of China's economy into the world, the interaction between the above two has strengthened, and China's economic transformation is directly included in the global economic rebalancing. During this process, all kinds of external shocks, including changes in the amount and structure of external demand, cross-border capital flows, the fluctuation of exchange rate, and commodity prices and unexpected risk events, will have a strong spillover effect on China's economy, which will increase the difficulties of promoting significant structural and institutional reforms.

In terms of the periodic changes in technological innovation and industrial revolution, a country is more likely to have asset bubbles and an economic and financial crisis when the real economy is in a period of structural adjustment and lacks new power for economic growth.[2] Some financial institutions, especially the small and medium-sized financial institutions, may encounter varying degrees of difficulties in their operations because of growing competition after interest rate liberalization. Hence, wrong policies may easily provoke a financial crisis. Under the background of the "three superimposed periods", China has gradually entered into a stage in which the economy and financial situation has become more sensitive to financial risks. It is more complicated and difficult to manage the financial risks, and the probability of accumulation and sudden outbreak of systemic financial risk is growing. These factors create new challenges for future interest rate liberalization reform.

A *Interest rate liberalization reform should be more cautious as economic growth is slowing down*

Global experiences show that the interest rate liberalization reform should be more prudent when economic growth is slowing down. Because interest rates had been controlled for a long time and were mostly lower than the market equilibrium level, the interest rates in most countries and regions rose to varying degrees in the early stage of lifting of controls. Out of 20 countries whose data are available, the nominal interest rates of 15 countries had risen, but only five countries had lower nominal interest rates; among the 18 countries with relatively complete data, the real interest rates of 17 countries was up and only one country's was down (Sa, 1996). Specifically, the interest rates of the United States rose quite rapidly at the initial stage of deregulation. The nominal interest rates on deposits and loans were 8.2 percent and 9.06 percent, respectively, in 1978, and then gradually increased to a high of 15.91 percent and 18.87 percent in 1981; the real interest rates rose from 0.6 percent and 1.46 percent in 1978 to 5.61 percent and 8.57 percent in 1981, and then began to decline and appeared to be stabilizing. During the second stage of interest rate liberalization reform in South Korea, the nominal interest rate on deposits grew from 8.5 percent in early 1993 to 9.81 percent at the end of 1996, while the real interest rates increased from 3.8 percent to 4.91 percent; the nominal interest rate on loans rose from 8.5 percent to 11.1 percent, while the real interest rate went up from 3.8 percent to 6.2 percent. In Chinese Taiwan, the weighted average nominal interest rates on deposits and loans rose from 5.96 percent and 9.18 percent at the end of 1985 to 7.22 percent and 10.5 percent at the end of 1990, but the real interest rates decreased from 5.99 percent and 9.21 percent to 3.12 percent and 6.4 percent during the same period. In Latin American countries that carried out radical reforms, the interest rates soared and experienced a lot of volatility and even encountered overshooting. For instance, the average real interest rate on deposits was 32 percent between 1976 and 1982 in Chile, and the figure in Argentina reached 52.57 percent in 1981.

In terms of the characteristics of China's economic development stage, the most important feature of the new normal is that the economy has shifted gear from the previous high-speed to a medium-to-high speed growth. At such a stage, in order to keep the economy running smoothly and orderly, we should fully consider the impacts of interest rate liberalization reform and avoid the excessive tightening effect caused by rising interest rates.

B   *The spillover effect of soft budget constraints is likely to weaken the practical impact of interest rate liberalization reform*

As far as the microstructure of China's investment and the sources of funding are concerned, the sectors and industries with soft budget constraints are not sensitive to the interest rate and have great demand for investments, thus taking more financial resources. First, the industries with low sensitivity of the interest rate have greater demand for investments. In China's fixed asset investments, the proportion of the infrastructure investment has always been above 20 percent and that of the real estate development investment has been about 18 percent since 2004. In 2013, China's infrastructure investment made up 21.4 percent of the fixed asset investments, 0.5 percentage points higher than 2012. And the real estate development investment accounted for 19.7 percent, the same as 2012 but up by 1 percentage point compared with 2009. Second, the investments in real estate and infrastructure were largely financed by domestic loans. Since 2006, the proportion of the domestic loans in real estate investments has been higher than that in the overall investments. The former average annual proportion was 1 percentage point higher than the latter between 2006 and 2013, and 2.4 percentage points higher in 2013. And 30.5 percent of the capital came from domestic loans in the municipal public facilities construction from 2004 to 2013, 14.2 percentage points higher than the proportion of domestic loans in the whole investments (among which were 13.9 percentage points higher in 2013). Third, the state-owned enterprises raised more funds with a high leverage ratio. The debt ratio of the state-owned industrial enterprises was 65.1 percent at the end of 2013, up by 7.3 percentage points than that of the industrial enterprises above the designated size. The debt ratio of the state-owned industrial enterprises increased by 0.63 percentage points from 2012 to 2013, while the ratio of the industrial enterprises above the designated size decreased by 0.03 percentage points. The state-owned enterprises occupied a large amount of loans, and the proportion of their outstanding loans in all loans was 46.5 percent at the end of 2013. Fourth, considering that RMB loans accounted for only about 50 percent of social financing, the infrastructure industry and the real estate industry actually occupied more financial resources. According to the National Audit Office, at the end of June 2013, local governments had a debt of 4075.6 billion RMB that was obligated to 7,170 financing platform companies, assumed the debt with guaranteed obligation of 883.3 billion RMB, and took on a debt that may bear some responsibilities for the debt relief of 2.0116 trillion RMB. The above three kinds of debts grew at an average annual rate of 11.0 percent, 3.3 percent, and 31.3 percent, respectively, from the end of 2010 to the end of June 2013. At the end of 2013, the outstanding trust funds had reached 10.3 trillion RMB, of which the money invested in the real estate was 1.04 trillion RMB (accounting for 10 percent), and the amount of money for cooperation between trust companies and government was 960.7 billion RMB (accounting for 8.81 percent), up by 3.5 and 2.1 percentage points compared with 2011 and 2012, respectively.

The major disadvantage of transition economies is the soft budget constraint. Although this situation has greatly improved since the reform and opening-up, the problem still remains. Currently, soft budget constraint is reflected in many aspects, including the rapid expansion of the financing platforms where the credits of government and enterprise are difficult to distinguish, the fast growing of housing credit, and the banks' excessive pursuit of assets and profits. Recently, there have been some discussions about the pace of interest rate liberalization reform, and both camps agree and emphasize the importance of strengthening the budget constraint. Otherwise, a misguided policy may further magnify the spillover effect brought by soft budget constraint, aggravate the distortion of the allocation of financial resources, and weaken the real effect of the interest rate liberalization reform.

C   *The rapid growth of money and credit increased the risk of interest rate liberalization reform*

The direct consequence of the stimulus efforts in the early stage to deal with the crisis is that China's bank credit and social financing have experienced a new round of rapid expansion since 2008. The outstanding loans of financial institutions (both RMB and foreign currency) increased from 32 trillion RMB to 76.74 trillion RMB from 2008 to 2013, an average annual growth rate of 19.1 percent, and total social financing rose from 6.98 trillion RMB to 17.32 trillion RMB, an average annual growth rate of 19.9 percent, while the average nominal growth rate of GDP was only 13.4 percent.

At the same time, the leverage ratios of China's household sector, non-financial enterprises, and government sector, especially non-financial enterprises, have seen rapid growth. According to estimates from different institutions, the liabilities of China's non-financial enterprises as a share of GDP is about 110~130 percent, while the above ratios of the United States, Britain, France, Germany, Japan, and Australia in 2012 were 72 percent, 109 percent, 111 percent, 49 percent, 99 percent, and 59 percent, respectively, which were all lower than China. The asset-liability ratio of 5,000 enterprises increased from 58.3 percent at the end of 2007 to 62 percent at the end of September 2014, rising by 3.7 percentage points, according to statistics of the People's Bank of China.

The high levels of indebtedness correspond to high investment. Given the strong external demand and high potential growth rate of the economy, the enterprises' returns on investment can cover the financing cost and help them to achieve sustainable development. However, many industries and enterprises will face challenges as China's economy is gradually transitioning from the original high growth model to a moderate growth model and focuses more on structural adjustments. The decline in the corporate profitability and its "hematopoietic function" results in the increased demand for external funds. Hence, the corporate financing is difficult to shrink in the short-term and the credit risks tend to be higher.

First, the corporate return on investment and the corporate profitability have declined. From a macro perspective, the output elasticity of investment in China has shown a downward trend and the incremental unit GDP brought by incremental unit investment decreased from 4.03 in 2000 to 2.08 in 2013. From a micro perspective, the cost to margins of 5,000 industrial enterprises has fallen to the current level of about 5.5 percent from more than 10 percent before the crisis, lower than one-year loan prime rates (LPR), according to a survey conducted by the People's Bank of China of those enterprises. In addition, in terms of cash flow management of the enterprises, the ratio of the demand deposits has been decreasing and the ratio of the time deposits has been rising since 2011, which also shows the decline in activities of the real economy and the insufficient impetus of enterprises to expand business.

Second, the real economy is more and more reliant on borrowing money. In recent years, the ratio of the matured debt instruments, such as wealth-management products, trusts, municipal corporate bond, policy financial bonds, and corporate bonds to the total new issues, has stayed at historically high levels. In 2013, 4.7 trillion RMB of the wealth-management products were due, 516.25 billion RMB of trust products were expired, nearly 1 trillion RMB of policy financial bonds were matured, and 2.03 trillion RMB of corporate bonds should be payable. The proportions of the above four kinds of maturing debts to new issues were 103.65 percent, 82.84 percent, 46.41 percent, and 55.16 percent, respectively, with an obvious feature of borrowing the new to repay the old. China's credit bonds market reached the first peak of expansion in 2009, and the payment of the long-term bonds peaked in 2014 because a large number of five-year bonds were issued in 2009. At the same time, the scale of interest payment also hit a record high in 2014 with the rapid expansion of the credit bonds market. According to rough estimation, the amount of the matured non-financial credit bonds reached 2.1 trillion

RMB in 2014, an increase of 16 percent compared with 2013, and 200 billion RMB of bonds entered the selling-back period. The total scale of interest payment of all the credit bonds was about 470 billion RMB in 2014, an increase of 24 percent compared with 2013, which revealed that a very substantial proportion of newly issued debts were used to repay the old or to extend the old.

Third, borrowing the new to repay the old, the Ponzi scheme, is the direct reflection of Minsky's financial instability hypothesis. Minsky (1975) divided capital raisers into three categories: The hedge-financed firms who only borrowed money to bridge funding gaps according to their cash flow in the future, so they were safe borrowers; the speculative-financed firms who did not have enough money to repay the principal, but can pay off the interest; and the Ponzi firms who did not have enough money to repay the principal and interest, and needed to borrow new debts or sold their assets for repayment. Then, Minsky (1975) interpreted the financial crisis within the framework that business cycles induce firms to run the business with high indebtedness: Most enterprises belonged to the hedge-financed firms at the start of a new cycle; the speculative-financed firms and Ponzi firms would increase rapidly with the further prosperity of the economy, because the enterprises' earnings were expected to rise and they tended to borrow more money on positive signs on the economy. As a result, the latter two types of borrowers whose risk was high became more and more, but the safe borrowers were getting less and less, which led to more serious financial vulnerability. Currently, the latter two types of borrowers are increasing in China, and the systemic risk behind it cannot be ignored.

Fourth, the risk of interest rate liberalization reform has increased due to the huge amount of money and credit and the hidden financial risks. On the one hand, according to international experiences, total amount of credit will increase because the rising interest rates and the narrower spreads stimulate the bank's lending after the deregulation of interest rates. The average annual growth rate of M2 was 9.7 percent from 1984 to 1990 in Japan, 3.4 percentage points higher than the level between 1984 and 1994. The loans and advances of commercial banks in Chinese Taiwan rose from NT$1745.33 billion in 1985 to NT$4645.2 billion in 1990, and the average growth rate was 21.6 percent, 4.6 percentage points higher than the 17 percent from 1980 to 1990. In South Korea, the average annual growth rate of M2 was 19.8 percent from 1990 to 1996, 2.7 percentage points higher than the level from 1990 to 2000. Even in the United States, which has developed financial markets, the growth rate of loans and money supply was also higher than the level in the 1980s. The average growth rates of loans and money supply were 9.35 percent and 9.32 percent, respectively, from 1980 to 1986, 1.05 and 1.89 percentage points higher than the levels between 1980 and 1990. Therefore, if there is a similar phenomenon in China during the process of interest rate liberalization reform, then it is against the current trend of deleveraging that is meant to absorb excess stock of money and credit. On the other hand, it is necessary to have a stable macroeconomic and financial environment to cope with the possible economic fluctuations and financial turmoil after the full liberalization of interest rates. China has entered a period that is sensitive to market risk and experiences the pain of reforms. Therefore, it is important to better deal with the relationship between the reform and risk prevention when promoting the interest rate market reform.

D   Shadow banking is developing rapidly, which increases the potential risk of the reform while promoting the interest rate liberalization reform

In recent years, one of the significant effects of the "three superimposed periods" on the financial sector has been the rapid development of the shadow banking system and its business. Due to the complexity of shadow banking products and the low transparency of the information disclosure, it is difficult for domestic and foreign institutions to accurately estimate the scale of shadow banking system. At the end of 2012, the total shadow banking assets that can be monitored stood at 20.7 trillion RMB, and the net assets were about 17.8 trillion RMB; at the end of 2013, the total assets reached 30.8 trillion RMB and net assets were about 24.2 trillion RMB; at the end of June 2014, the total assets rose to 37 trillion RMB and net assets were about 27.8 trillion RMB.

Table 4-4 Size of shadow banking business in China

Shadow banking within the traditional financial system				Shadow banking outside the traditional financial system			
Organization type	Asset quantity (100M RMB)			Organization type	Asset quantity (100M RMB)		
	06/2014	2013-end	2012-end		06/2014	2013-end	2012-end
Bank off-balance-sheet wealth-management	74,512	63,157	46,984	PE	15,100	25,000	24,000
Fund trust investment program	119,015	103,089	70,697	Financing guarantee companies (estimate)	12,145	10,400	15,000
Security company asset management	68,200	43,750	672	Small-sum loan companies	9,626	8,856	6,701
Fund company asset management	54,274	38,505	29,086	Pawn shop	1,402	1,382	950
Of which: Securities investment fund	39,241	29,612	28,662	Non-bank financial leasing company	9,500	9,500	13,000
Insurance asset management	6,300	4,500		Third-party payment entity	1,302	1,302	

Notes: 1. Data for third-party payment entity as of 2013-end; 2. Estimated data for financing guarantee companies, non-bank financial leasing companies and pawn shops

China's capital market woke up late and asset securitization is still in the infancy stage, so China's shadow banking, including their projects, funding sources, product sales, and liquidity guarantee, basically rely on traditional commercial banking systems. In this sense, shadow banking actually is a substitute for bank credit business. In addition, shadow banking in China is largely within the regulatory system, and there are few institutions, businesses, and products outside this supervision except for some private lending. Overall, the development of China's shadow banking is driven in large part by the spontaneous reforms of the financial system from bottom to top, which plays a positive role in promoting financial liberalization reform and satisfying the diversified demands for investment and financing. Moreover, the shadow banking is regulated and subject to supervision to some extent, and the risks are also under control.

The scale and risks of China's shadow banking differ greatly from the formal banking system and are far below the level of Europe and the United States. But the actual risks of China's shadow banking are greater than what it seems, which partly limited the further promotion of the interest rate liberalization reform, reminding us that we have to take the possible consequences of the reform fully into consideration.

First, the wholesale business model causes the maturity mismatch of assets and liabilities of shadow banking products, thus leading to default risks. Investors have strong pricing power under this model, and shadow banking institutions would rather raise short-term funding at a low cost by issuing securities than choose expensive long-term financing. In order to search for higher yields, shadow banking institutions buy underlying assets and all kinds of securities that have higher expected return and longer-term from different sources, which results in the maturity mismatch of shadow banking products, with many short-term liabilities but a lot of long-term assets. Once instability emerges in the financial markets, investors will panic and withdraw their money, which may lead to liquidity difficulties of shadow banking products because the shadow banking institutions cannot immediately realize their illiquid long-term assets or will suffer great loss if they liquidate those assets quickly. In such circumstances, shadow banking institutions will face the risk of runs similar to commercial banks, thus leading to default risk of shadow banking products.

Second, the high degree of risk of underlying investments could trigger default. Shadow banking deploys large amounts of capital to the underlying assets with high risks such as real estate, local government financing platform, stock market, and offshore financial market assets. Such asset allocation confronts shadow banking with high risk and high yields. Once the price of the underlying assets enters the downward path, the returns on shadow banking products will decline significantly and maybe fall even lower than the expected rate of return, thus leading to the default risk. For instance, six trust products worth 972.7 million RMB in Shanxi Fu Yu Energy Project of Jilin Trust Songhua River No. 77, which was consigned and managed by Shanxi branch of China Construction Bank, defaulted in March 2014.

Third, connected transactions accelerate the contagion of the default risks within the shadow banking system. In recent years, the boundary between the proprietary business of financial institutions and shadow banking business has become increasingly blurred with the development of the financial system's mixed-business, and both kinds of businesses depend and step on each other. The commercial banks usually provide financial support for the maturity and liquidity conversion of shadow banking business through their proprietary business, and also invest in various shadow banking products. This kind of connected transaction increases the possibility of the risk contagion. With the ample liquidity and the rising prices of assets, the connected transactions have a positive effect on improving the efficiency of resource allocation, but the risks will spread between the shadow banking business and proprietary business once the financial markets experience fluctuations and the prices of assets fall sharply, which may trigger a reversal in market liquidity.

Fourth, the over-long credit chain accelerates the spread of the default risk in the financial system. The default risk of shadow banks will be transmitted to every related investor through the complex chain of credit; the risk of shadow banking products may spread quickly and develop into systematic default due to the vulnerability of the financial system, which could result in turmoil in the financial system. First, the default risk of shadow banking products will be transmitted to investors, causing tight liquidity and increasing default risk of investors. Second, the higher default risk of investors will further tighten the liquidity of creditors and increase creditors' risk of default on debt. This vicious circle repeats itself again and again and may affect the stability of the financial system if not managed properly.

After analyzing the characteristics of different stages of economic and financial development, the requirements for interest rate liberalization and its effects on the reform, we can conclude that interest rate liberalization reform in China is the inherent requirement for economic growth, and the country is ready for it with the development of its economy and financial system. However, the process faces challenges from "three superimposed periods". On the one hand, the country needs to accelerate interest rate liberalization; on the other hand, it is necessary for China to effectively guard against risks.

Notes

1 The meaning of "three superimposed periods" is that China has to simultaneously deal with the slowdown in economic growth, make difficult structural adjustments, and absorb the effects of previous economic stimulus policies (Translator's note).
2 When the economy moves from recovery to prosperity, technology innovation and revolution will promote the industrial revolution and then boost economic growth. At the same time, it will promote the prosperity of the capital market. When the technology enters the mature stage and then evolves to a recession period, thus leading to the slowdown of growth or recession of real economy, returns on investment will decrease. But the prosperity of real economy at the early stage will stimulate the desire of the whole society to chase high profits and also greatly augment the investment funds which are eager to find the fields of investment. When there is no new growth point and profitable projects in the real economy, investors will be eager for quick success and invest in the financial and real estate market that can "get instant benefit" to obtain high profits. When

large amounts of investment funds pour into the stock market and housing market, the phenomenon in which the virtual market departs from the real economy becomes more and more remarkable, resulting in bubble boom and false prosperity; then, the bubble burst and the crisis breaks out, which has a negative effect on the real economy in turn (Fang Kun, Causes and Rules of Financial Crisis and Economic Recession in the USA and Japan – Based on the Theory of the Industrial Revolution Period, *Journal of Financial Research*, No. 82011).

5 Market-based interest rate reform and the construction of related systems

China's institutional reform and the process of transitioning to a market economy is a systemic transition that demands extensive and interrelated supporting reforms. There is a full range of issues that should be considered when pursuing the reforms. A macro-prudential policy framework, market entry and exit mechanisms, deeper financial markets, exchange rate reform, capital account convertibility, consumer finance protection, risk education, and other related mechanisms are needed in order to carry out systemic reforms (Zhou, 2012). Hu Xiaolian (2012) points out that a multitude of preconditions should be considered for the interest rate reform. Only when the essential requirements are met, such as improved corporate governance, self-discipline, and hard budget constraints of financial institutions, can a fair and competitive environment be maintained after the market-based interest rates take effect. As increased competition after the realization of market interest rates may cause some financial institutions to exit from the market, there is a real need for deposit insurance systems to guarantee smooth exit, protect depositors, and avoid systemic financial risks. In addition to the supporting facilities to the financial system, Zhou Kunping (2012) believes that reform should go hand in hand with the reform in the real economy and the taxation system. If there are no effective budget constraints in place after the realization of market-based interest rates, government departments and large enterprises with significant investment, and those relying heavily on banks for funding, will be profoundly affected by interest rate fluctuations. Such a situation is not conducive to macroeconomic stability. Currently, a unified taxation system is adopted for commercial banks; the government does not differentiate between different risk levels just to protect small and medium-sized banks. These factors restrict the interest rate reform and must be addressed in future reforms.

Of course, it is not necessary to promote the reform until all the conditions are mature (Zhou, 2012). Without the necessary supporting systems, however, the comprehensive interest rate reform will be restricted. Thus, it is of vital importance to manage the relationship between the interest rate reform and the reform of relevant supporting systems. At present, the interest rate reform is constrained by underdeveloped system supports. This chapter discusses several unresolved issues to provide the basis for furthering the reform.

I Strengthening budget constraints for microeconomic entities and market-based interest rate reform

A key condition for market-based interest rate reform is the reform of relevant economic entities. Economic entities must operate as real market participants; they must have internal ownership restraints and external market competition constraints and participate in the fund market on principle of profit maximization and cost minimization. Only in this way can a market-based interest rate mechanism and interest rate levels that reflect the supply and demand of funds be formed; economic entities will then be sensitive to interest rate changes, adjust their production and management behavior in a timely manner, and take effective measures to manage interest rate risks. Ultimately, the process of formation of market-based interest rates → market transmission of interest rates → optimal allocation of financial resources → effective macro-level regulation can be realized.

However, both in theory and in practice, microeconomic entities have not become real market players. This is exemplified by the existence of soft budget constraints. For example, as the supplier of funds, soft budget constraints of financial institutions have led to blind increases in deposit interest rates regardless of costs, producing the vicious cycle of bad money driving out the good. As funds users, state-owned enterprises (SOEs) and financing vehicles of local governments lack effective budget constraints, so they are not responsive to interest rate fluctuations. They only care about the availability of funds, but not about the cost of funds. This has distorted the relationship between the supply and demand of funds and is not conducive to the formation of a real market interest rate. At the same time, both the suppliers and receivers of funds exercise soft budget constraints, causing a blind expansion of credit, irrational credit structure, and the concentration of credit. This not only goes against market-based optimal allocation of financial resources but also leads to greater financial risks. Therefore, in order to further promote the market-based interest rate reform, strengthened budget constraints for microeconomic entities are needed. Hard financial constraints will help these entities become more price-sensitive and steadily push forward the market-based interest rate reform.

A The definition and manifestation of soft budget constraints in microeconomic entities

Kornai's 1980 study of centrally planned economies introduced the concept of soft budget constraints (Kornai, 1980). According to him, a soft budget constraint occurs when economic organizations have financial difficulties and are dependent on external help for survival. In contrast, a hard budget constraint is the survival of the fittest, meaning that all activities of the organization are limited to its intrinsic resource constraints.

Soft budget constraints involve two economic entities: Budget constraint body and budget support body (Kornai, 2009). The budget constraint body refers to an organization that cannot survive on its own resources without external assistance when income is less than expenditure – for instance, SOEs. However, when losses occur at an SOE, the government provides fiscal or financial support in various ways; the enterprise that would have normally been eliminated by the market survives. The budget support body is under the control of the government; it can directly transfer funds to help organizations with financial difficulties. In general, supporters of state-owned banks are the government and the central bank, whereas supporters of the SOEs are the government and the state-owned banks.

An examination of China's economic development shows that the investment-driven growth model and the scarcity economy in the early development stage led to soft budget constraints for microeconomic entities. Although corporate governance has improved and the status of the market has been enhanced, SOEs and local governments as well as other microeconomic entities still operate under the soft budget constraints.

a *SOEs' soft budget constraints are the inevitable outcome of government seeking policy returns beyond economic interests*

At present, the SOE reform in essence pursues a balance between policy interests and the resolution of SOE problems such as soft budget constraints and moral hazard. As SOEs assume part of the government functions, the government will consciously uphold and strengthen the monopoly status of the SOEs and enhance their profitability, thus creating the problems with soft budget constraints. Soft budget constraints have hindered SOEs' capital structure adjustment. Studies have shown that the more substantial SOEs' soft budget constraints become, the slower the pace for capital structures to adjust, and the further the actual capital structure deviates from the target capital structure. The existence of soft budget constraints results in the weakening of SOEs' ability to improve capital structure, impeding recapitalization and giving rise to the inefficiency of the SOEs. Soft budget constraints have caused SOEs to become indifferent to managing investment costs and slowed their responsiveness to the cost of capital and market supply and demand, resulting in low elasticity of demand for loans, making it difficult for SOEs to adjust the investment strategy and financing plan based on interest rate signals.

b *Local governments' soft budget constraints derive from the Chinese style of decentralized governance and competition among local governments*

After the reform and opening-up, China's unique governance structure and its assessment system for local government officials greatly stimulated local economic development initiatives. This has played an important role in China's rapid economic growth. However, there are many negative by-products, such as excessive competition among local governments for resources. With the tax-sharing system, there is serious asymmetry between local governments' financial decision-making powers and obligations. Based on competition needs among local governments, local governments and the central government are engaged in a game. If local governments are unable or pretend to be unable to compensate for debt losses, the central government will intervene; thus, the debt of local governments will be passed on to the central government. Local governments obtain resources in a top-down manner to break through budget constraints, passing on their debt to the organizations and individuals in their jurisdictions, which gives rise to soft budget constraints. On the one hand, local government's debt and budgets are not fully integrated into budget management, and debt regulation is not in place. Some regions and industries have weak debt-paying ability and may have hidden financial risks. However, the risk has been lessened by the expectation that local governments will be bailed out by the central government. On the other hand, due to the lack of effective democratic supervision, taxpayers cannot control the flow and use of financial resources, and the government monopolizes the discretion of public financial resources; thus, soft budget constraints have become a common phenomenon in local government budget.

The soft budget constraints of SOEs, local governments, and other micro-economic participants caused firms to produce regardless of costs as well as the excessive debt of local governments; these weakened the regulatory role of interest rate instruments in allocating resources and regulating economic activities. This not only makes it difficult for funds to flow to more productive projects but also weakens the role of the interest rate in optimizing the distribution of resources and leads to financial risk and difficult economic transition. This hinders the implementation of the interest rate reform.

B   The relationship between microeconomic entities and market-based interest rate reform

The goal of market-based interest rate reform is to enable financial markets to guide the society's capital toward different entities and different sectors, achieve equilibrium of the supply and demand of funds, and match the funds with risk–return objectives. Soft budget constraints do not strictly adhere to the rule of expenditure based on income; those enterprises are thus not sensitive to the price of funds, and interest rates cannot reflect the real relationship between supply and demand of funds, which hinders the market-based interest reform process. The soft budget constraints of microeconomic entities influence the interest reform in the following ways.

a   Soft budget constraints cannot respond to capital supply and demand and hinder the formation of market-based interest rates

Interest rate formation mechanisms directly determine the reasonability of the price of funds and the effectiveness of capital markets, and thus it has a profound impact on the financing structure and financial stability. The objectives of forming a market-based interest rate are two-fold. First, the establishment of market-based benchmark interest rates; second, determination of market equilibrium interest rates by the pricing capacity of market entities and market competition. At present, the market basis for the interest rate formation mechanism is weak; interest rates lack the ability to reflect the relationship between supply and demand in the capital market. Benchmark interest rates are not in place, and there is disagreement over the diversification and unification of the benchmark interest rates. The discovery of the equilibrium exchange rate is still in the exploration stage due to factors such as calculation methodology and sample size.

Therefore, to promote the formation of market-based interest rates, characteristics of economic growth, financial needs of the real economy, and the influence of the dual-track interest rate system should be taken into consideration, and a reference system that can reflect the natural equilibrium of capital supply and demand should be found. For example, the interest rate in the credit market, which is the target of the most critical reform at the current stage, should be in line with the potential economic growth rate. However, soft budget constraints of China's microeconomic entities mask their real preferences for financing. The investment-driven economic growth model also hampers the formation of a market-based interest rate that reflects true supply and demand of capital.

First, the SOEs with soft budget constraints change their investment behavior as monetary policy changes, affecting economic efficiency and the formation of market-based interest rates. Indirect financing dominates in China, and the SOEs are the main receivers of credit. Compared with the naturally hard budget constraints of non–state-owned firms whose investment strategies are sensitive to market prospect, price changes, and cost of capital, the state-owned firms have the problem of ambiguously defined proprietary rights, which distorts the principal–agent relationship and the governance structure. There exists a political symbiosis between the SOEs, government, and commercial banks, resulting in apparent soft budget constraints. Investment decisions often deviate from the goal of profit maximization, and managers' remunerations and promotions are closely related to the scale of operations, so the SOEs have strong incentives to expand even against rational market expectations. SOEs, with this type of investment decision-making mechanism and the financing capabilities under the soft budget constraints, are the main channel to achieve monetary policy targets, which can be seen from the simultaneous movement of credit expansion and the increase of investment by the SOEs. However, the soft budget constraint means that investment often is irrational and does not reflect the real investment preferences or the demand for funds in the real economy and, therefore, severely affects capital supply and demand, causing the interest rate to deviate from the equilibrium level.

Second, with insufficient constraint from budget law, local government financing vehicles incur too much debt, which distorts the supply and demand of funds and affects the formation of market equilibrium interest rates. Under the tax-sharing system, the financial power and responsibility of local governments are not symmetrical. The governments are struggling to meet their financial obligations and raise funds for economic transition and development, which has brought about a large number of financing vehicles at the local level. Using the government credit as collateral and fiscal revenues as source of repayments, these financing vehicles have no budget constraints, do not take costs into consideration, and do not adjust the scale and direction of their investments according to the market interest rate, creating excessive demand for capital. According to the National Audit Office's (NAO's) *National Government Debt Audit Report* issued on December 30, 2013, total debt held by local government debt vehicles reached RMB 6.97 trillion as of end of June 2013, accounting for 38.96 percent of total local government debt. The artificially high demand for funds is caused by the lack of budget constraints. It not only increases the level of debt and financial risk but also distorts the relationship between capital supply and demand. Under such circumstances, it is difficult to form a market equilibrium interest rate that is scientific and accurate.

b   Soft budget constraints result in insensitivity to credit costs and hinder transmission of market-based interest rates

Economic players under both soft and hard budget constraints may exist simultaneously. However, these two types of entities do not have the same sensitivity toward the price of funds, which creates a dual-track system of fund prices. On one hand, because of fiscal subsidies, deduction of dividend payments, and the absence of a repayment obligator, local governments and SOEs, which are subject to soft constraints, only consider the availability of funds, are not sensitive to the cost of funds (interest rates), and can withstand even dramatic changes in the interest rates. On the other hand, under the current credit system, most private firms as represented by small and medium-sized enterprises are adversely affected in the face of interest rate risks. Fluctuations in credit prices change financing costs and greatly influence the normal operation of business, so these firms must consider both the cost and timing of repayment; as they are extremely sensitive to the cost of credit (change in interest rates), even minor changes in the interest rate will affect their credit demand, thus forming the naturally hard budget constraints.

The essence of the interest rate reform is to let the market determine the interest rate and regulate the supply and demand of credit. The dual-track pricing of funds and the soft budget constraints cause a new liquidity trap and weaken the role of the market in regulating the supply and demand of credit. Companies that are not sensitive to interest rate changes have low interest rate elasticity; rising interest rates have little impact on their demand for funds. Thus, interest rate changes have no effect on these companies. To some extent, their demand for funds is almost infinite and doesn't decrease as interest rate rises. No matter how the price of funds fluctuates, it only affects the small and micro-sized enterprises with hard budget constraints. Those firms with soft budget constraints play a dominant role in the economy, but their demand for capital does not respond to changes in the interest rate. The interest rate cannot regulate the supply and demand of funds and the effectiveness of the interest rate reform is weakened.

c   *Microeconomic entities with soft budget constraints crowd out*
    market-oriented participants, leading to imbalanced distribution of
    financial resources

Under the dual-track system, entities that are not sensitive to interest rates push up the overall price of credit, and commercial banks under the pressure of profits are sure to distribute more resources toward these sectors. In this way, market-based entities such as small and medium-sized enterprises that are sensitive to interest rates are crowded out, which restricts the process of the market-based interest rate reform.

First, SOEs' use of credit does not match their profit contribution. Because the SOEs enjoy preferential treatment in getting credit and lack budget constraints and interest rate elasticity, they use resources inefficiently. The excessive use of credit lowers the contribution that credit expansion makes to economic growth. In 2013, the SOEs' outstanding loan accounted for 46.5 percent of all the loan balance. That same year, state-owned industrial companies' total profit accounted only for 38.3 percent of total profit of all industrial companies. Meanwhile, the debt ratio of the SOEs was higher than the social average level. At the end of 2013, the debt ratio of state-owned industrial companies was 65.1 percent, 7.3 percentage points higher than the average debt ratio of large-scale industrial companies.

Second, local governments have a strong impulse to take on debt. Over the past 30 or more years, when the interest rate in China was subject to strict controls, local governments would directly participate and intervene in the distribution of credit funds, causing more credit to be invested into local businesses. With the deepening of the financial reform, the degree of participation and intervention of local governments has been curbed; however, the fact that local governments are still competing for credit resources remains unchanged. The local government debt vehicle is an innovation to circumvent rules and regulations and obtain more credit. As long as soft budget constraints of local government investment exist, the hunger for capital will remain, and their interest rate elasticity will be low. According to the findings published by the NAO, as of the end of June 2013, 56.6 percent of local government debt funding came in the form of bank loans. Credit funds are still the main source of debt financing.

Third, commercial banks have strong credit rationing. Regardless of whether or not commercial banks are market players, given that local governments and SOEs will not default, commercial banks will compete to offer loans to them. Under market-based interest rates and a lack of interest rate elasticity, local governments and SOEs may have more access to credit than under non–market-based interest rates, because they can provide higher returns than other borrowers.

d   *Soft budget constraints obscure credit risks and increase*
    interest rate risks

Evidence shows that the recent spikes in interest rates are not cyclical; instead, they are structural and relevant to the asymmetric risks and returns of China's market-based interest rate reform process. Individuals seeking return on investments, banks seeking profits, and the investment-driven behavior of local governments will eventually lead to the rise of interest rates, increase of the society's financing costs, and concentrated debt risks. The SOEs and local government debt vehicles have the credit backing of the government; banks which are under pressure to produce profits will be enticed to distribute resources to them. However, the operational efficiency of these sectors is low and ability to repay is weak, which increases the financial system's vulnerability, and there is an increased risk of default. With the advance of market-based reform, interest rates will return to the normal level in the long run. However, over the short-term, rise in interest rates will be a great probability. This will increase the debt serving pressure for local government debt vehicles. According to findings published by the NAO, as of end of June 2013, debt of governments at all levels reached a total of RMB 20.69 trillion. Of this, debt of local governments was RMB 10.88 trillion. Local government financing vehicles gradually enter into a peak period for debt repayment; about 37.5 percent of loans are set to expire between 2013 and 2015. If interest rates rise sharply over a short period of time due to furthering of the interest rate reform, it will impact the debt repayment by local government debt vehicles. Second, the risk caused by downward economic pressure is increasing. The role of credit funds in stimulating economic growth has already weakened considerably, and this situation will only exacerbate as the economy slows down. From 2003 to 2007, China's elasticity of economic growth to credit growth was 0.73, that is to say, if growth of RMB loans increased by 1 percent, economic growth would increase by 0.73 percentage points. During 2008 to 2013, China's elasticity of economic growth to credit growth was 0.47, that is to say, if growth of RMB loans increased by 1 percent, economic growth increased by 0.47 percentage points.

Overall, soft budget constraints of microeconomic entities have caused a number of problems, such as borrowing regardless of cost, insensitivity to price of funds, and firms not showing their real preference of demand for credit. This in turn has caused the market interest rate to deviate from the equilibrium level and misallocation of capital between entities, sectors, and time periods. Therefore, soft budget constraints should be changed. Hard budget constraints can force firms to act as true market players which will effectively help promote the reform of interest rates.

C   *Proposals for strengthening hard budget constraints and promoting the market-based interest rate reform*

The proposal to strengthen hard budget constraints "could make SOEs and local government financing vehicles sustain real losses and earn real profits while bearing real risks, and this is the key for market-based interest rate reform" (Guan, 2014). To become a market entity, businesses should implement hard budget constraints and strengthen budget supervision and management with a market-based risk compensation mechanism. To these ends, we recommend the following.

a   *Improving the governance structure of the SOEs and strengthening*
    hard budget constraints

Researches show that the SOEs' soft budget constraints are the result of weak government accountability, policy burdens, and insider controls. Solving these problems and strengthening the hard budget constraints of the SOEs require a modern corporate system and a better governance structure of firms, and a strengthened check and balance among shareholders, boards of directors and supervisors, and managers. Multiple types of investors, mixed ownership, incentives, and discipline mechanisms to eliminate weak enterprises and support strong ones should be introduced. At the same time, ending the implicit relationship between the SOEs, state-owned banks, and local governments and reducing subsidies will transform the SOEs into true market players, enhance their sensitivity to the price of funds, and force them to make financing plans based on the cost of funds, so as to avoid problems such as excessive accumulation of debt and increased financial risk and overcapacity, and lay the foundation for the steady advance of interest rate reform.

b   *Clarifying boundaries between the fiscal rights and responsibilities*
    of central and local governments, changing the assessment model
    of local governments

The 1994 tax reform aimed to increase the fiscal authority of the central government. Decentralization led to impetus of the local governments to increase investment and spur economic growth, which was the key cause of the soft budget constraints of local governments. To this end, strengthening the hard budget constraints of local governments should focus on solving the debt problem caused by investment expenditure and mismatch between responsibility and fiscal powers, forcing local governments to spend within a budget that is reasonably based on tax revenue. First, we must change the performance assessment model of local governments which uses GDP as the core indicator; gradually switch to a model that uses other indicators, such as people's well-being and cultural, social, and sustainable development; and factor the resolution of local government debt into the evaluation system, to control the investment thirst of local economies. Second, we must further clarify the fiscal powers and responsibilities of central and local governments, replace the sales tax with value-added tax, and implement structural tax reductions to allow room for local governments to adjust and change their behavior with budget constraints. Third, now that the government is going through transformation of functions and reform of performance-based budgeting is being implemented, we should take this opportunity to speed up the restructuring of fiscal expenditures, reduce government investment in competitive industries, emphasize the feature of government spending of being public finance, and strictly manage the scope and direction of local government investment. Fourth, in accordance with the revised Budget Act, local government should clean up existing debt, take on a reasonable amount of new debt, and continue to roll out pilot programs on innovative market-based investment and financing mechanisms such as the pilot issuance of bonds. Market mechanisms have greater transparency, and market signals can impose more effective supervision of government borrowing, which is conductive to hardening budget constraints.

c Establishing a risk compensation mechanism for the SOEs to carry out corporate social responsibility

The SOEs carry out the will of the state. As the backbone of the state economy, the SOEs play an irreplaceable role supporting and guiding economic and social development. The unique characteristics of the SOEs require them to play a role in social welfare, such as implement macro controls, create jobs, promote environmental protection, and carry out the going global strategy. The social responsibilities of the SOEs should be properly classified and the performance of SOEs in carrying out these responsibilities should be effectively reviewed. In addition, risk compensation mechanisms need to be set up based on the degree of budget constraint, to reasonably protect the interests of the SOEs. This will speed up the transformation of the SOEs to become true market players who take full responsibility for their profits and losses and survive based on their strength and competitiveness.

d Strengthening the protection of the rights and interests of microeconomic entities during the marketing process

Fluctuations of the price of funds caused by market reform of the interest rate will inevitably influence businesses and local governments with financing arrangements. To ensure the advancement of reform and protect the rights and interests of microeconomic entities, relevant mechanisms need to be set up. The deposit insurance system officially launched in May 2015 is an effort in this direction. On one hand, the deposit insurance system is conducive to the protection and risk sharing of depositors based on changes in the operations of financial institutions. On the other hand, it also helps maintain the credibility of banks, keep financial order, and stabilize the value of money, thereby stabilizing the expectations of borrowers so they can make better financing plans, and carrying out productions more effectively. In addition, we must encourage banks to integrate loans and investment, give commercial banks free reign in pricing specific products, ease market-access restrictions to financial institutions, develop structured financial products to promote market stratification and integration, smooth the pricing and transmission channels of funds, and provide more financing and price options for microeconomic entities with hard budget constraints. Thereby, optimal financial arrangements could be realized on the basis of matching cost, risk, and returns.

II Market-based interest rate reform, level of bank competition, and bankruptcy system

The level of competition, the bankruptcy mechanism, and cost allocation in the banking sector are worthy of consideration as we promote market-based interest rate reform. First, fair market interest rates can only be established through sufficient competition in the capital markets. Second, the existence of a system which allows banks to declare bankruptcy is very important. Without an institutional mechanism for bankruptcy, there exist moral hazard and distortion of the price levels. Furthermore, with liberalized interest rates, the competition in the banking sector will intensify, causing banks with poor management to become insolvent. Whether or not the banks are allowed to declare bankruptcy will have a significant impact on the risk management and future operations of other banks. Learning from the experience of the recent global financial crisis, externalities associated with banks means that cost-sharing of bank failures remains a key issue. The moral hazard associated with deposit insurance and recapitalization of banks by the state merits further study. However, at present, big state-owned commercial banks still dominate China's credit markets, which has led to inadequate competition and made it hard to form a market-based interest rate that truly reflects supply and demand of funds. Meanwhile, in the absence of a deposit insurance system, with the long-standing implicit state guarantee, financial institutions rarely go bankrupt, causing much moral hazard and adverse selection. Therefore, how to enhance diversity of financial institutions and strengthen the external constraints on these institutions is a prerequisite for further reform.

A The degree of competition in China's banking sector and its influence on interest rate reform

a Theoretical analysis of banking competition and its impact on interest rates

The 3rd Plenum of the 18th CPC Central Committee decreed that the market should play a decisive role in the allocation of resources; the level of competition and social efficiencies of businesses vary greatly under different market structure. In a perfect competition market, enterprises are market price takers, the demand curve for an individual enterprise is a horizontal line, businesses produce goods in accordance with the principle of marginal cost pricing, and the long-term profit is zero with optimized resource allocation and no loss of social welfare. In a completely monopolized market, the firm's demand curve is downward sloping, the monopoly price is higher than the market price at equilibrium, and the monopoly output is lower than the output level under perfect competition; the firm obtains the monopoly profit and creates a net social welfare loss.

Banking services are competitive but not fully competitive. Financial services in any country are a type of franchise; start-up banks must be qualified by way of approval, bidding, or tender. China's banking sector includes the five big commercial banks, Industrial and Commercial Bank of China, Agricultural Bank of China, Bank of China, China Construction Bank, and Bank of Communications, as well as the joint-stock commercial banks such as China Merchants Bank, Shanghai Pudong Development Bank, and Citic Bank. Many urban and rural credit cooperatives have been reformed into urban commercial banks, rural commercial banks, community banks, rural banks, and other micro-financial organizations. For this reason, in China's monopolistic competitive market structure, the banks are not interest rate takers, because they have a certain power over interest rate setting and obtain a certain monopoly profit.

In a monopolistic competitive market, we can assume there are two oligopolistic banks that conduct Cournot competition. The market demand curve for funds is as follows: $p = A - BQ = A - B(q_1 + q_2)$, where p is the market interest rate, Q is aggregate bank credit, and q_1, q_2 are the total amount of bank loans for each bank, respectively. The marginal revenue for the two banks is: $MR_1 = A - 2Bq_1 - Bq_2$, $MR_2 = A - Bq_1 - 2Bq_2$. Assuming that the marginal cost of funds for both banks is the same C, then at equilibrium, the aggregate loans and profits for both banks are the same, represented by: $q_1^* = q_2^* = \dfrac{A-c}{3B}$, $\pi_1 = \pi_2 = \dfrac{(A-c)^2}{9B}$. The market equilibrium interest rate is: $p^* = \dfrac{A+2c}{3}$, and total bank loans are $Q^* = \dfrac{2(A-c)}{3B}$.

Now let's assume that there are N banks in the market for which the marginal cost of funds is C, the demand curve for market funds is $p = A - BQ = A - B\sum\limits_{i=1}^{N} q_i$, the marginal revenue of an individual bank loan is $MR_i = (A - BQ_{-i}) - 2Bq_i$, where Q_{-i} is the aggregate loans of the financial market excluding bank i. At equilibrium the total loans for each bank is $q_i^* = \dfrac{A-c}{(N+1)B}$, the equilibrium interest rate is $p^* = \dfrac{A}{(N+1)} + \dfrac{N}{(N+1)}c$, and total bank loans in the market is $Q^* = \dfrac{N(A-c)}{(N+1)B}$. As the number of banks increases $N \to \infty$, the market equilibrium interest rate converges toward marginal cost $p^* \to c$, and the total number of market loans approaches the level of perfect competition $Q^* \to \dfrac{(A-c)}{B}$. Thus, increasing the number of banks and the level of competition among financial institutions can effectively improve the financial market structure, reduce the level of market equilibrium interest rate, increase the total amount of bank loans, and effectively reduce social welfare loss.

Compared with the joint-stock commercial banks and other banking institutions, the scale of loans, total assets, and number of customers in the banking sector are all dominated by the five main commercial banks. Therefore, a more reasonable assumption is that there are two monopolistic competitive banks in the financial market; the first is a large commercial bank, the "leader" of the monopolistic competition, and the second is a joint-stock commercial bank, or the "follower" of the big commercial bank. In the credit market, two banks are engaged in Stackelberg competition. The market demand curve is $p = A - BQ = A - B(q_1 + q_2)$; bank 2's response function is $q_2 = \dfrac{A-c}{2B} - \dfrac{q_1}{2}$. By substituting the response function of the follower into the market demand curve, we can obtain the leader's demand curve $p = \dfrac{A+c}{2} + \dfrac{Bq_1}{2}$. When profits are maximized, the leader's total loan is $q_1^* = \dfrac{(A-c)}{2B}$; inserting the leader's total loan into the follower's response function will produce the equilibrium loan amount $q_2^* = \dfrac{(A-c)}{4B}$. Thus, at Stackelberg's equilibrium, the amount of total bank loans is $Q^* = \dfrac{3(A-c)}{4B}$, which is higher than the Cournot equilibrium output level; the equilibrium interest rate is $p^* = \dfrac{A+3c}{4}$, which is lower than the Cournot equilibrium interest rate.

b Market structure and competition of China's banking sector

In the planned economy period, China only had one bank, which was the People's Bank of China (PBOC), acting as both the central bank and a commercial bank. Since reform and opening-up, China's banking market structure has undergone significant changes. From 1979 to 1984, the four state-owned banks were restored or established, breaking the PBOC's monopoly over the traditional financial system. Each of the four state-owned banks performed a specific role. Their businesses were divided so there was no competition. In the mid-1990s, policy credit was gradually separated from the four banks to establish policy banks; meanwhile, a number of local banks and non-bank financial institutions were set up. After 2002, the majority of state-owned banks began to carry out joint-stock reform based on commitments made upon accession to the WTO. Entry barriers and operational restrictions in China's banking sector for foreign banks were gradually reduced. Overall, after the reform and opening-up, the level of concentration in China's banking industry was reduced; the banking system has become more robust, with the type and quantity of banking institutions increased. According to

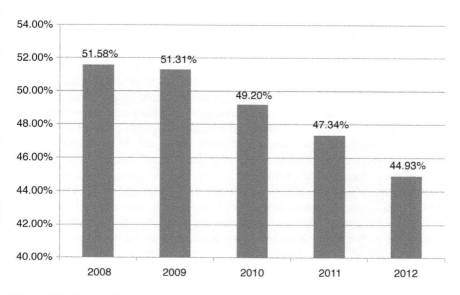

Figure 5-1 Assets of the five major commercial banks as a percentage of total banking assets in China

China Finance Yearbook 2013, at the end of 2012, there were a total of 144 urban commercial banks, 337 rural commercial banks, 147 rural cooperative banks, 1,927 rural credit cooperatives, and 876 village banks. Among them, the assets of the five major commercial banks accounted for more than 44.93 percent of total assets, down 2.41 percentage points from 2011.

The method of measuring the competitiveness of the banking industry mainly includes the H index and the Lerner index. The H index calculates the competition degree of the banking industry using macro data, whereas the Lerner index is based on micro data, which can estimate the competition degree of every bank. Zhang Xiaomei and Pan Ling (2013) found that from 2004 to 2010, HHI index of the banking industry's deposit and loan business declined continuously, with competition increasing, indicating that China formed a banking sector structure with the big commercial banks as the main body; joint-stock commercial banks, city commercial banks, rural commercial banks, and foreign banks coexist. The Lerner index reported by Yang Tianyu and Zhong Yuping (2013) showed that between 1995 and 2010 the average Lerner indexes for state-owned and joint-stock banks increased, while the average Lerner indexes for urban and rural commercial banks and the industry as a whole declined. Zhang Xutao and Hu Ying (2010) used the h-statistic based on the Panzar-Rosse model and concluded that between 1996 and 1999, China's banking sector was in a state of monopolistic competition. From 2000 to 2005, China's banking market had greater demand than supply, and the banking sector tended to be an absolute monopoly market. After 2005, it again entered into the state of monopolistic competition.

c   The impact of China's banking market structure on resource allocation and market-based interest rate reform

The market structure of the banking sector is an important field in the research of financial structure, and the research on the relationship between the market structure and the efficiency of resource allocation is becoming more in-depth. The SCP (structure–conduct–performance) paradigm theory, based on industrial organization, argues that market power or concentration will have a negative impact on credit supply and cost. This is because in a highly competitive market with a high degree of market concentration, monopolistic banks can set prices higher than marginal costs, thus reducing the amount of credit supply, paying lower deposit rates, and receiving higher lending rates and earning excessive profits. Thus, high market concentration will lead to lower market efficiency and social welfare loss. Now China's urban and rural commercial banks have been established. Due to the operational characteristics of these banks, China's banking industry is seeing a decline in both concentration and competition; this has led to increased competition for large SOE clients and sustained financing difficulty and high costs for small and medium enterprises. Therefore, in the current context of advancing the market-based interest rate reform, China should optimize its banking structure, vigorously develop regional small and medium-sized banks, reduce the market share of big commercial banks, and improve the market share of small and medium financial institutions so as to optimize the credit structure and improve the efficiency of credit allocation.

Considering the impact of the market structure on interest rate reform, small and medium-sized banks are in a relatively unfavorable position in a monopolistic competition market environment. In the case of full liberalization of interest rates, there may be excessive competition for deposits among some small and medium-sized banks, which will cause increases in financing costs and worsen the financing condition for small and medium enterprises. In addition, according to relevant research, the market structure has a significant impact on the spread of interest rates in the banking industry, i.e. the market structure is one of the key factors affecting price-setting at commercial banks. Thus, measures to improve the market structure such as lowering entry barriers should be taken to push forward interest rate reform.

d   Policy recommendations

I   CREATE A POLICY ENVIRONMENT TO PROMOTE ORDERLY COMPETITION IN THE BANKING INDUSTRY AND IMPROVE OPERATIONAL EFFICIENCY

We need to reduce the government's intervention and strengthen the independence of banks so they can have more decision-making power. In addition, controls of the banking industry should be gradually relaxed, barriers for private capital to enter into the banking sector should be reduced, relevant legal systems should be improved to create a competitive and flexible market environment, and diversified development of the sector should be promoted.

II   CONTINUE TO OPTIMIZE THE MARKET STRUCTURE OF THE BANKING SECTOR AND SOLIDIFY THE EFFECTIVENESS OF MARKET-BASED INTEREST RATE REFORM

We need to actively promote the development of commercial banks with diversified operation scales, locations, and ownership structures; lower entry barriers to small and medium commercial banks; clarify the positioning of small and medium banks, especially urban commercial banks; and improve the banks' fund supply models to effectively meet the financing needs of enterprises. In addition, we need to improve the current dual-track financial structure in China under which banks in cities face more competition and less market concentration, whereas banks in the country side face less competition and more concentration, which is further deteriorating the financing condition of small and medium enterprises in the rural area.

III   IMPROVE COMMERCIAL BANKS' CAPABILITIES FOR INTEREST RATE SETTING AND RISK MANAGEMENT

We should urge commercial banks to carry out research on the macroeconomic and financial trends and set up interest rate risk management goals which properly factor in their own situations, formulate a scientific interest rate decision-making mechanism, implement asset-liability management centered on interest rate risk management, and explore new tools and methods. We should urge banks to perform in-depth studies on the influence of risk compensation, cost-sharing, early repayment, and probability of default on interest rates, lower the probability of mismatch between interest rates and risks, and provide more training to professionals on interest rate setting and risk management.

IV ACCELERATE TRANSFORMATION .OF BUSINESS MODELS AND IMPROVE THE OVERALL COMPETITION LEVEL

The banks should create universal financial services platforms that integrate deposit, loan, exchange, credit cards, agent, leasing, trusts, and bond businesses to accelerate the transformation of the business models. Active use of new media tools such as the Internet will boost retail services to small and micro businesses and individuals. The banks should also provide differentiated services to customers, actively innovate businesses, accelerate the development of asset-backed securitization, supply chain finance and accounts receivable-backed loans, innovate, and promote wealth-management services to realize a win–win outcome for both customers and banks while ensuring compliance and effective risk controls. In addition, banks could provide more intermediary services such as agent businesses, mobile banking, and advisory services.

B   *Interest rate liberalization and bankruptcy system for banks*

a   *Moral hazard and its impact on interest rate liberalization*

Moral hazard has long existed in economic activities. Early in 1776, Adam Smith (1827) mentioned in *The Wealth of Nations*:

> In any case, since the directors of these companies manage other people's money, it is difficult to expect them to watch over the money with the same care and vigilance with which they watch over their own. Negligence and profusion, therefore, must always prevail, more or less, in the management of the affairs of such a company.

In the 1980s, Arrow widely applied the concept of moral hazard in the *Collected Works of Kenneth J. Arrow*. In the principal–agent relationship of economic activity, the principal is unable to observe all of the agent's activities due to high monitoring costs. Therefore, the principal can only determine the agent's remuneration based on the results, which makes it possible for the agent to harm the principal's interests as a consequence of the feature of being the economic person.

Moral hazard is caused by the conflict between soft restraints and maximization of an individual's profit, and is prevalent in the financial industry. Moral hazard is more difficult to prevent and control in banks than other types of risks. It refers to the situation where, under information asymmetry, managers or staff do not fully bear the risks and consequences of their actions and use privileged access to information to maximize their own interest, causing damage to the interests of shareholders. Moral hazard is one of the causes of market failure and affects the progress of interest rate reform.

From the principal–agent relationship perspective, with the completion of ownership reform of most commercial banks in China, these banks' corporate governance structure is further improved, and the ownership and management (actual control) of the banks are gradually separated, resulting in the principal–agent relationship. Shareholders are the owners of bank assets and the principal in the principal–agent relationship. The management and staff of banks run the daily operations at the banks. Shareholders use contracts to incentivize and discipline the agents. Management and staff are economic persons with opportunistic thinking and behavior. Information asymmetry exists between the shareholders and the management and general staff. The latter enjoy advantages of information access over the shareholders who are not directly involved in the banks' operations. Thus, they are in a weaker position in terms of obtaining information. The management and staff will maximize their own interests by using the information advantage, and shareholders have to accept the risk. If the shareholders incur excessive costs monitoring the behavior of management and staff, then the problems of moral hazard will be inevitable. The management and staff may increase their risk tolerance level and give priority to the businesses with higher returns. Accelerating interest rate reform blindly may exacerbate the moral hazard problem. After realizing market-based interest rates, management and staff of the banks will prefer high-risk business to improve their performance.

From the perspective of incomplete contracts, because the management team and staff of the banks have bounded rationality, information is incomplete during the process of providing financial services and the outcome is uncertain. Thus, it is impossible to create completely clear contracts. Incomplete contracts are a universal phenomenon in market economies. If a contract has to clarify all eventualities, then transaction and enforcement costs will be too high. To minimize costs and maximize benefits, market participants frequently sign incomplete contracts. In the course of modern commercial banks development, contracts between commercial bank shareholders and the management team, and commercial bank staff and customers are always incomplete contracts. Commercial bank shareholders are concerned with long-term benefits. The management team needs to produce contractually obligated profits but are also concerned with their own interests. Because the costs of a complete contract are too high and too difficult to enforce, the costs of monitoring moral hazard and incentivizing management and staff to avoid moral hazard are very high. If the interest rate reform is carried out in a blind way, management at the commercial banks may use loopholes in the incomplete contract to pursue personal interests, which will worsen the problem of moral hazard.

Problems with moral hazard at commercial banks are unavoidable in a market economy and will adversely impact interest rate reform. International experiences suggest that excessive market competition can distort prices of capital. After the

US liberalized its interest rates and banking competition, there was increased conversion of demand deposits to time deposits and institutional deposits, which increased bank liability costs. Because bank management and staff tended to increase their risk tolerance for personal gain, they would select clients and financing entities with higher returns but higher risks to increase the interest spread. At the same time, it should not be ignored that under the deposit insurance system, there will be moral hazard between commercial banks and clients. If a commercial bank has non-performing loans, part of the banks' debts will be covered by the deposit insurance system. Commercial banks may prefer assets with higher risk in order to raise lending rates and increase risks and volatility of interest rates. Therefore, how to guard against the banks' moral hazard during the process of interest rate reform must be considered.

b   Interest rate liberalization will intensify bank competition and the survival of the fittest

Market-based interest rate reform is conductive to improving the pricing ability of commercial banks; banks can adjust the interest rates according to their needs and market environment to enhance market competitiveness and capacity for risk management. At the same time, with further reform, price competition will become an important means for commercial banks to compete for funds, customers, and market share. Banks and financial products that lack competitiveness will lose market share and customers in the competition. For a long time, interest rate regulations have caused distortions in the price of funds; the interest rates could not accurately reflect market supply and demand. In recent years, the rise of shadow banking, internet finance, and other new financial services has increased the momentum of financial disintermediation, which has diverted deposits from banks. The traditional model with deposits as the core business has been challenged. After the completion of market-based interest rate reform, commercial banks are likely to raise interest rates to attract savings and customers and curb the diversion of deposits. It can be predicted that after the completion of interest rate reform, price competition between commercial banks and new types of financial services will be intensified.

Interest rate liberalization will impact the traditional business model of domestic commercial banks which relies heavily on deposit and loan spreads, and will intensify their competition on financial products, services innovation, and intermediary businesses. Interest rate spread has always been a main source of income for commercial banks. After the completion of the interest rate reform, commercial banks need to raise interest rates to attract more funds and clients, which will cause increase in costs; on the other hand, banks will be enacting differing loan rates for different customer groups. Given prime customers' higher bargaining power, banks will be forced to offer them more favorable interest rates to attract or retain them. Meanwhile, although increasing loan interest rates for high-risk clients is necessary, high-interest rates will increase the adverse selection for loans and increase the risk of loan default, thus limiting the space for commercial banks to increase the loan interest rate. Overall, once interest rates are liberalized, the lending rate to high-quality customers is expected to be reduced; financing costs of high-risk customers will be on the rise but to a limited degree. International experience shows that interest rate reforms usually lead to increased competition among commercial banks, a significant reduction in interest income, and a significant increase in non-interest income. Market-oriented interest rates will challenge commercial banks' reliance on interest rate spreads, bringing with it an era of meager profits. Commercial banks can succeed in the post-reform era only by accelerating the transformation of the business model, forcefully developing the intermediary business and off-balance-sheet business, searching for new sources of profit, actively increasing the proportion of non-interest revenue, and building competitive and sustainable business models and business types.

Market-based interest rate reform will require better pricing and risk management ability of commercial banks. After the interest rate is liberalized, the volatility and amplitude of the market interest rate will increase, and interest rate structure and pricing management will become more complex. Setting interest rates must take into account factors such as the macroeconomic and financial situation and the degree of competition in the market; properly judge trends of interest rates; and prevent revenue losses and operating risks resulting from abnormal fluctuations in interest rates. After the completion of the interest rate reform, banks will diversify their asset-liability structure, and at the same time large fluctuations in the short-term interest rate will worsen the maturity mismatch problem caused by the phenomenon of borrowing short and lending long, making it more difficult to manage portfolios. Improving the management of fund pricing and asset-liability is an important means that commercial banks can use to cope with the challenges brought about by the interest rate reform. Banks need to reform existing systems, mechanisms, and processes, and build a modern asset-liability management system.

Market-based interest rates will also make liquidity management more difficult for commercial banks, increasing the risk of small bank failures. After the completion of interest rate reform, depositors will be more sensitive to interest rate fluctuations and will deposit and withdraw money more frequently, making it more difficult to manage liquidity. Banks will finance projects and enterprises with higher risks, which will increase credit risks. If funds cannot be paid back in full in a timely manner, a liquidity risk will result. At the same time, the small scale of capital, imperfect management systems, and inadequate pricing and risk control capabilities will force small and medium banks into a poor position in a more complex and dangerous operating environment. International experience shows that after the completion of interest rate liberalization, small and medium-sized banks typically experience operational difficulties and bankruptcy. This may happen in China as well.

c   *Influence of implicit guarantees and bailouts on the interest*
    rate reform

Implicit guarantee for commercial banks is a historical issue in China's reform and development. Under the planned economy, the development of the domestic banking sector lagged significantly behind. In accordance with the highly central-ized planned economy, banks primarily serve the fiscal departments. After the reform and opening-up, with the transformation of the planned economy to mar-ket economy, China has established a number of state-owned banks in order to give full play to different types of funds to promote economic growth. China also provided implicit guarantees against bankruptcy for banks with the credit of the nation in order to mobilize national savings. At the same time, the government used administrative intervention to provide funds to SOEs to solve their financing problems, and the domestic banking sector expanded very quickly with the gov-ernments' implicit guarantees. This kind of implicit guarantee with national credit solved China's financial bottleneck during this specific period.

With the development of modern commercial banks, deposits are an important bank liability; however, they also carry risks, which originate in the operational model of these banks. In the past, the government's implicit guarantees caused market players to ignore deposit risks. By borrowing short and lending long, banks absorb short-term deposits at low rates, then transfer the fund to other individuals or enterprises for long-term investment for higher returns. Since loans take a longer period to recover, there is always a risk for asset-liability mis-match. At present, most savers believe that their deposits are under the implicit guarantee of the government, and deposits are an absolutely risk-free asset; the deposit interest rate is basically the risk-free interest rate. Savers' deposits will always get bailout from the government. Implicit guarantees have boosted mar-ket players' confidence and minimized the risk of bank runs to the greatest possible extent; however, at the same time it also created the psychological assumption that the government would foot the bill for any losses, thus throw-ing out internal incentives and constraints necessary to control risks. Although the majority of bank wealth-management products are non-guaranteed, market participants expect a bailout, and thus the market for wealth-management prod-ucts have been developing at full tilt in recent years. Even though principles and earnings are not guaranteed, most products are viewed as having the implicit guarantee of the bank, and most of the products have not experienced losses. Many investors mistakenly believe that wealth-management products are equiv-alent to bank deposits with no investment risk, and the expected return will be received upon expiry. That clients purchase wealth-management products as if there were deposits, and banks sell them as if there were loans, has become an unspoken rule in the market.

Due to historical factors, commercial banks in China are weak in dealing with risks. In the traditional view, market participants generally believe that banks are too big to fail. Even if banks do go bankrupt under special circumstances, the state would use its administrative authority to formulate the appropriate support policies to help banks during tough times. At present, the laws governing finan-cial institutions' bankruptcy include *Enterprise Bankruptcy Law*, *Law on People's Bank of China*, *Law on Commercial Banks*, *Law on Supervision Over Banking Industry*, *Draft Regulation on Prevention and Disposition of Payment Risks of Financial Institutions*, and *Regulation on Shutting Down Financial Institutions*.

Bankruptcy of banks should follow the general proceedings set by the *Enterprise Bankruptcy Law*. The degree and level of bankruptcy legislation in China is still far behind that of the western countries. At the same time, because of public interest, once a commercial bank goes bankrupt, it is difficult to enforce the legal procedures. China's current bankruptcy law at the center of the bankruptcy regulation overlooks the special characteristics of banks and lacks practical operation; bankruptcy standard, the selection and supervision of bankruptcy overseer, the order of debt repayment and liquidation, and the subrogation rights of deposit insurers are not clear. Hainan Development Bank collapsed in 1998 but has not yet been liquidated, which vividly illustrates how difficult it is to go through the bankruptcy system in China.

Implicit guarantees and bailouts, as well as the lack of a mechanism for market exit, have inevitably resulted in the lack of effective restraints for commercial banks and distortions of the market interest rate. This is not conductive to achieving the central bank's interest rate goals; rather, it will even hinder the construction of the market interest rate formation mechanism and will increase risk, which is not conducive to the advancement of market-oriented interest rate reform. One of the key supporting conditions for the reform is to switch deposit protection from implicit guarantees to explicit guarantees, establish and perfect the deposit insurance system, stop bailouts, and establish and improve the bankruptcy system for commercial banks.

d Recommendations

I CREATE A COMPREHENSIVE DEPOSIT INSURANCE SYSTEM AS SOON AS POSSIBLE

Gradually improve compatible incentive systems such as the risk differentiated fee rates to guard against moral hazard and create a sound financial safety net for interest rate and other financial reforms.

II CLARIFY THE BANKRUPTCY STANDARDS AND SET PREPOSITIONAL PROCEDURES FOR INSOLVENCY

China should improve the existing laws and regulations and improve special technical standards for insolvency judicial procedures. Three-way cooperation between the People's Bank of China, regulatory bodies, and deposit insurance companies should determine the extent of banks' crisis, and develop and implement specific assistance measures. According to the *Law on Commercial Banks*, regulatory authorities should carry out insolvency prepositional procedures and avoid initiation of judicial procedures arbitrarily.

III IMPROVE THE COMMERCIAL BANK INSOLVENCY SYSTEM

First is to improve the bankruptcy trustee system for commercial banks and clarify credentials and composition of trustees and other specific provisions; second is to improve the system of commercial bank reorganization; third is to improve the bankruptcy liquidation system for commercial banks.

IV   STRICTLY DEFINE CONDITIONS FOR BANK BAILOUT MEASURES

If the state bails out commercial banks that are about to go bankrupt without restrictions, it is bound to increase moral hazard of commercial banks. Thus, when taking rescue measures for banks, the government should strictly limit the conditions for the implementation of bailout.

III   Development of financial markets and the interest rate reform

A   *The importance of financial market development to the interest rate reform*

Many researchers have shown that the development of financial markets is important to interest rate liberalization. For example, in Fan Weidong's (2002) opinion, the existence of comprehensive, structured, and efficiently operating financial markets is the key to forming market-based bank deposit interest rates; Xu Jian (2003) believes that financial market infrastructure and financial regulation are prerequisites for market-based interest rate reform. Specifically, only in developed money markets is it possible to form a short-term benchmark interest rate and for the central bank to use monetary policy tools to guide market interest rates; only with a complete set of financial instruments, a reasonable market structure, and adequate competition among market players can there be a system of complete and correlated market interest rates, and can the central bank's rate adjustment measures be effective. Therefore, the development of financial markets is an important foundation for interest rates liberalization.

International experience shows that the development of financial markets is a catalyst for interest rate liberalization. After the Second World War, Japan experienced more than 20 years of high-speed development, but then the economic slowdown caused firms' demands for funds to decline. To improve the efficiency of capital, firms transferred a large amount of funds to the freely tradable bond repo market, resulting in a rapid expansion of the market. In 1978, the trading volume already exceeded four trillion Japanese yen. At the same time, to stimulate economic growth, fiscal expenditure increased constantly, and the government became the main demander for funds. Hence, increasing the issuance of treasury bonds became the most convenient choice (Zhang et al., 2012). Since 1975, the treasury market started to expand as the Japanese government tried to make up its fiscal deficit by issuing bonds. This promoted the development of the variety and scale of financial market transactions, and the Bank of Japan also tendered bonds traded in the secondary market. The development of the treasury bond markets facilitated the process of interest rate liberalization. In April 1977, the Japanese

Ministry of Finance officially approved commercial banks to sell bonds on the market after holding them for a period of time and liberalized interest rates for bond trades and issuance; in April 1978, the Bank of Japan permitted interbank borrowing interest rates to float and in July liberalized interest rates for interbank commercial bill transactions.

Based on the experience of the United States and a few other countries, even though interest rate liberalization was triggered by financial innovation and disintermediation, it also reflected the development of new financial products and markets. In the 1960s, against the backdrop of high inflation, the separate-business operation of banks and interest rate controls in the US led to a decline in the competitiveness of commercial banks, and a large amount of savings flowed to the securities markets. As financial disintermediation became more severe, commercial banks made great efforts to develop off-balance-sheet business and expand foreign branches in order to circumvent controls and cope with disintermediation. This contributed to the transformation of commercial banks' business strategies and operations and marked the beginning of interest rate liberalization in the United States. Since the 1970s, development of financial products and creation of new demand took place mainly in the capital markets, and direct financing via the securities market played an increasingly important role. The indirect financing function of the loan market has gradually been shrinking; the amount of assets controlled by commercial banks in total financial assets has fallen from more than 60 percent to less than 25 percent. Non-bank financial institutions, especially investment banks, gradually replaced commercial banks as the dominant player in the financial sector, and the capital market became the core of the US financial system.

Learning from the international experience, China has attached importance to the development of financial markets in its interest rate reform. China first developed its money market and liberalized money market interest rate as a starting point. Furthermore, the development of financial markets has always been an important part of the reform. Deposit and loan interest rate liberalization was pushed forward through the liberalization of financial market interest rates.

At present, a multi-tier capital market system has taken shape in China, and the stock market, bond market, futures market, derivative market, and wealth-management markets flourished with increasingly diverse products. Securities companies, fund companies, and futures companies and other capital market intermediaries developed rapidly. As of October 2014, there were over 2,584 companies listed on the Shanghai and Shenzhen exchanges with market capitalization of RMB 30.05 trillion and 135 million active stock trading accounts; as of the end of September of 2014, the "new third board" for small and medium-sized businesses had a total of 1,153 listed companies and had raised a total of RMB 9.285 billion. There are more than 32 regional stock transfer exchanges nationwide, with over 7,400 listed companies and an ever-expanding service coverage; 15 securities companies have launched over-the-counter business pilot programs and made obvious progress. China's bond market includes the interbank market, exchange market, and commercial bank counter market, similar to the structure of mature markets with on-floor and off-floor markets. Judging from the total number of bonds under custody, the interbank market is the main body of China's bond market, and the exchange market is also an important part. As of the end of September 2014, the face value of bond under custody had reached a total of RMB 34.14 trillion, with the volume in the interbank market accounting for about 90.82 percent, exchange market about 6.97 percent, over-the-counter market 1.70 percent, and the remaining 0.51 percent. At the same time, the bond market has developed steadily with an ever more enriched product system covering government bonds, local government bonds, central bank bills, government-backed agency debt, financial bonds, corporate bonds, medium-term notes, SME collective notes, commercial papers, private placement notes, corporate bonds, convertible bonds, equity warrants bonds, and SME private placement bonds. Asset securitizations developed steadily. From the financing structure point of view, the proportion of RMB loans as a proportion of total social financing decreased year by year. In 2002, new RMB loans accounted for 91.9 percent of total social financing, and by 2013 this had fallen to 51.4 percent. The steady development of financial markets and direct financing have gradually altered the dominant position of China's banking industry, and a diversified multi-tier financial system and financing structure are being formed.

At present, however, China's financial market doesn't satisfy the requirement for interest rate reform completely. In Li Yang's (2010) view, the proportion of direct financing in China is low; the money market is underdeveloped, and hence there is no core market in the money market system, making it difficult to further interest rate reform. Specifically, China's financial market and infrastructure are not sound; markets are segmented with multiple regulators, and information is not transparent. Financial products are not rich enough, the standards for financial markets need yet to be improved, and the depth of financial markets needs to be expanded. The transmission efficiency of the financial markets is low, with no sufficient linkages between interest rates of various products; the interest rate signals of some products are even contradictory, which needs to be rectified. The benchmark interest rate system is not complete; as transactions in the money market are not sufficient, the mid- to long-term Shibor interest rates have yet to solidify their benchmark position. Some key types of government bonds have yet to be issued on a rolling basis, and a reference for pricing of mid- to long-term financial products is not in place. Financial markets do not provide enough information for pricing, and the interest rate transmission mechanism is imperfect. Under these conditions, it is difficult for the central bank to adjust interest rates through the financial market. Therefore, in order to further advance the market-based interest rate reform, we also need to develop the financial market. First, the bond market needs to be further developed. Now the market has relatively small-scale, limited product offerings with a distorted and segmented structure. All these need to be improved. The development of the bond market needs to be coordinated with the need of monetary policy operations to form a better benchmark interest rate system. Second, multi-level financial markets should be developed to form a financial system that is diverse, competitive, and deep enough to reflect the needs of the real economy and provide a market basis for interest rate reform.

B   *The mutually reinforcing relationship between financial market development and market-based interest rate reform*

The development of financial markets is fundamental to the interest rate reform, and there are different views on how to develop financial markets and liberalize the interest rates. Here we mainly focus on whether or not direct financing should be allowed to develop to a certain degree before moving forward with market-oriented interest rate reform.

One view is that market-oriented interest rate reform can be achieved through the improvement of external conditions. Fan (2002) believes that in a sense, the basic condition for market-oriented interest reform to be successful is that financial markets' development changes commercial banks' position as the dominant financial intermediary in social financing activities. A financial system with a reasonable and efficient structure is imperative. Huang Jinlao (2013) believes that the dominance of indirect financing is the main obstacle to liberalizing deposit interest rates. Thus, the only path to market-oriented interest rate reform is to promote the transformation of financing models, and to rapidly liberalize loan and deposit interest rates through the development of direct financing tools. Li Yang (2010) believes that direct financing must be developed first, and liberalization of bank interest rates is realized through pressure and competition outside of the banking sector. Second, the money market needs to be developed to establish a core market for the financial system and form a short-term benchmark interest rate. Third, China should develop the shadow banking system and form market-oriented interest rates through a variety of financing channels. Miao Jianmin (2010) believes that in order to advance the market-oriented interest rate reform, the Shibor mechanism must first be perfected to form a core market transmission mechanism for interest rates; second, the intermediary business should be developed to reduce banks' dependence on deposit and loan spreads. Some also suggest that the offshore RMB markets should be used to promote domestic market-oriented interest rate reform.

Another view is that under bank interest rate controls, developing financial markets to force the banks to carry out market-oriented interest rate reform will only increase their risks; the bank crisis in the United States in the 1980s is an example (Lu, 2011). Yao Yang et al. (2015) think the negative effects of the market-oriented interest rate reform in China shouldn't be ignored.

> In recent years, China's financial innovation has been to circumvent administrative control. This gave rise to the rapid expansion of the shadow banking system, and the accumulation of financial risks. The financial system and real economy are increasingly disconnected, with financing to the real economy becoming ever more difficult and expensive.
>
> (Yao Yang et al., 2015)

Even though they believe that the primary cause for this problem lies in the large number of entities that are not sensitive to interest rates in the real economy and the lack of deposit insurance, it also shows that under the present condition, promoting market-oriented interest rate reform through the shadow banking system presents great risks. Huang Jinlao (2013) also believes that direct financing at this stage of development is too fast and irrational; as he said, "implicit market-based interest rate formation should be regulated".

Re-examining other countries' experiences on interest rate liberalization, we find that even though the development of financial markets is very important for market-oriented interest rate reform, it is not necessary to wait for financial markets to mature before liberalizing the interest rates; financial market development and interest rate reform have a mutually reinforcing relationship. Interest rate liberalization requires the development of financial markets; on the other hand, interest rate reform will promote the development of financial markets. For example, after interest rate liberalization, the structure of social financing in the UK featured more direct financing such as stocks, and stock capitalization increased quickly as a percentage of GDP. In 1981, the ratio of bank loans to GDP was 42 percent, while the ratio of stock market capitalization to GDP was 39 percent; in 1995, the stock market capitalization to GDP ratio was 123 percent, surpassing the ratio of bank loans to GDP (120 percent). From Japan's experience, on the one hand, the development of government bonds accelerated the interest rate reform. On the other hand, canceling the controls on government bond interest rates and other non-price restrictions on the bond market boosted the expansion of bond issuance and trading. Interest rate liberalization also helped the development of other forms of direct financing. Judging from the structure of financial institutions' assets, the share of assets held by savings institutions, including banks, was on the decline. Among them, bank assets have declined from 54 percent in 1979 to 39.3 percent in 1999; savings institutions' total assets fell from 65.5 percent in 1979 to 52.5 percent in 1999; the share of insurance and pension funds' assets increased from 9.2 percent in 1979 to 15.2 percent in 1999; and the assets of other financial institutions such as investment trusts, financial traders, and brokerages also rapidly increased from 25.3 percent in 1979 to 32.3 percent in 1999.

In addition, the mutually supporting relationship between financial market development and the market-oriented interest rate reform does not necessarily manifest fundamental changes in the financing structure. Take Germany as an example: The social financing structure is dominated by indirect financing. After the realization of market-oriented interest rate reform, the scale of direct financing expanded; however, bank loans still dominated in the non-financial sector. In 1970, bank loans accounted for 55.2 percent of non-financial sector liabilities in Germany; by 1995 this proportion was as high as 52.8 percent. Among corporate liabilities, bank loans increased from 51.3 percent in 1970 to 56.5 percent in 1995. The role of interest rate liberalization in promoting financial market development is characterized by significant changes in the structure of households' financial assets; savings deposits were transformed into insurance assets and securities assets; bank assets fell from 56.5 percent in 1960 to 32.8 percent in 1990; insurance assets increased from

15.9 percent to 29.5 percent; and securities assets increased from 13.7 percent to 28.9 percent. Meanwhile, in order to adapt to this change, commercial banks made an adjustment to the structure of assets and liabilities, with banks paying more attention to stocks and bonds issuance among other means of financing and becoming the primary institutional investor in the securities market.

By comparing the influence of liberalization of deposit and lending rates on the financial system in Germany, Japan, and the United States, we can see that whether deposit and lending rate liberalization will bring about greater risks to the banking sector does not depend on whether the liberalization was started within or outside of the banking system; a sound financial system and adequate regulation are the decisive factors which determine financial risk. In China, the institutional reform of banks should be continued; developing direct financing can, to some extent, promote banking sector's reform and operational transformation. But in China's real economy, there are still some prominent problems, such as soft budget constraints; financial regulation and risk prevention mechanisms are imperfect, so developing financial markets can't solve the problem completely. During this process, the development of financial markets may become distorted. At present, the distortions in China's financial structure are the consequences of non-market factors. One is the administrative restrictions on financial institutions' entry to certain markets. Second is the administrative approval requirement for various financial products, including bond and stock issuance. Meanwhile, a few spontaneously emerged market-oriented financial activities lack regulation. Therefore, in order to promote the interest rate reform successfully, we must vigorously promote the market-oriented reform of microeconomic entities, standardize the market operating system, strengthen financial supervision, and improve basic conditions of the market from various aspects.

Introducing new financial products that are not under interest rate controls is an important strategy for market-oriented interest rate reform; however, the existence of dual-track interest rate systems needs to be properly handled. If the arbitrage between the two tracks causes significant distortions in resource allocation, then it should be corrected in a timely fashion. In order to properly manage the relationship between financial innovation, financial market development, and market-oriented interest rate reform, the latter two should be pushed forward simultaneously so as to form a relationship of mutual promotion and support.

IV Market-oriented interest rate reform and financial regulatory reform

Market-oriented interest rate reform is a systematic project, which involves macro and microeconomies, systems, and institutions, as well as monetary policy and financial regulation, etc. International experience shows that during the process of market-oriented interest rate reform, if regulators cannot follow up in a timely fashion, it could trigger a banking crisis or even a serious economic crisis. In order to promote market-oriented interest rate reform successfully, there must be an all-round reform of financial regulation, including the concepts, rules, means and methods, and organization. Specifically, as shown by the last international financial crisis, the traditional price-based monetary policy framework of a single tool (the interest rate) and a single objective (price stability) has been challenged. The macro-prudential concept has been further strengthened. We should learn from the lessons of financial crises and push forward the market-oriented interest rate reform together with financial regulatory reform, on the basis of guarding against systemic financial risks and maintaining financial stability.

A The market-oriented interest rate reform puts forward new challenges to the financial regulatory system

a Improving the financial regulatory system is a practical need to adapt to the trend of mixed operations of financial institutions under interest rate liberalization

At present, China's financial innovation has become increasingly vibrant; the process of market-oriented interest rate reform will undoubtedly further accelerate the trend of integrated operation of financial institutions. In this context, banks' off-balance-sheet business has expanded rapidly in recent years. Excess capacity in the real estate market and potential risks with local government debt accumulation have required sound coordination of financial supervision and regulatory reform. At the same time, with the rapid development of China's financial industry, cooperation between banks, securities firms, and insurance companies are prevalent and financial holding companies with comprehensive businesses and shadow banking activities have emerged. The Internet and other non-financial businesses continue to integrate deeper with the financial industry, gradually breaking through the boundaries of separated operations. However, due to the lack of overall institutional arrangements, China's current regulatory system has two obvious drawbacks. First, the regulatory vacuum caused by separate regulation: Financial holding companies (groups), financial products with mixed features, and Internet finance platforms that sell these products are mostly in the regulatory blind spot. Second, regulatory segmentation caused by institutional regulation: Institutional regulation means different agencies regulate different types of financial institutions. Regulation is segmented and regulators focus only on their own area and generally emphasize development over regulation and ex-ante approval over ex-post regulation, resulting in a low level of financial regulation. Moreover, China's current financial regulatory structure cannot prevent systemic risks that emerge from financial innovation; the capability to properly handle the relationship of innovation, development, and risks should be improved.

b Improving the financial regulatory system will allow timely and effective crisis management with interest rates liberalized

International experience shows that during the process of market-based interest rate reform, commercial banks' operational risks will increase. Rising loan interest rates led to adverse selection and increased moral hazard, severely affecting small and medium-sized financial institutions. According to the research by Hu Xinzhi and Yuan Jiang (2011), the US officially started market-based interest rate reform in 1980, and the year became a watershed for the banking sector. Prior to this, less than 20 banks went bankrupt each year. However, with the interest rate reform in full swing, the number of banks that went bankrupt and banks that received the FDIC's assistance increased significantly. By 1989, there had been 531 bank failures in the US, a historical record. Therefore, constructing a financial safety net and improving the coping mechanisms for systemic risks are crucial to the reform. Financial liberalization and deregulation in the 1980s led to the trend of removing mandates other than monetary policy from the central bank. This culminated in two types of central banks: One with a total removal of the central bank's role in financial regulation, e.g. the UK, and the other with the unduly weakened power of the central bank in financial regulation, e.g. the US. The reform assumes that the financial market is effective and that therefore the central bank can maintain financial stability just by keeping the inflation rate low. There is no need for the central bank to perform any supervisory function over the financial markets. But the global financial crisis has exposed the deficiency of this arrangement. Eliminating the regulatory powers of the central bank makes it difficult to obtain accurate financial information, which in turn will affect the central bank's authority and power in crisis management and thus make it impossible to function fully as the lender of last resort in maintaining financial stability. In this sense, while speeding up interest rate reform, how to construct a new financial regulatory framework to improve the timeliness and effectiveness of crisis management is an issue worthy of attention.

c *Perfecting the financial regulatory system is necessary to execute coordinated macro-prudential management and micro-prudential supervision under market-based interest rates*

Under market-based interest rates, the potential risks of the financial industry are likely to increase. The risk may be at the micro-level or at the macro-level. In the relationship between micro-financial supervision and macro financial stability, the traditional view is that as long as a single micro body is healthy, the entire financial system is bound to be healthy. But this crisis tells us that the entire system, which is the sum of healthy individuals, is not necessarily healthy; and sometimes strengthening the supervision over individual institutions may lead to instability of the macro financial system due to cyclicality. For example, in the original regulatory framework with adequate capital, when there is an economic downturn and increased financial risk, all the individual institutions should increase capital adequacy at the same time; the systemic effect is a recession of the entire financial systems' balance sheet, which endangers overall financial stability.

Moreover, China is faced with another special problem; that is, the micro regulatory functions are sometimes generalized to become macro-control measures, making it difficult to adjust interest rates. Within the macro financial management and supervision coordination mechanisms, the organizational structure of the central bank and regulatory bodies and corresponding regulatory functions remain to be defined. The rights and responsibilities are unbalanced, and the institutions are not compatible. In practice, there are cases when the micro regulatory functions are generalized to become macro-control. The current mechanism, consisting of one central bank and three regulatory commissions, lacks clear orientation or clear responsibilities and means; the market interest rate is interfered with by many factors. All these increase the difficulty for regulation. For example, because financial institutions are highly dependent on deposits as a result of regulatory requirements, including deposit–loan ratio, the money market is not yet an important source of financing for financial institutions. This has increased the difficulty of the transmission of money market rates to bond markets and credit markets. In addition, in recent years, the regulatory authorities have adjusted the regulation over wealth-management products and interbank business, which also had a great impact on the market interest rates.

The experience and lessons from this crisis show that the combination of macro-prudential management and micro-prudential supervision is an effective way to maintain financial stability. Traditional micro-regulation puts too much emphasis on individual institutions' security and does not have macro perspectives; it ignores the importance of supervision and coordination, which leads to regulatory overlap and regulatory loopholes that make it impossible to recognize and protect against systemic risk, which ultimately leads to disastrous consequences. Macro-prudential management and micro-prudential supervision, however, are not fully compatible with each other, especially when the two functions are implemented by different regulators separately. Information asymmetry and sectoral interests may affect the decision-making on recognition and prevention of systemic financial risks. In addition, the basis of macro-prudential management is macro-prudential analysis, which is based on the judgment of systemic financial risks. It requires a centralized, unified, and efficient source of information and micro-prudential regulatory support and coordination. Therefore, it is necessary to further improve the macro-prudential policy framework and establish a higher-level regulatory and coordination mechanism to ensure smooth communication between macro-prudential management and micro-prudential regulatory bodies, and to prevent regulatory conflicts and oversight so as to guard against systemic financial risks effectively.

d   Improving the financial regulatory system is critical to defining
the responsibilities of central and local financial supervision and
accelerating the transformation of government functions under
market-based interest rates

The core issue of the financial system reform, including the market-based interest rate reform, is to properly handle the relationship between the government and the market so that the market can play a decisive role in the allocation of resources, and the government can play a better role as well. In the process of market-based interest rate reform, the key to the reform of the financial management system is to solve the problem of excessive government intervention and inadequate supervision. From the perspective of China's central and local financial management system, the financial management authority is too centralized and cannot adapt to local economic development. There is still too much administrative intervention by local governments, and some local governments are the source of capital demand for accelerating local economic development. This will either directly or indirectly intervene in the allocation of financial resources and affect the independence of financial institutions, and, to some extent, may intertwine fiscal and financial risks. At present, against the backdrop of fostering steady growth, adjusting economic structure, and advancing reforms, the financial regulatory system should be further reformed so as to fully mobilize the initiatives of both the central and the local governments, accelerate the transformation of government functions, form a long-term and stable institutionalized financial system, and create a matching financial services system for real economy development.

B Reform of China's financial regulatory system under market-based interest rate reform

a Strengthening the regulatory principles of fair competition, functional regulation, and unified standards

Fair and effective market competition is the fundamental means to control financial risks under the market-based interest rates. The financial industry, as a competitive services industry, should function in accordance with the negative list of market entry and the requirements of a more open services industry. It should provide a fair competition market environment for various types of investors, introduce different risk preferences, and establish a multi-tiered, wide-coverage system of financial institutions. The system should conform to the trends of financial innovation and deepened integration; financial businesses with similar businesses such as trusts, bonds, stocks, and funds should be placed under unified regulation to reduce regulatory arbitrages, including access standards, information disclosure, risk isolation requirements, and definition of investor qualifications; and the focus should be on clarifying the rights and responsibilities and risk undertaking of market participants and regulators.

b Establishing a sound macro-prudential management policy framework

The government should draw lessons from international experiences and combine them with China's national conditions, further build and improve the counter-cyclical macro-prudential management policy framework, and effectively prevent systemic financial risks. The credit and liquidity management and regulation of monetary aggregates will strengthen the macro-prudential management and further improve the differential dynamic reserve adjustment mechanism. We should improve the monitoring and evaluation framework of systemic financial risks, establish a forward-looking early warning system of risks, and build a system of risk management and liquidation. It's necessary to formulate evaluation models of the importance of financial institutions and improve the management system for financial institutions of systemic importance.

c   Reforming and improving the financial regulatory framework to adapt to the development of modern financial markets

In recent years, the development of China's financial industry has accelerated with the formation of a diversified system of financial institutions, complex product structures and digital transaction systems, and more open financial markets with an evident trend of comprehensive operation by financial institutions. However, financial holding companies (groups), all types of cross-category financial products, and the Internet finance sector involved with multiple cross-category financial products are not being regulated, which creates great challenges for the current system of separated supervision. The recent frequent exposures of local risks, especially the volatility in capital markets during June–August 2015, reveals the weakness of institutional regulation and the separation of monetary policy and prudential regulation under the current regulatory framework. High leverage in the A-share market affected many other markets, financial institutions, and non-financial organizations. Single regulators and separated statistics monitoring systems cannot identify the sources of risks and cannot judge the degree of risk expansion; thus, such a system is unable to manage market liquidity effectively.

Since the global financial crisis, major economies have carried out significant financial regulatory reforms. The main approach is to coordinate regulatory systems for systematically important financial institutions and financial holding companies, especially those responsible for the prudent management of the financial institutions; coordinate the regulation of key financial infrastructure, including important payment systems and clearing institutions, financial assets registration and depository institutions, and the maintenance of financial infrastructure; coordinate responsibility for comprehensive statistics for the financial industry by collecting data covering the entire financial industry; and strengthen and improve macroeconomic regulation and control to maintain financial stability. China should adhere to the direction of market-based reform, accelerate the establishment of an effective and coordinated regulatory framework that adapts to the development of modern finance, and keep the bottom line of zero systemic risk.

d   Perfecting the legal framework of financial regulation

A sound legal system is the guarantee for the effective operation of the financial regulatory system. Within China's current system of separate supervision, both macro and micro-prudential regulatory authorities, as well as the central and local regulatory authorities, have introduced laws and regulations to prevent risks from their respective perspectives. But some laws and regulations are not consistent or well-coordinated. In the future, an improved legal system for financial regulation should be established.

e Defining regulatory and risk management responsibilities of central and local regulators

China needs to adhere to the centrally unified management of the financial sector, urge local governments to change the tendency of emphasizing development and neglecting regulation, and execute their duties based on their regional mandates. China should clarify the responsibilities of local governments in supervision and management of local financial institutions and markets, as well as their responsibilities in financial risk management, strengthen routine regulation and regional financial risk prevention, and standardize the responsibilities of local government to financial institutions so as to avoid administrative interference in the business operations of financial institutions.

V The relationship between interest rate reform, exchange rate reform, and opening-up of the capital account

How to deal with the relationship between the market-based interest rate reform and the reform of exchange rate formation mechanism as well as the opening-up of the capital account is a key problem that many countries need to face during the process of interest rate reform. It is also a long-standing controversial issue in China and a problem that must be resolved at the current stage of reform.

A International experience and theories on the sequencing of interest rate reform, exchange rate reform, and opening of the capital account

The classical theory on the relationship between interest rates, exchange rates, and the opening of the capital account is embodied in Mundell's impossible trinity theory and related theories on interest rate and exchange rate parity. According to these theories, if the capital account controls are removed before market-based interest rate reform and exchange rate formation mechanism reform, funds for cross-border arbitrage will flow into the domestic market unhindered, which will weaken the efficacy of domestic monetary policy. Therefore, the optimal sequencing of financial reform is to carry out market-based interest rate reform first, followed by the reform of the exchange rate formation mechanism and capital control removal. Sachs (1987), McKinnon (1984), and Fischer (1987) argue that the ideal sequencing of financial reform is to move from "internal to external", that is, to stabilize the domestic economy first and then carry out the reform of external sectors. McKinnon (1991) summarized the experiences of Argentina, Chile, and Korea as well as Eastern Europe, Vietnam, and Russia and other transitional economies' experiences of financial liberalization in the 1970s and 1980s. He discovered that there is an "ideal sequence" for economic liberalization . . . after successfully liberalizing trade and finance domestically, the liberalization of foreign exchange markets will see appropriate progress. Opening the capital account and currency convertibility is the final step of this sequence. However, Guitian (1997) argues capital account liberalization should not wait until all the conditions are met; instead, he believes that the opening of the capital account is conductive to the formation of such conditions. Johnston and Sundararajan (1999) summarized the financial sector reform experiences of multiple countries and discovered that in reality many countries did not follow the approach of internal first and external latter in financial reform but instead utilized a coordinated and comprehensive pace of financial reform.

From international experiences, we can see that different countries adopted different sequencing options. Below are several countries' specific experiences.

a   Japan

Japan has gone through a long process of reforms of the capital account, interest rate, and exchange rate as well as the domestic financial sector. Generally speaking, Japan first completed the exchange rate reform, followed by the gradual reforms of the interest rate, capital account, and domestic financial sector. However, the liberalization of deposit interest rates was more prudent and took a longer time.

Japan's reform process can be roughly divided into two phases, the 1970s and post-1980s.

The first phase (in the 1970s): The main feature of this phase is transforming the yen from a fixed exchange rate to a floating exchange rate, frequent changes to capital controls in line with short-term capital flows, and a partial undertaking of interest rate and domestic financial sector reform. After the war the yen had been pegged to the dollar; however, entering into the 1970s, with the collapse of the Bretton Woods system, the yen's dollar peg was replaced by a floating exchange rate. Nonetheless, the Japanese government continued to intervene with the yen's exchange rate. Due to the high degree of uncertainty in the international economic environment during this period, especially after the two oil crises, Japan experienced two instances of massive capital inflows and outflows, making the exchange rate increasingly volatile. In response to this situation, the adjustment of capital control policy became a coping mechanism for the Japanese government. By loosening or tightening controls on capital inflows and outflows, the Japanese government attempted to control the size of inflows and outflows when faced with exchange rate fluctuations and capital flows.

The second phase (post-1980s) saw the rapid liberalization of the capital account and the advancement of domestic financial reform and more prudent deposit interest rate reform. After the Plaza Accord, the exchange rate saw a significant one-time appreciation. In 1980, Japan modified its capital control law substantially and achieved free convertibility in the capital account in a very short period of time. The liberalization of deposit rates began in May 1979, and Certificates of Deposit issuance without interest rate controls was permitted. Subsequently, in

Table 5-1 Sequence of financial reforms in Japan

Year	Interest rate reform	Exchange rate reform	Capital account liberalization	Supporting reform
1970			Allowed outbound securities investment, opening-up of FDI continued	
1971		Yen's peg to the US dollar ended, but still with significant foreign exchange intervention		
1972				
1973				
1974				
1975				
1976				
1977				
1978				
1979				
1980			Transition from the examination and approval system to the registration and recording system	
1981				
1982		Since 1978, yen became freely floating		
1983	Gradually alleviated deposit rate limit, from large to small amount, and from long-term to short-term deposits			
1984			Alleviated the upper limit for yen's exchange amount	
1985				
1986				
1987				
1988				
1989				
1990				
1991				
1992				
1993				
1994				
1995			Capital account fully liberalized	
1996				
1997				

1985, large time deposit interest rates were liberalized. The deposit rate was fully liberalized till 1994. The liberalization of the domestic financial sector is reflected in the emergence and reform of a range of new markets and products, including the commercial paper market and the corporate bond market.

There are two important problems in this stage of reform. First, reform asymmetry. Capital account liberalization and development of other financing vehicles meant many institutions might no longer need bank financing. In bond, stock, and overseas financing markets, the main fund providers were non-bank financial institutions. Bank deposits were still a major investment tool for many Japanese households due to the slow pace of new market and product liberalization for retail customers. This asymmetry has created an imbalance in the growth of bank assets and liabilities, forcing banks to start a substantial increase in loans to real estate and small businesses. Second, the failure of macroeconomic policy after the Plaza Accord. The yen's sharp appreciation after the Plaza Accord caused the Bank of Japan to maintain a very loose monetary policy. Even during the real estate bubble, the Bank of Japan still did not tighten monetary policy in time, resulting in further expansion of the bubble. In the early 1990s, with the collapse of the housing bubble and a sharp decline in economic growth, the balance sheet problems of Japanese banks exposed the banking sector to a crisis. Since then, the Japanese economy has entered a period of low growth and deflation.

b   Chile

Chile's exchange rate, interest rate, capital account, and financial liberalization reform is a more successful example. The sequence of Chile's reform was to first reorganize the domestic banking system and then to gradually increase the flexibility of interest rates and exchange rates without opening up the capital account and developing domestic financial markets at the same time. Finally, following the basic completion of the interest rate, exchange rate, and supporting reforms, Chile opened up the capital account and implemented a free-floating exchange rate regime at the same time.

After the setback in liberalization and crisis in the early 1980s, Chile once again undertook reforms. The reform first focused on the restructuring of domestic banks and the opening of a few selected capital inflow accounts. After the reorganization of the banking sector, Chile shifted the focus to developing domestic financial markets (currency, bond, and stock markets), as well as the gradual increase in interest rate and exchange rate flexibility. Capital accounts were also gradually opened. However, measures were taken to limit the inflow of specific types of capital during the process of opening-up. Chile's experience with reform of the exchange rate, interest rate, and capital account is, first of all, gradually increasing the flexibility of the exchange rate and maintaining a certain degree of control over the capital account. This guaranteed the smooth completion of the interest rate reform and relevant adjustments to the monetary policy framework with indirect tools. On this basis, the flexibility of the exchange rate was further increased, which led to the realization of a free-floating regime. The opening of the capital account was completed only after the domestic financial market was allowed to develop for a period of time. In the face of a large number of short-term capital inflows, Chile introduced a number of temporary control measures. However, there were debates about the effectiveness of these measures. Another important fact is that the peso was constantly under depreciation pressure in the 1980s, but during the 1990s it was under appreciation pressure. Chile has allowed

Table 5-2 Sequence of financial reforms in Chile

Year	Interest rate reform	Exchange rate reform	Capital account liberalization	Supporting reforms
1985		Multiple valuation adjustments of the peso and gradual expansion of float range	Measures to encourage capital outflows	Bank capital-ization, reorga-nization, and privatization
1986				
1987	Central bank notes' interest rates determined at auction			
1988				
1989	Independent central bank			
1990	Overnight interbank rate as reference rate, mon-etary policy with explicit inflation targeting			Continuously increase types of products in the capital market
1991				
1992			Measures to encourage capital outflows and limit inflows	
1993				
1994				
1995				
1996				
1997		Reduction in the float range		
1998				
1999		Free float	Removal of mea-sures to prevent inflows	
2000	Inflation targeting			

the gradual devaluation and appreciation of the peso at a controllable pace and has carried out a number of one-time currency adjustments.

c   Korea

South Korea's interest rate, exchange rate, capital account, and domestic financial reform were incomplete before the Asian financial crisis, and from the beginning it lacked a unified plan. Korea's reform sequence featured limited interest rate liberalization, accompanied by a significant liberalization of the capital account, and a still relatively fixed exchange rate system.

In the 1980s, banks were privatized in Korea. However, as a result of the priva-tization, several large corporations took ownership of the banks. At the same time, several non-bank financial institutions were also under these corporations' control and were subject to very weak regulations.

In 1990, the Korean won was originally pegged to a basket of currencies, then it switched to the market average rate system (MARS), the floating range of the won to the US dollar was expanded, and more market mechanisms were introduced to determine the won's exchange rate. However, the rate was still highly regulated.

In 1993, Korea started to gradually liberalize its interest rate. However, the lib-eralization was incomplete. The government kept its interventions on the interest

Table 5-3 Sequence of financial reforms in Korea

Year	Interest rate reform	Exchange rate reform	Capital account liberalization	Supporting reform
1983				
1984				
1985	Gradually allevi-ated deposit rate limit, from long-term to short-term deposits		Encouraged capital outflows	Gradually opened the market to for-eign banks
1986				
1987				
1988				
1989				
1990		Exchange rate largely determined by the mar-ket, expanded free float range, but with limited flexibility	Encouraged capital inflows	
1991				
1992				
1993				
1994				
1995				
1996				

rate largely because some sectors in Korea's economy were sensitive to interest rates.

Capital accounts were opened at a gradual pace. However, the sequence of capital account controls was wrong. Korea first eased control over short-term inflows, and at the same time maintained controls over long-term inflows. This directly led to the accumulation of a large amount of short-term foreign debt.

The Asian financial crisis in 1997 exacerbated the mistakes made during the reform process. A huge amount of short-term debt matured, banks mistakenly lent to corporate affiliates which could not repay, and non-performing loans piled up. The won depreciated and non-bank financial institutions' currency mismatch problems became ever more prominent. For these reasons Korea experienced double crises – balance of payment crisis and domestic financial crisis.

d   Mexico

In the wake of Mexico's debt crisis in the 1980s, interest rate, exchange rate, the capital account, and domestic financial reforms advanced rapidly and simulta-neously with little or no sequence. The capital account and interest rates were completely liberalized, while the exchange rate regime never moved away from a rather inflexible system. In 1994, Mexico suffered a peso crisis.

Mexico allowed the peso to gradually devalue and increased the floating band, but never fully abandoned the fixed exchange rate regime. This, to some extent,

Table 5-4 Sequence of financial reforms in Mexico

Year	Interest rate reform	Exchange rate reform	Capital account liberalization	Supporting reform
1988			Largely opened up capital account, maintained restrictions over FDI, interbank market and money market	
1989	Liberalization of the interest rate	Free float range expanded, but still under relatively strict control		
1990				
1991				Privatization of 18 banks, strengthened regulation
1992				
1993				
1994				

eased the Mexican peso's overvalued exchange rate. However, due to the difference in inflation rates, the peso was still overvalued after depreciation.

In terms of capital accounts, Mexico liberalized foreign direct investment (FDI), portfolio investment, and government bond investment between 1989 and 1993.

In terms of interest rates, Mexico abolished the control over interest rates in 1989. Moreover, between 1991 and 1992, 18 banks were privatized in Mexico and regulation strengthened. However, the regulatory reform was not fully in place and had much oversight.

The peso crisis was, to a large degree, a macro crisis – overvalued exchange rate, huge current account deficit, and excessive rise in external debt. However, since regulation was not in place, the currency mismatch issue was exposed and exacerbated the crisis.

e Indonesia

Indonesia hoped that a package of reforms for exchange rates, interest rates, the capital account, and the domestic financial system could help improve the vitality of its private economy, reduce the dependence on the oil sector, and transform Indonesia into an export-oriented economy. Before the reform, Indonesia liberalized capital outflows but strictly controlled capital inflows, the interest rates were strictly controlled, and credit was limited. The government intervened heavily in the lending of the five state-owned banks. These banks were major players in Indonesia's banking industry. The sequence of the reform was to first carry out interest rate liberalization, followed by gradual liberalization of capital inflows and increase of the flexibility of the exchange rate. However, the fixed exchange rate regime was not fundamentally changed.

The first stage of the reform was from 1982 to 1986. This period saw large currency devaluations (1983 and 1986) which caused the exchange rate to return to a competitive level. The interest rate was liberalized and bank loan controls were partially removed in 1983. Money market instruments were introduced to the domestic financial market in 1984.

The second stage of the reform took place between 1987 and 1992. This phase primarily targeted the domestic financial system and the opening-up of the capital

Table 5-5 Sequence of financial reforms in Indonesia

Year	Interest rate reform	Exchange rate reform	Capital account liberalization	Supporting reform
1983	Liberalization of interest rates			
1984				Continuously liberalized financial market, promoted competition, and strengthened regulation; although still with obvious loopholes
1985			Increased liberalization of capital inflow; fewer restrictions on capital outflow	
1986		After the one-time depreciation in the 1980s, the exchange rate remained relative stable; reform mainly focused on increasing free float range		
1987	Increased interest rate flexibility, maintaining government intervention			
1988				
1989				
1990				
1991				
1992				
1993				
1994				
1995				
1996				

account. Domestic financial reform included reducing intervention in banking operations, reducing restrictions on foreign banks, and increasing the level of regulation. Major capital account reforms took place relatively late, restrictions on capital inflows to financial institutions were relaxed in 1989, banks were allowed to borrow from abroad, and foreign investment was allowed in the domestic stock market.

Indonesia's reform was successful in the early stage, but the governance of banks was not effectively improved in the reform process, with a large number of loans flowing into affiliated enterprises and overcapacity sectors. Banks had weak risk management. After the opening-up of the capital account, a large amount of short-term capital flowed into the country through banks, and the banks took on huge exchange rate risks.

Credit risk, term, and exchange rate mismatch caused a systemic banking crisis in Indonesia in 1997. A large number of banks went bankrupt. Even banks that were performing well had to receive large recapitalization from the government in order to survive.

f Sweden

Sweden's reforms of the interest rates, exchange rates, capital accounts, and domestic financial sector took place mainly from the late 1970s to early 1990s. The sequence of these reforms was interest rate reform first, followed by the opening-up of capital accounts, accompanied by domestic financial reform and removal of capital controls. Sweden had maintained a relatively fixed exchange

Table 5-6 Sequence of financial reforms in Sweden

Year	Interest rate reform	Exchange rate reform	Capital account liberalization	Supporting reform
1978	Gradually alleviated the restriction on interest rates and credit volumes	Maintained the less flexible exchange rate regime, with slight changes in currency band and values		
1979				
1980				
1981				
1982				
1983				
1984				
1985				
1986				
1987			Accelerated the opening of capital account	Gradually alleviated the regulation over foreign banks in Sweden
1988				
1989				
1990				
1991				
1992				

rate; the reform was focused on the adjustment of the floating band and ladder-like changes in currency value.

From 1978 to the early 1980s, Sweden gradually liberalized interest rates and restrictions over the scale of lending. By 1985, basic controls over interest rates and credit were largely liberalized. Sweden accelerated the opening of its capital account in 1986, mainly by eliminating restrictions on the scale of capital inflows and outflows. By 1989 Sweden had removed all capital controls.

The problem with Sweden's reform was surge in lending after credit controls were eliminated, which was followed by large capital inflows; the inflexible exchange rate led to an asset bubble. Risk began to accumulate due to imperfect regulation. Ultimately, with the burst of asset price bubbles, Sweden suffered dual crises in the early 1990s – banking crisis and currency crisis. Sweden was not alone; two other Nordic countries – Finland and Norway experienced similar crises during their reforms.

By studying the sequence of reforms in Japan, Korea, Indonesia, Chile, Mexico, and Sweden, we find that China can learn from the experiences of these countries, although they are located in different regions and at different development stages with different timing, methods, and sequences of reforms, and though some even experienced crisis during their reforms.

The first lesson is that there is no universal rule for the reform sequence. It is unwise to follow other countries' sequences without careful thought. Different conditions, domestic and international political environments, and reform strategies require that the reform sequence be in line with national conditions. Reform must be undertaken flexibly based on the specific cases. There is no fixed reform model.

Second, we must have an overall plan for the speed and sequence of reforms of interest rates, exchange rates, and opening of the capital account, and coordinate all these reforms. Countries that experienced crisis all made mistakes with regard to the speed and sequence of the reforms. In Korea, opening of the capital account adopted the improper sequence of short-term first and long-term later, leading to a significant increase in high-risk short-term external debt; the exchange rate remained fixed even after the capital account was opened. Domestic financial reforms lagged behind, banks and enterprises had very close relationships, and a large number of loans made to affiliated companies turned into non-performing loans. The above-mentioned factors together contributed to the crisis. In Sweden, the strengthening of regulation lagged behind the loosening of financial controls and liberalization of the interest rate, which led to massive capital inflows and credit expansion that in turn triggered banking and currency crises. In Japan, reform measures for bank assets and liabilities were asymmetric and adopted a wrong sequence. This led to the loss of high-quality assets, whereas deposits continued to grow. As a result, banks were forced to invest in the high-risk real estate sector and small businesses, which planted the seeds for the crisis. In Indonesia, corporate governance reform and regulation severely lagged behind reforms in other areas; massive risks accumulated and led to a crisis. Experiences of these countries show that a rational choice of reform sequence and coordination between the various reforms are crucial to the success of the reforms.

Third, many countries chose the reform sequence of internal first, external later and parallel advancement. The arrangement of internal first and external later prioritizes interest rates, exchange rates, and other related reforms, and then allows for the opening of the capital account. The advantage of this sequence is that it protects domestic reform from the influence of fluctuations in international markets and capital flows, as appropriate capital controls can provide enough time and create the conditions for successful domestic reform. The arrangement of parallel advancement is the concurrent advancement of multiple reforms. For example, before the capital account is completely opened, interest rate and exchange rate reforms can be carried out at the same time since cross-border capital flows are limited and interest rate and exchange rate reforms will not stand in each other's way. Chile is an example of success of the reform sequence. In the 1990s, Chile retained measures to limit capital inflows. By restricting capital flows, Chile improved the flexibility of the exchange rate and interest rate, established an inflation targeting the monetary policy framework, and developed the domestic financial market and products. By the end of the 1990s, the exchange rate was allowed to float freely and the capital account was opened completely.

Fourth, the level and flexibility of the exchange rate are very important. If the exchange rate deviates from the equilibrium level, it is important to adjust it first. As vulnerability grows, or when the economy suffers internal or external shocks, the risks may turn into crises. Mexico was an example. Before the crisis, Mexico accelerated exchange rate and capital account reforms; however, the peso was overvalued, the capital account was in massive deficit, foreign debt continued to increase, and there were severe currency mismatches in the banking system. As the peso devalued due to massive capital outflows, the banking system experienced a crisis. Contrary to Mexico, Chile and Indonesia (early stage of the reform was successful) largely adjusted its currency exchange rate toward the equilibrium level at the beginning of their reforms and then carried out radical reforms on the exchange rate system. On the other hand, exchange rate flexibility is also very important, even if the exchange rate does not significantly deviate from the equilibrium level. If the exchange rate were not flexible, it would then be hard to respond to shocks from short-term capital flows and changes in domestic and international interest rate spreads; this will undermine monetary policy independence. Korea, Indonesia, Mexico, Sweden, and Argentina all adopted a relatively inflexible exchange rate system and experienced currency crises.

Fifth, crucial reforms are more easily undertaken when the macroeconomic environment is stable, and the opening of the capital account must serve the financial reform and stable operation of the domestic economy. Improper monetary, fiscal, exchange rate, and other macroeconomic policies will increase economic risks and harm the advancement and coordination of reforms. These risks will be embodied in the financial system; for example, over-expansionary monetary policy will result in excessive liquidity, and financial institutions may take on greater risks, undermining stability of the financial system in the end. Therefore, where the macroeconomic situation isn't supportive or macroeconomic policy isn't appropriate, the chances of reform derailment will increase greatly. Mexico initiated reforms with an overvalued currency, high inflation, and fiscal deficit, which directly triggered a peso crisis. This proves that the reform must wait for the appropriate time to be initiated; reform will easily derail if the conditions aren't mature. Waiting for stable conditions in the domestic and international economy and financial systems will help crucial reforms to succeed. The volatility, unpredictability, and massive scale of international capital flows may affect domestic economic stability, which is why delaying the opening of the capital account or reinstating some of the capital controls should be taken as countermeasures. In the 1990s, Chile brought in capital control measures to cope with large-scale capital inflows. During 2013–2015, Brazil and other countries also used capital controls to respond to large capital inflows and currency appreciations. The IMF points out that capital controls can be used as a policy tool to manage capital inflows.

Sixth, supporting reforms for the real economy and financial infrastructure must be in place. The exchange rate, interest rate, and capital account convertibility reforms are important reforms that affect the entire macro-economy and financial system. The success and failure of the reforms is not only dependent on themselves, but also on many supporting factors. These supporting factors include reforms of the real economy, the basic institutional environment, improvement of the corporate governance structure, regulation, macro-prudential measures, and the development of financial markets. The common feature of the countries that had crises during reforms is that supporting reform measures were insufficient.

Korea's large corporations were extremely cost sensitive, which meant that changes in the interest rate had a big impact, which limited the process of market-based interest rate reform. The financial systems in Korea and Sweden had regulatory loopholes for non-banking financial institutions. Mexico's accounting standards were flawed; banks' exposure to foreign currencies was not recorded correctly to reflect the risks of currency mismatch. The failure of Korea and Indonesia emphasized the importance of the domestic institutional environment and corporate governance. Lack of good corporate governance distorted the behavior of banks and businesses severely and reduced their incentives and ability to control risks; these problems, which were exacerbated with the opening of the capital account and capital inflows, became important factors that caused crises.

B Analyzing the sequence of interest rate reform, exchange rate reform, and capital account liberalization

a Overview

Some hold the view that China's exchange rate and interest rate reforms should be completed before the opening of the capital account. Yu Yongding (2011) believes that

> the most urgent task is to adjust the exchange rate policy to realize external balance, next is to shift monetary policy from adjusting aggregates to adjusting prices, i.e. liberalizing interest rates, then to liberalize the capital account, and the internationalization of the RMB should be the last.

Yu believes that in the financial sector, the obscure expression of creating momentum for reform through opening-up may lead to a repeat of past mistakes. Xue Hongli (2003) argues that while China's financial markets are dynamically opening-up, the exchange rate system should be actively reformed. The IMF and World Bank Financial Sector Assessment Program of China (2011) indicate that China should complete exchange rate and interest rate reforms; liberalizing the capital account should be the final step. However, along with the development of financial markets and institutional improvement, China should implement opening-up in a gradual manner.

Still, others believe that capital account liberalization will improve the efficacy of monetary policy and promote domestic reforms, and could be pursued appropriately. Xie Ping (2013a) believes that interest rate liberalization and exchange rate liberalization need not be pursued in a specific order, and one should not be treated as a precondition for the other; both are part of the market infrastructure and the loosening of political limitations on financial transactions and behavior. In the area of the exchange rate and RMB convertibility, RMB convertibility targets foreign exchange demand of the capital account; it influences the formation of the exchange rate but shouldn't be a fundamental condition for the market-based exchange rate. Interest rate parity theory is the basis for determining the sequence of RMB convertibility or interest rate liberalization. Trial and error may be used. The current interest rate system could be maintained and adjusted based on changes taking place after the capital account becomes convertible. In reality, the situation may not be that complicated, because flexible controls and market-based adjustment measures can be used on interest rates domestically. Li Bo (2014) believes that a close examination of the details will show that the relationship between capital account convertibility and other reforms isn't a simple matter of sequence; instead, the relationship is a mutually supportive one. Whether to achieve interest rate liberalization or exchange rate liberalization, foreign exchange controls must be removed, and removing foreign exchange controls is a concrete step toward capital account convertibility. Without capital account convertibility, there is no way to streamline supply and demand in the foreign exchange market, and market participants will find it difficult to have confidence that the exchange rate has really been liberalized. The sequence of reforms cannot completely adhere to the teaching in the textbooks; there must be some flexibility to adapt to the real situation and the market. In the past few years, there has been a large demand for RMB in the international market. If capital outflow is not allowed until the exchange rate reform and capital account convertibility are achieved, then an opportunity will be missed. While controlling risks, we should open some of the easily manageable channels such as trade settlement and FDI, which in turn will promote capital account convertibility.

Some others think that the reforms must be carried out sequentially in accordance to the real conditions. Jin Zhongxia (2013) and others believe that exchange rate equilibrium and interest rate equilibrium share a close relationship, and that interest rate policies and exchange rate policies affect each other; interest rate disequilibrium will lead to exchange rate disequilibrium, and exchange rate disequilibrium will be reflected in the disequilibrium of the interest rate. Optimal dynamic adjustment pathways should be based on the level of disequilibrium of the two; the one with greater disequilibrium should be adjusted first, followed by the other. Zhao Xijun (2012) thinks that the sequencing of exchange rate liberalization, interest rate liberalization, and capital account liberalization is unimportant. Priority should be given to the reform to which conditions are most suited. If the fundamentals for exchange reform are better, then it could potentially be carried out more quickly; China has made impressive progress in opening the capital account and has the capability to achieve more. However, market-based interest rate reform could be more difficult.

At present, more and more experts believe that there is no correct sequential order for executing these reforms; execution of the three can be coordinated. Sheng Songcheng and some others (2012) believe that the sequence of internal first and external later has its limitations. First, the theory does not fully take into account the situation of large economies. For large economies in the world, the exchange rate is mainly influenced by the competitiveness of products, the structure of trade, the purchasing power of its currency, and inflation expectations; interest rates in the large economies are largely determined by changes in the domestic financial environment. As a result, variations of the interest rate and exchange rate in large economies are not mainly determined by international capital shocks and flows but instead by domestic economic conditions and terms of trade with foreign countries. Second, the market is not perfectly competitive. Interest rate parity theory holds that there is only one type of financial product in the market, or that all financial products in the market are interchangeable, so there is only one type of interest rate. In reality, there are many types of interest rates. Scholars have conducted theoretical studies into interest rate parity theory; some studies confirmed the theory, but many have refuted it. The interest rate parity theory and the impossible trinity theory are perfect in theory but do not correspond to reality. Third, attention to the middle state was insufficient. The impossible trinity consists of capital controls (or free capital flows), fixed exchange rate (or floating exchange rate), and effective monetary policy (or ineffective monetary policy). However, these terms are relative, not absolute. Today, few countries implement a fixed exchange rate, and few nations implement a true free float exchange rate regime. China's exchange rate is not entirely fixed, nor is it fair to say that it is a floating one. Its current state is somewhere in the middle. Using countries that have completed financial reforms as examples, the US has executed the sequence of external first and internal later; Japan implemented internal first followed by external; the sequences of reform of the UK and Germany were essentially the same, but with opposite outcomes. There is no fixed sequence for financial reform and opening-up. Practice shows that China's financial reforms are implemented in a coordinated manner. Interest rate and exchange rate reforms and capital account liberalization should be coordinated to protect against the risks of opening the capital account. Guan Tao (2012) believes that capital account convertibility, exchange rate liberalization, and market-based interest rate reform shouldn't be pursued in a specific sequence but should be conditional on each other and mutually supportive. For a period of time, a great deal of arbitrage-seeking capital was flowing into China because of the expectation that the RMB would appreciate, and the RMB interest rate was high relative to the USD. These two differentials made China a very attractive destination for arbitrage. On the other hand, exchange rate reform is slow because the capital account is not fully convertible, affecting the overall market environment. The international balance of payment adjustment mechanism in a mature market is based on a floating exchange rate and capital flows. A surplus in the current account must have a corresponding capital account deficit, and as of today there exist many limitations on capital outflows from China. If the exchange rate is allowed to float freely, then there is a high probability that the exchange rate will overshoot against the background of trade surplus.

b   Current state of interest rate reform, exchange rate reform, and
capital account liberalization

China began to explore ways to liberalize the interest rate a long time ago, but more substantial development started after the exchange rate reform took place. In January 1994, the official exchange rate and the foreign exchange swap price

Table 5-7 Progress of financial reforms in China

	Market-based interest rate reform	Reform of exchange rate formation mechanism	Opening of capital account
1979		Dual-track exchange rate regime (internal trade settlement price was set besides official prices)	Established four special zones; enacted Joint Venture Enterprise Law, attracted FDI
1985		Official exchange rate and foreign exchange swap rates coexisted	
1993	Interest rates on working capital loans were allowed to float 10% below and 20% above the benchmark rates	Official exchange rate and swap exchange rate unified	
1996	Liberalization of the inter-bank offered rate; market-based treasury rates reform		Current account convertibility
1997	Liberalization of interbank repo rates and spot trading rates		
1998	Liberalization of discount, transfer discount interest rates; issuance of financial bonds by policy banks		
1999	Liberalization of RMB borrowing rates by foreign banks; liberalization of deposit rates for insurance companies		
2000	Liberalization of foreign currency loan rates; liberalization of foreign currency deposit rates for amounts over US$3 million		
2002			Introduction of Qualified Foreign Institutional Investor (QFII)
2004	Removal of the upper limit on lending rates of financial institutions (not including urban and rural cooperatives); allowed deposit rates to float downward while maintaining the upper limit		

(*Continued*)

Table 5-7 Continued

	Market-based interest rate reform	*Reform of exchange rate formation mechanism*	*Opening of capital account*
2005		Implementation of a managed floating exchange rate regime with reference to a basket of currencies	
2007	Creation of money market benchmark rate (Shibor)	Floating band of spot rate of RMB against US dollar enlarged from 0.3% to 0.5%	Introduction of Qualified Domestic Institutional Investor (QDII)
2008		De facto peg of RMB to US dollar	
2009			Pilot programs of cross-border use of RMB
2010		RMB managed floating regime re-implemented	Development of HK offshore RMB market; opening-up domestic bond market.
2011			Introduction of RMB Qualified Foreign Institutional Investor (RQFII)
2012	Upper bound of deposit rates expanded to 1.1 times of the benchmark rate; lower bound of loan rates expanded to 0.7 times the benchmark rate	RMB–USD exchange rate floating band expanded to 1% from 0.5%	Initiation of offshore RMB market in London; QFII and RQFII quota expanded; domestic banks allowed to issue offshore RMB loans
2013	Removal of lower bound of loan interest rates		Pilot program of Shanghai Free Trade Zone
2014	Upper bound for deposit interest rate expanded to about 1.2 times the benchmark rate	RMB–USD exchange rate floating band expanded to 2% from 1%	Shanghai-HK Stock Connect

were merged; a single managed floating exchange rate regime based on market supply and demand was established. In April 1994, the foreign exchange settlement and sales system was established and a unified national interbank foreign exchange market was founded. Interest rate reform didn't see any breakthroughs until 1996, when the interbank interest rate was liberalized. Capital account liberalization wasn't implemented until 2002, after China's accession to the WTO, while the current account was liberalized in 1996. Subsequently, the RMB interest rate, exchange rate, and capital account reforms were implemented alternately.

Although great progress has been made in all three areas, none has been completed. Table 5-7 shows that in the early stage, China's reforms followed the basic sequence of exchange rate–interest rate–capital account. At present, these three reforms are being pursued in a coordinated manner.

c   An analysis of the preconditions for the interest rate and exchange rate reforms and capital account liberalization

The relationship between the RMB exchange rate, interest rate, and capital account liberalization is very complex. However, based on the conditions necessary to the smooth implementation of each of the three reforms, it can be said that the implementation of one reform may require partial or complete implementation of the other two. From this perspective, the relationship between the three reforms becomes clear, and the correct sequence of the reform becomes more apparent.

This section will analyze the preconditions for the successful implementation of the three reforms and explore their relationships.

I   BASIC PRECONDITIONS FOR IMPLEMENTING THE MANAGED FLOATING EXCHANGE
    RATE REGIME

First, the exchange rate reaches to a more or less equilibrium level. There are no strong market expectations for one-sided appreciation or depreciation. Otherwise, once the managed float is instituted, there will be pressure on the currency to fluctuate. Foreign trade, control over inflation, operation of monetary policy, and financial stability will be adversely affected, hurting the macro-economy and financial stability.

Second, domestic businesses, residents, and other microeconomic entities are capable of effectively sustaining shocks from exchange rate fluctuations. Under a managed floating exchange rate regime, the fluctuations of bilateral exchange rate and nominal effective exchange rate are typically large, and this will increase the exchange rate risk facing financial institutions, businesses, and individuals. This necessitates the balance sheets of microeconomic entities to be free from obvious currency mismatch or other problems sensitive to the exchange rate; it also requires microeconomic entities to have acquired significant experience in managing exchange rate fluctuations, and the capability to deal shocks from currency fluctuations. A mature foreign exchange market with diverse participants and products, a large amount of transactions, and ample liquidity can efficiently discover market prices and decrease the excessive fluctuations in the exchange rate, satisfying the needs of various economic entities in managing foreign exchange settlement and risks.

Third, appropriate macro-prudential management and financial regulation are in place. With increased exchange rate fluctuations, the accumulation of risks for some businesses, sectors, and financial products is unavoidable; macro-prudential management and financial regulations must be in place so that risks can be identified and eliminated before they break out.

First, the exchange rate basically reaches the equilibrium level. If interest rates are liberalized when the exchange rate is not at the equilibrium level, it will lead to conflicts between domestic equilibrium and equilibrium in the international balance of payments. This is because market-based interest rate reform is beneficial to domestic equilibrium but could cause disequilibrium in the international balance of payments and macroeconomic instability. For example, if the exchange rate is undervalued, the current account surplus will expand, speeding up capital inflows and intensifying domestic inflation. Under these conditions, any increase in interest rates, although beneficial to curbing inflation, will stimulate more capital inflows and cause further disequilibrium in the international balance of payments. In this case, a more severe problem would be that it is hard for the interest rate to reach the equilibrium level when the exchange rate is in disequilibrium. Under such conditions, even if the interest rate can be liberalized, it may not have any obvious benefits and may even have the adverse effect of worsening the structural disequilibrium.

Second, an effective monetary policy transmission mechanism needs to be in place. The realization of market-based interest rates does not necessarily mean the central bank gives up guidance and management over interest rates. After interest rates are liberalized, direct determination of the deposit and loan benchmark interest rates by the central bank is replaced by the indirect adjustment of rates by adjusting the quantity and price of money. Furthermore, the benchmark interest rate can affect other interest rates in the market; this transmission will rely on an effective transmission mechanism of monetary policy.

Third, the interest rate must be close to the equilibrium level. Large changes in the market interest rates will not benefit macroeconomic and financial stability. Before interest rates are liberalized, they should be close to the equilibrium level already, and the macro-economy should also be relatively stable, guaranteeing that there won't be any major fluctuations after interest rates are liberalized.

Fourth, financial institutions, businesses, and individuals and other microeconomic entities should be capable of dealing with sharp interest rate fluctuations. Interest rates fluctuate according to market conditions and have different impacts on different microeconomic entities. Moreover, rational responses of microeconomic entities to interest rate fluctuations are necessary conditions for macroeconomic controls through price tools. However, if the asset-liability structure of microeconomic entities isn't appropriate, and the entities lack the ability to manage interest rate risks, then interest rate volatility may lead to undesired adverse results and financial risks.

Fifth, appropriate macro-prudential management and financial regulation are needed. High-interest deposits, over competition, over-lending to high-risk industries, rapid credit growth, and term mismatch may appear over the course of market-based interest rate reform, which will increase financial risks. To protect against the excessive accumulation of risks in the financial sector, we must strengthen macro-prudential management and financial regulation to detect and manage risks in a timely manner.

III PRECONDITIONS FOR REALIZING CAPITAL ACCOUNT CONVERTIBILITY

First, the exchange rate must be flexible and close to the equilibrium level. When the capital account is freely convertible, in order for the monetary policy to remain independent, the exchange rate needs to be around the equilibrium level, and could float freely. This is the basic conclusion of the impossible trinity theory.

Second, the interest rate is basically liberalized. When the capital account is freely convertible, interest rate controls will become ineffective as financial institutions, businesses, and individuals channel money through overseas financial markets to avoid the controls. Non–market-based interest rates will cause problems such as disintermediation and arbitrage, pushing the exchange rate further away from the equilibrium level. Even though capital account convertibility can promote the interest rate reform, a complete opening of the capital account before realization of market-based interest rates will make the liberalization process untenable and will lead to instability.

Third, financial institutions, businesses, individuals, and other microeconomic entities must be capable of managing shocks from volatility of the exchange rate, interest rate, and capital flows. Capital account convertibility will lead to increased volatility in the exchange rate, the interest rate, and capital flows; therefore, microeconomic entities must be able to effectively respond to these risks. Otherwise, economic instability is unavoidable.

Fourth, the internal control, corporate governance, market development, and accounting standards of the financial system must be in line with international standards. Capital account convertibility means the domestic financial system not only faces domestic risks but also risks from international financial markets. International experiences show that capital account convertibility will exacerbate the existing problems within the financial system and create new ones. Demand for better internal controls, corporate governance, market development, and accounting standards will increase.

Fifth, appropriate macro-prudential management and financial regulation are needed. With the opening of the capital account, the financial system faces increased and more complicated risks, and the consequences of any problems are much greater. Only an effective macro-prudential management and regulation system can alleviate these risks.

d   The relationship between exchange rate reform, interest rate
   reform, and capital account liberalization

Figure 5-2 summarizes the relationship between reforms of the exchange rate, the interest rate, and capital account convertibility. In summary, exchange rate reform is the precondition for interest rate reform and capital account convertibility. Interest rate reform creates the conditions for capital account convertibility, while capital account convertibility will in turn promote the interest rate reform. Having appropriate supporting reforms in place is a necessary precondition for the smooth implementation of each of the reforms.

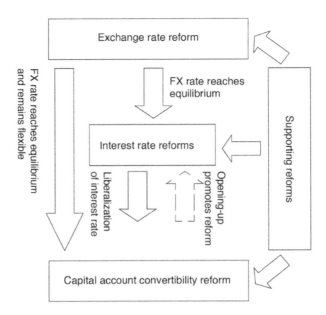

Figure 5-2 Relationship between exchange rate reform, interest rate reform, and capital account convertibility

C   *Basic principles for coordinating the three reforms*

When designing the sequence of the reforms, consideration must be given to the internal logic of each reform as well as the coordination between all the reforms; there should also be clear principles for how to carry out the reforms. We believe that any reform sequence should adhere to the following principles.

First, financial development should adapt to the development of the real economy and make timely adjustments according to the development and reform needs of the real economy. It is discernable that over the course of China's financial reform, the sequence of important financial reforms has followed the basic rules of financial reforms and complied with the development needs of the real economy. In the early stage of the reform and opening-up, China adopted the export-oriented development strategy; therefore, the financial reform saw its first breakthrough in the exchange rate regime. At the same time, China set up economic special zones and attracted FDI. With the development of the domestic economy and advancement of reforms of enterprises, price, and financial institutions, market-based interest rate reform sped up correspondingly. In 2005, when external imbalance became pronounced, China took steps to advance the exchange rate reform and orderly opening-up of the capital account. Meanwhile, taking note of the relationship between internal and external imbalances, China actively sought to create conditions to speed up the reform of deposit and lending interest rates. In the future, we should continue to adhere to the principle of tailoring financial reforms to economic development and reforms.

Second, strengthened financial regulation and an improved monetary policy framework are required to maintain financial stability and the autonomy and effectiveness of monetary policy. If financial stability and the independence of the monetary policy are adversely affected, then the reforms cannot be regarded as successful. These are the basic premises of any reform. To achieve this, in addition to promoting reforms in a reasonable manner, we must constantly strengthen financial supervision and improve the monetary policy adjustment framework.

Third, China must coordinate implementation of the reforms, focusing on the easy tasks first; create momentum for reforms through opening-up; and gradually push forward capital account liberalization and RMB internationalization to advance China's financial reform and development while controlling risks. Based on other countries' experiences and the intrinsic requirements of reforms of the exchange rate, interest rate, and capital account convertibility, it's easy to see that these three reforms need to be advanced holistically; this is the only way to minimize risks and guarantee the orderly and steady advancement of the reforms. Because resistance will be encountered over the course of these reforms, it's necessary to execute easy tasks before the difficult ones and create momentum for the reforms through opening-up to guarantee smooth progress of reforms. The priority is to improve the exchange rate formation mechanism and realize the two-way fluctuations of RMB at a reasonable equilibrium level. Because the interest rate reform can create the conditions for capital account convertibility, and capital account convertibility in turn can promote interest rate reform, the two initiatives are mutually supportive and should be advanced in a coordinated manner.

6 Overall evaluation and policy recommendation on China's interest rate reform

I Overview of China's interest rate reform

The essence of the interest rate reform is to let the market rather than monetary authorities determine the interest rates. Specifically speaking, the interest rate reform has three components. First, supply and demand of funds decide the level, risk structure, and term structure of interest rates. Second, interest rates are correlated with the benchmark interest rate taking a key and leading role. Third, monetary authorities influence interest rates through market operations. In 2003, the 3rd Plenum of the 16th CPC Central Committee adopted the *Decision on Some Issues Concerning the Socialist Market Economy*. The decision identifies the objective of China's interest rate reform as steadily pushing forward interest rate liberalization and building a market-based interest rate formation mechanism where the central bank uses monetary policy instruments to guide the interest rates.

To this end, the reform must remove controls over the interest rates. However, the reform does not simply mean that the market and financial institutions, instead of the government, will be determining the interest rate; the reform also requires orderly market competition according to market disciplines. Moreover, the reform does not completely rule out the necessity of intervention by the central bank. In other words, while removing controls over the interest rates, market mechanisms for interest rate determination and adjustment should also be established. Therefore, while gradually relaxing controls over deposit rates, technical preparatory measures should be taken to nurture a benchmark interest rate system, form market-based mechanisms for interest rate adjustment and transmission, establish a deposit insurance system, and develop new risk management tools (Zhou, 2013b).

In relaxing controls, China should take a gradual approach and take into consideration the varied degree of influence on the allocation of financial resources by financial markets at different tiers. The reform should start with the market which has the least influences. As "indirect financing plays a dominant role in China's financial system, interest rate liberalization in the wholesale market does not affect enterprises' financing cost and helps improve the efficiency of capital allocation" (Yi, 2009). Therefore, China's interest rate reform sees its first breakthrough in the wholesale market. In 1996, the control over interbank offered rates was removed, and by 1999, interest rates in the bond issuance and secondary markets had been mostly liberalized. "While maintaining the overall control, we introduced market-oriented interest rates as a complement. Therefore, the reform was like a Pareto improvement that improves the allocation efficiency of bank resources without harming the real economy" (Yi, 2009). Therefore, in the process of interest rate liberalization, China adopts a dual-track system of controlled rates in the banking system and market-oriented interest rates outside the banking system. The dual-track system has evolved in a way that market-oriented interest rates kept expanding and controlled interest rates gradually shrank. In 2012 the control on lending rates was removed, and in October 2015 the cap on deposit rates was lifted. Since then the control on interest rates has basically phased out.

While easing controls and introducing market-oriented interest rates, the PBOC made great efforts to improve infrastructure to facilitate the development of a market-based interest rate formation mechanism. On one hand, the pricing mechanisms of financial institutions have been strengthened; on the other hand, efforts have been made to push forward the construction of the benchmark interest rate system. Currently, the pricing mechanisms of commercial banks include funds transfer pricing (FTP) and risk pricing. With the deepening of reforms, domestic banks have strengthened relevant organizational structure, improved rules and regulations, developed new pricing models, established support systems, and enhanced managerial arrangements. In developing the benchmark interest rates, China has established a short-term rate system with Shibor as the prime rate and a medium and long-term rate system with the government bond yield as the prime rate. After removing the control on lending rates, China set up a centralized quote and publish mechanism for the loan prime rate (LPR). At present, the LPR mechanism operates smoothly and plays an increasingly important role in pricing credit products and derivatives. According to empirical studies, market rates and prime rates are positively correlated and the interest rate gap reflects the risk structure. However, the position of Shibor as a benchmark for short-term rates needs to be enhanced. At the same time, China needs to further develop the financial market to produce a complete yield curve in order to establish the medium and long-term rate system. Generally speaking, the level, risk structure, and term structure of interest rates are to a large extent determined by supply and demand in the financial market. However, before controls over interest rates were completely lifted and the financial market lacked width and depth, China's interest rates were still not completely decided by the market and the risk and term structure still needed improvement. In addition, hindrances still existed in the interest rate transmission mechanism as different interest rate systems were not sufficiently linked. Since the control on deposit rates has just been removed, China still needs to improve the interest rate formation mechanism and the transmission between different rate systems.

During the process of interest rate liberalization, the PBOC on one hand adjusts interest rates and their floating bands for deposit and lending; on the other hand, it uses open market operations (repo, reverse repo, issuance of central bank bills) and monetary policy instruments (e.g. reserve requirement ratio) to indirectly adjust liquidity and interest rates. The central bank base rate can also guide market rates. However, PBOC's rate adjustment operation still needs to be enhanced and the mechanism of using the central bank base rate to guide market rates needs to be established. Meanwhile, the transmission of interest rates from the money market to the credit market is not smooth. As a result, the central bank's ability is limited in using monetary instruments to guide market rates and further the lending and deposit rates of financial institutions. As hindrances exist in interest rate transmission, the influence of interest rate policies on the whole economy is weakened. Moreover, the decision-making process on interest rates is inflexible; adjustments of deposit and lending benchmark rates need to go through a long and complicated process. Therefore, interest rate adjustments often lag behind market changes. Besides, interest rate policies need to incorporate multiple goals and balance multiple interests. As a result, the policies are often compromised and mitigated and fail to achieve the desired effects.

In general, from the three aspects of control relaxation, price formation, and rate adjustment, China has made tremendous progress in interest rate liberalization. In particular, China has almost entirely relaxed the control on interest rates. However, China has not yet completed the reform and still needs to build and improve the interest rate formation and adjustment mechanisms and enhance the effectiveness of the central bank's rate adjustment measures. It is worth noting that the liberalization of interest rates takes place while China continuously pushes forward the overall economic reform and the financial sector keeps growing and opening up. Therefore, the interest rate reform is an integral part of building a socialist market economy and an important symbol of the progress of China's economic reform and development. The progress made and gaps to close both reflect the characteristics of China as a transitional and developing economy.

II   Overall evaluation of China's interest rate reform

A   *Different assessments of China's interest rate reform*

Currently, people have multiple opinions on the progress of China's interest rate reform. The mainstream holds a positive view, thinking that the reform has relaxed financial control, optimized the allocation of financial resources, and improved the transmission mechanism of monetary policies. For instance, Huang Jinlao (2013) believes that over the past 16 years, the reform has been much criticized but carried forward nonetheless; that the reform has achieved great results without leading to financial crises and economic regressions; and that just like the liberalization of RMB exchange rate, the interest rate liberalization can be regarded as a model of financial price reforms in developing countries. Currently, the lending rates by financial institutions are already liberalized. On the other hand, fundraising is achieved through multiple channels, and increasingly at market rates and RMB deposit rates are no longer unified. Yi Gang (2013) argues that many enterprises complain about high financing cost and small and medium-sized enterprises face difficulties in fundraising; according to previous analyses, further liberalization will push the lending rates higher and will not necessarily be beneficial to enterprises. For households and individuals, the current deposit rate is favorable.

China's current one-year deposit rate is 3.3 percent, the highest level among reliable currencies in the world. Financial institutions have gained a large amount of capital. From 1998 to 2000, many banks were on the brink of bankruptcy technically; but nowadays, five of the ten most profitable banks in the world are from China. The development of the banking sector also increases the government's tax income. Therefore, the current interest rate system is beneficial to enterprises, households, banks and other financial institutions, and the government.

As the interest rate reform involves multiple interests and has not been completed, two opposite views currently exist regarding the progress. One view holds that the reform is still not yet completed after such a long time; that this slow process has hindered the development of China's financial sector, which cannot match China's status as the world's second largest economy; and that the lagging reform has adverse effects. For instance, Xie Ping (2013b) believes that although gradually liberalized, the control on deposit and loan rates is still strict. Deposit rates cannot keep up with inflation, resulting in depreciated savings and booming "shadow banking" services such as wealth-management and bank–trust–cooperation products; loan rates cannot curb the investment impulse, reducing the efficiency of resource allocation; and banks can easily make high profits as the lending-deposit spread is protected, leading to dissatisfaction with the disproportionately high profits and salaries of the banking industry and the deviation of the financial sector from the real economy. Nicholas Lardy (2013) maintained that interest rate liberalization was suspended from 2004 to June 2012. Since 2003, financial repression has been strengthened and the PBOC's policy of maintaining a low interest rate has curbed the growth of resident income and consumption, leading to imbalances in growth and other aspects of the economy, including the stubbornly high investment rate since 2003. Low interest rates have also contributed to the high-speed growth of real estate investment. Hong Pingfan (2012), director of the Global Economic Monitoring Unit of the UN Department of Economic and Social Affairs, argues that China's financial repression, caused by interest rate control, is rather severe and has distorted the economic structure, in which some industries suffer overcapacity while others are underinvested. Zhang Ming (2013) holds a similar view that the deposit rate control was an important contributor to China's financial repression, an important channel for the wealth transfer from residents to the government and enterprises, and a cornerstone of the traditional growth mode driven by investment and foreign trade. The research group of the World Bank and the Development Research Center of the State Council (2013) points out that excessively low deposit rates led to the excessive credit supply and demand, distorting the risk pricing mechanism and the incentive mechanism of financial institutions and hindering the development of the capital market. As a result, the monetary authority has to rely on quantity methods and intervene in market operations to rectify the distortion of price signals.

The other view holds that currently China does not have the conditions to liberalize the deposit rate – if China rushes to do so, fundraising will be even more costly and difficult against the backdrop of economic slowdown, and the real economy will be affected. Furthermore, narrowing the deposit-loan spread may lead to a potential financial crisis. For example, many scholars (i.e. Wu Xiaoling, 2013; Xu Gao, 2015) have pointed out that currently, local government financing platforms, state-owned enterprises, and the real estate sector are not sensitive to interest rate changes and rely more on the shadow banking system for financing. This reliance raises the actual interest rate level across the society. As a result, even with interest rate liberalization, allocation of financial resources cannot be optimized. Meanwhile, as the equilibrium interest rate will inevitably rise during the liberalization process, the difficulties with and high cost of obtaining credit will lead to broader concern during the economic downturn. As such, the side effects of interest rate liberalization should not be ignored (Wan, 2014). Meanwhile, international experiences indicate that competition will become fiercer as the rate spread narrows in the state-owned banks, and small and medium-sized financial institutions will be hit hard. Rushed measures for interest rate liberalization may cause vicious competition and systemic risks in the financial sector (i.e. Lian, 2014). Wang Guogang (2014) believes that China needs to be cautious, as the liberalization of loan and deposit rates may have an influence on the entire financial system, and conditions for the reform are not ripe yet. Instead, China should take surgery-like measures and develop alternative products to deposits and loans (i.e. corporate bonds, asset-backed securities, and wealth-management products). By taking a gradual approach and nurturing favorable conditions, China could establish the market-based formation mechanism of lending and deposit rates step by step.

B   *Analysis of assessments*

The analytical approaches used to evaluate China's interest rate reform can be divided into two categories. The first focuses on whether the interest rate is fully liberalized. Some recognize the achievements while maintaining that China currently does not have the conditions for liberalization; others believe that the liberalization is not fast enough as the process is far from being completed. The second approach takes into consideration China's overall economic and financial development and income distribution when evaluating interest rate policies. Some believe that the interest rate reform lags behind, invoking economic problems, especially the prominent structural imbalances in recent years; others recognize the positive influence of interest rate reform in improving resource allocation and promoting economic and financial development, citing China's recent achievements. Both approaches are valid and simply adopt different perspectives.

Determining whether the reform is successful is a very complicated issue. Focusing on whether interest rate is fully liberalized, we could figure out where China stands now and how much still needs to be done; but it risks simplifying the analysis if other factors are ignored. On one hand, not only the interest rate reform but also many other reforms are not completed yet; it is unrealistic to evaluate a reform based on the distance to the ultimate goal. On the other hand, completely lifting interest rate control does not necessarily mean a success. Although many countries once removed interest rate control, their interest rate reforms turned out to be a failure and finally they had to re-impose such control. This shows that interest rate liberalization is not as simple as just lifting the control. To determine whether the liberalization succeeds in countries that have relaxed interest rate control, we need to see whether the relaxation has caused turbulence to the financial market or resulted in banking and financial crises or fierce economic fluctuations. Therefore, when evaluating interest rate reforms, we should not only look at the interest rate system itself, but also consider the overall economic and financial development.

When the overall reform is not completed, can interest rate liberalization be achieved first? Will removal of interest rate control lead to severe economic and financial volatilities? These also need to be taken into consideration when evaluating the reform. Under the current institutional arrangements and economic conditions, if further interest rate deregulation will not lead to economic and financial fluctuations or increase potential financial risks, then it is fair to say that the current reform has lagged behind; if further deregulation will lead to dramatic fluctuations and increase potential risks, then we should retain a certain degree of control. Therefore, interest rate reform should be evaluated based on actual conditions rather than against the ideal state.

Considering economic problems (especially prominent structural imbalances in recent years), some believe that interest rate control is the main reason for the structural imbalance. This analytical approach is also questionable. First, a consensus has not been reached on whether China's consumption rate is too low. Many scholars believe that China's consumption rate is underestimated. If the imbalance between investment and consumption is not serious in China, the accusation of the interest rate system loses its foundation. Second, even with structural imbalances, we still need to assess whether such imbalances are entirely caused or to what extent are caused by interest rate control. Macroeconomic problems are often caused by multiple factors, not just one single factor. Structural imbalances appear due to a series of factors, including the enterprise system, government's role, investment and financing mechanisms, financial system, fiscal and taxation policy, income distribution policy, land policy, etc. Interest rate systems and policies are only one factor, and it is inappropriate to blame structural imbalances solely on interest rate control. Third, the interest rate system and interest rate policy should not be considered as the same. Whether the interest rate has been too low for a long time and whether the interest rate adjustment has lagged behind are more closely related to interest rate policies rather than the interest rate system. And people tend to have different opinions on central banks' interest rate policies. For example, people often criticize the policies of the Federal Reserve.

C How to properly evaluate China's interest rate reform

a International comparison

As a gradual approach was adopted, China's interest rate reform has taken a comparatively long time. It has been 18 years since 1996, when China lifted the control on the interbank offered rate. If we include early explorations, the reform has lasted even longer.

International experiences show that the process is usually long for countries that have taken a gradual approach. For instance, the rate liberalization of the US took 16 years to complete from the relaxation of the control on the deposit interest rate for CDs (less than 90 days and above US $100,000) in 1970 to the cancelation of Regulation Q in 1986; it also took Japan 16 years to complete interest rate liberalization, allowing treasury bonds to be traded in 1977, lifting the control on interbank offered rates in 1978, and finally removing all limits on deposit rates in 1994; South Korea also went through 16 years from the liberalization of the discount rate of commercial papers in 1981, two rounds of market-based reforms, to the full liberalization of the interest rate in 1997 (Zhang et al., 2012). France spent 19 years, canceling the cap on rates for deposits of six years and longer in April 1965 and fully rolling out the liberalization in 1984. India also went through 19 years of liberalization, starting the reform in 1992 and lifting limits on deposit rates and achieving full liberalization in October 2011. Actually, as early as 1985, India allowed banks to freely set up interest rates under the cap of 8 percent for deposits with the term of 15 days to one year. Although the policy failed rather quickly, it shows that India's interest rate liberalization indeed took a very long time.

However, China and these countries are not exactly comparable. As the world's largest developing and transitional economy, during the process of interest rate reform, China also needs to transform microeconomic entities, including enterprises and banks, into market players that operate independently and take responsibility for their own risks. The most important and difficult task during this transformation is the property right reform of state-owned enterprises, which have not finished yet. In addition, China needs to reform the pricing mechanism of the general goods and resources. Pricing of general goods has been basically liberalized, while the reform on pricing of resources is still underway. In addition, as China started relatively late in establishing its financial system, the foundation of financial development is weak and financial institutions lack competency in pricing and risk management. China needs to make a greater effort to develop financial infrastructure and establish market mechanisms. Considering all these factors, it cannot be said that 20 years of interest rate reform is an excessively slow process. Even France, which enjoys a high level of financial development, and India, which does not face the difficulties posed by economic transition, have both gone through about 20 years to accomplish interest rate liberalization.

Unlike Russia and other transitional economies that have taken a radical approach, China has chosen a different path. Seen from the current development of Russia and China and international opinions, China's gradual approach has more advantages.

b   *Interest rate reform and economic and financial development*

Interest rate reform aims to reduce financial repression. Under interest control, the interest rate remains at a low level, which has led to low deposit levels and strong investment incentives. Through lifting the controls, the interest rate will be liberalized so it can fully reflect the real demand for and supply of funds and rise to the equilibrium level. The liberalization will help promote the growth of savings and investment and achieve a virtuous circle between the financial system and economic development.

Since the reform and opening-up, and especially in the past decade, China's savings and investment rate have both been on a rising trend; this has boosted industrial growth, infrastructure investment, and real estate development. China has accumulated a large stock of fixed capital and laid a foundation for economic growth. From 1978 to 2013, the annual growth of China's capital stock was as high as 10.8 percent (at the constant price), one percentage point higher than GDP growth. The capital stock in 2013 was 36.4 times as much as that of 1978, while the GDP of 2013 was 26.1 times that of 1978. It was this accumulation of capital that has boosted China's rapid growth of nearly 10 percent annually. Therefore, from the perspective of savings, investment, and economic growth, the situation where financial repression hinders economic growth does not exist in China. Lardy and some IMF officials explain that Chinese residents have their target amount for savings; therefore, when the deposit interest rate decreases, the residents may just deposit more money. Yi Gang (2013) argues that the explanation is controversial because many counter-examples exist and that more data are needed as proof. Lardy (2013) also acknowledges such controversy and recognizes that the trends of the real interest rate and the deposit level can only show the existence of correlation but not a causal relation. Wei Shangjin (2013) also disagrees on the argument that lower real interest rates stimulate savings. He believes that China's high savings rate can be attributed to factors other than precautionary savings such as the accession to WTO and the

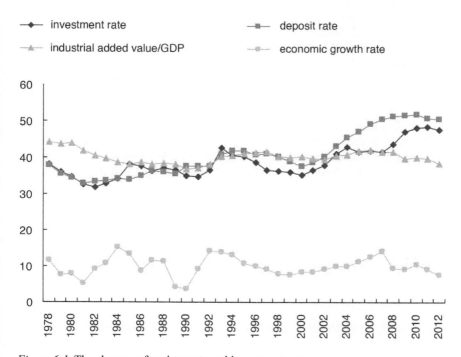

Figure 6-1 The changes of savings rate and investment rate

imbalance of sex ratio before marriage. Therefore, the evidence is not sufficient to conclude that China's interest rate reform has lagged behind based on the relationship between savings, investment, and economic growth.

In terms of the influence on financial development, as pointed out in the first chapter, China's interest rate reform takes place simultaneously with development of the financial sector. Since the reform and opening-up, China's financial institutions have mushroomed, the financial market has been established from the scratch, and financial products have become increasingly diversified. In the meantime, China has continuously pushed forward interest rate reform and properly addressed its relationship with financial development and stability. Take the banking industry as an example: From 1994 to 2000, due to institutional constraints many banks in China had solvency problems and were facing technical bankruptcy. The 2003 reform centered on corporate governance and introduced a shareholding system to state-owned commercial banks. In addition, a large amount of foreign exchange reserve was injected into those banks to replenish their capital. Even so, the banks were still very weak. Thanks to the gradual approach for interest rate liberalization, the ceiling on lending rates and the floor on deposit rates were relaxed step by step, which protected the rate spread of commercial banks for a while. As a result, the banks were able to replenish their capital with profits, which substantially enhanced their growth. During the subsequent financial crisis, China's banking industry was able to support overall economic development while maintaining its own steady growth. Currently, among the ten most profitable banks around the world, the majority are from China. It is safe to say that China achieved such results because it properly handled the relationship between reform, development, and stability of the financial sector.

It is worth noting that the gradual approach has not only protected and boosted the growth of banks but has also changed the way they operate and improved their efficiency. Thanks to the removal of interest rate control, interest rate elasticity of banks has increased; commercial banks have adapted to competition of interest rates, enhanced their capabilities for risk management, expanded sources of income, and improved the income structure. Although interest income is still the main source of income for banks in China, revenue from intermediary businesses grows rapidly. According to analysis of data from 16 listed banks, the proportion of non-interest income in total income has risen from less than 2 percent in 2001 to around 10 percent. For banks, especially those small and medium-sized ones, traditional businesses, including bank card service, account settlement, and agent services, are still the main source of non-interest income; for large banks, the proportion of the income from investment services is rising rapidly. All these are closely related to the transformation of operations of commercial banks under interest rate liberalization.

c Interest rate reform and the economic structure

Theoretically, interest rate reform is beneficial to both the allocation of resources and the improvement of economic structure. But it remains to be proven whether and to what extent partial liberalization or deviation of the interest rate from the equilibrium level would cause imbalance of the economic structure.

Looking around the globe, we could tell that China's structural imbalance is not unique but rather part of a worldwide issue and mirrors the economic imbalance in the United States. Studies show that the causes of such imbalance are the high savings rate in China, the high consumption rate, and the resultant high debt level in the US. Studies also show that after 9–11, the inappropriate monetary policies and long-lasting low interest rate in the US caused excessive growth of consumption. The situation is different in China as the low rate policy has led to insufficient consumption. Therefore, the interest rate alone cannot explain the rates of consumption and savings. It also shows that China's structural imbalance is influenced by the global economy; we should not ignore the impact of international labor division on a country's economic structure.

Domestically, the high savings rate and high investment rate can be attributed to institutional, economic, and cultural factors. Culturally, Chinese people have the tendency to save; demographic structure, income distribution, and the pension and social security system all influence the savings rate, and interest rates exert an influence that should not be ignored. However, we still need to find out whether low or high interest rates lead to an increase of savings. In terms of investment rate, industrialization and urbanization have greatly boosted the demand for investment. Specifically, China is a manufacturing power in the world and thus has a very high degree of industrialization. Meanwhile, the high-speed of investment growth is maintained by a series of institutional and policy factors, including the government's role, investment and financing mechanisms, exchange rate regime, financial policy, fiscal and taxation policy, income distribution, factor price, and land policy. Among these factors, the fiscal system and local governments' influence should not be ignored. A large amount of literature indicates that under the unique system of fiscal decentralization and administrative centralization, growth is the major criterion in promoting local officials. This model of high-powered incentives is thus the key to understanding the Chinese growth miracle since the reform and opening-up (Zhou, 2007). As GDP growth is the top priority, local governments mainly make medium and long-term investments, including infrastructure construction, real estate development, or heavy and chemical industry projects (Zhang et al., 2007; Zhang, Xia and Zhang, 2010). Therefore, all these factors should be taken into consideration when analyzing the influence of interest rates on the economic structure.

It is worth noting that as interest rate control is gradually relaxed, the function of interest rates as a leverage in optimizing resource allocation has been significantly enhanced. The liberalization of interest rate and the rise in lending rates have curbed the demand for credit. In particular, with the structural adjustments and slowdown in potential growth, enterprises' effective demand for loans also weakens. As a result, banks have to examine projects carefully in order to invest in the industries with high return, high efficiency, and a growth prospect; they also have to further balance loans' risk and returns. Previously, less effective industries with excessive capacity could get large amounts of loans; now they are facing further restraints. Banks are becoming more cautious in lending to real estate enterprises and high-risk local financing platforms; they now favor high-tech enterprises that grow rapidly and can offer high returns. Meanwhile, as the service industry (especially modern service industry) enjoys huge potential, banks will offer more loans to this sector. With further optimization of the industrial structure and improvement of the quality of economic growth, credits and loans will be more effective in helping resource allocation. In recent years, medium and long-term loans have grown more rapidly in the service sector than in the manufacturing sector; within the manufacturing sector, loans to the light industry grew much faster than loans to the heavy industry. The credit environment for small and micro-sized enterprises has been significantly improved. In the third quarter of 2014, the growth rate of medium and long-term loans in the service sector was 12.6 percent, nearly 6 percentage points higher than that of loans in the secondary sector; the long-term loans to the light industry increased by 12.3 percent, nearly 6 percentage points higher than the growth of loans to the heavy industry; the growth rate of loans for small and micro-sized enterprises was up 13.5 percent, 4 and 1.8 percentage points higher than that of loans to medium-sized and large enterprises, respectively. All these reflect the role of the interest rate in economic restructuring.

III   Policy recommendation

Under the State Council's guidance, the interest rate reform should be carried out based on the following principles, serve the needs of economic development based on national conditions, focus on market-oriented institutional arrangements, take a comprehensive and gradual approach, balance multiple needs with supporting measures, and manage potential risks without crossing the bottom line. The overall direction is to establish an interest rate formation mechanism based on market supply and demand, and the focus will be on improving the market-oriented interest rate system and transmission mechanism. To facilitate the process, the PBOC's capabilities for macro management should be enhanced. As China has basically relaxed interest rate control, the next step would be to establish interest rate formation and adjustment mechanisms suited to market conditions and enhance the effectiveness of PBOC's adjustment measures. When answering questions about lowering the benchmark interest rate and the reserve requirement ratio and removing the cap on deposit rates, PBOC officials pointed out that

> specifically, we aim to establish and improve the system of policy interest rates so as to guide and adjust market rates. Meanwhile, we will facilitate the establishment of benchmark rates and yield curve in the market which will provide a base for the pricing of financial products. We will further streamline the transmission channels between the PBOC's policy rates and benchmark rates in the various markets (i.e. the monetary market, bond market, credit market, and other markets) and finally to the real economy. We will build interest rate formation, transmission, and adjustment mechanisms in which

the market plays the decisive role, the central bank takes the guiding position, and all types of financial markets will be covered. Then the market will truly play a decisive role in resource allocation and interest rate formation.

(2015 PBOC officials answering questions raised
by China Securities Journal)

This clearly lays out the tasks of future reform. To achieve these tasks, future reforms should focus on the following.

A   Establish a comprehensive framework for the central bank's interest rate adjustment

First, optimize the targets of monetary policy. Considering the need for opening-up and economic transformation, we should properly handle the relationship among price stability, structural adjustment, growth, and risk prevention. Price stability is the top priority and should be dealt with from a broader perspective. Second, improve the decision-making mechanism for monetary policies. The PBOC's Monetary Policy Committee should play an important role in policy formulation and adjustment. Third, improve implementation of monetary policies. The authorities should consider economic and financial development and the need for transformation when determining the tool mix, term structure, and magnitude of monetary policies. They should also enhance the coordination of policy tools and be more proactive in liquidity management. Fourth, build an interest rate corridor based on the equilibrium rate. Fifth, establish an effective communication mechanism, enhance the transparency of monetary policy. and proactively guide public expectations.

B   Nurture and improve the benchmark rate system in the financial markets

On one hand, we should draw upon international practices to optimize the price formation system of Shibor and strengthen the supervision of quoting banks. We should expand the use of Shibor, encourage product innovations using Shibor as the benchmark rate, and enhance Shibor's credibility. On the other hand, we should improve the evaluation of the quality of LPR quotation through annual assessment. We will also continue to expand the application of LPR. At the same time, we should complete the construction of the yield curve of treasury bonds and give full play to its role as the reference for pricing bonds and other mid- and long-term financial products. Through the above measures, we can establish a comprehensive system of benchmark rates and form a transmission channel that consists of Shibor in the money market, the yield curve of treasury bonds and LPR in the credit market, and functions in all types of financial markets. This will create favorable conditions for PBOC's interest rate policies to influence the bond market, the credit market, and the real economy. These efforts are also conducive to future elimination of PBOC's benchmark rates for deposits and loans.

C Improve the pricing ability of financial institutions and enhance market participants' sensitivity to interest rate changes

We should improve the pricing ability of financial institutions and encourage commercial banks to establish internal check and control systems centered on shareholders' interest and based on modern banking systems. Through improved corporate governance structure, we can offer institutional guarantees for improved pricing ability. We should gradually establish the pricing systems for internal fund transfer and potential risks. We should offer technical support for interest rate pricing and improve the ability to identify, quantify, and eliminate risks. We should also accelerate the transformation of government functions so that the government will not interfere excessively in resource allocation and government credit and commercial credit will be separated. Then debtors and borrowers will be aligned and those who use the money will be the ones who borrow it. All market players should see their credit status decided based on their financial performance and enjoy equal rights to financing. Through these measures, the efficiency of financing will be improved.

D Accelerate complementary reforms

a Push forward the transformation of growth model, accelerate the transformation of government functions, and strengthen budget constraints on enterprises

Over the past 30 years, China pursued an extensive development model that is government-dominated and features high investment, resource consumption, and export. This model has laid the foundation for China's long-term and high-speed growth and also led to the imbalance of supply of and demand for production factors (land, labor, capital, etc.). This is the major reason behind the disequilibrium in the capital market and the interest rate system. Currently, investment is still the main driving force for growth and mainly covers infrastructure construction and the real estate sector. For domestic investments, local governments and government-controlled SOEs take the dominant position, leading to problems such as redundant construction and excessive capacity and hampering the efficiency of resource allocation. In recent years, the rapid increase and related risks of loans borrowed by SOEs and local government financing platforms have drawn widespread concern. As SOEs and local government financing platforms enjoy soft budget constraints and are insensitive to interest rate changes, the market cannot truly play the decisive role in interest rate formation. Therefore, we should adopt a development model and mechanisms suited to the scientific mode of development. We should properly handle the relationship between the market and the government, respect market laws, and improve government functions. We should also enhance the budgetary constraints of SOEs. By doing the above-mentioned, we will achieve economic growth that is more efficient, more equitable, and more sustainable.

b   Improve the deposit insurance system and the entry and exit mechanism of financial institutions

We should improve the deposit insurance system and align it effectively with existing financial stabilization mechanisms so as to prevent and manage financial risks in a timely manner and maintain financial stability. We should improve the bankruptcy procedures for financial institutions, market-oriented mechanisms for preventing and managing financial risks, and a system that effectively prevents and controls systemic risks. By clarifying exit rules of financial institutions, including those concerning risk compensation and sharing, we can enhance the protection for depositors and effectively prevent bank runs. We should push for a gradual introduction of budgetary discipline in depository institutions and avoid irrational price competition among those institutions. We should also nurture more competent market players and further clarify the boundary between the market and the government. In addition, we should strengthen market discipline and prevent moral hazards to get rid of the accumulation of risks in the financial system.

c   Establish a scientific concept of development and transform the business philosophy and growth model of commercial banks

The development of China's banking sector over the past 30 plus years shows that rational and prudent operation is the key guarantee to sustainable development. Against the backdrop of interest rate liberalization, commercial banks should establish effective structures and mechanisms for corporate governance. They should transform their business philosophy and growth model based on scientific concepts of development and promote standardized, prudent, and rational operations. They should further strengthen the awareness of capital, cost, and risk control, pay attention to the coordination of development speed, scale, quality, and revenue, and emphasize the balance between cost and revenue, risk and return, and short-term and long-term interests. Banks should adhere to a growth model that features capital constraint, value orientation, and long-term development. They should also transform their operation by adopting a model that saves capital, promotes innovation, and optimizes the business and income structure so as to achieve steady and sustainable development.

d   Build a multi-tier financial market that is more competitive and inclusive

With deepened market-based reforms, financial institutions will be increasingly exposed to interest rate risks. As the financial markets become more mature, risk management tools are constantly being developed and innovated. This can open up new channels of investment and financing for financial consumers, help financial institutions transform their business model, and actively participate in market competition; it also offers a necessary channel for financial institutions to effectively manage and tackle interest rate risks. In addition, we should further enhance the inter-connectivity among various financial markets and nurture more effective market prime rates, providing favorable conditions for the formation of the equilibrium rate and the transmission of monetary policy.

e   Advance the reform of exchange rate regime, capital account convertibility, and factor pricing in a coordinated way

Interest rate liberalization, reform of the RMB exchange rate, and capital account convertibility are at the core of financial reform and are essential for China to utilize resources of both the domestic and international markets, increase the level of opening-up, promote economic transformation, and sustain healthy growth. These three reforms are interrelated. Thus, we need to take a gradual and coordinated approach and seek synergies wherever possible. In addition, as interest rate is a key element of factor prices, interest rate liberalization should be advanced in coordination with the pricing reforms of other factors such as resources and energy. In this way, the market can play the decisive role in resource allocation on a larger basis.

References

Allen, F. and Gale, D. (1999). Diversity of Opinion and Financing of New Technologies. *Journal of Financial Intermediation*, (8), pp. 68–89.

Arrow, K. J. (1984). *Collected Papers of Kenneth J. Arrow, Volume 4: The Economics of Information*. Cambridge: Belknap Press.

Barro, R. (1986). Reputation in a Model of Monetary Policy with Incomplete Information. *Journal of Monetary Economics*, 17(1), pp. 3–20.

Bech, M. L. and Klee, E. (2011). The Mechanics of a Graceful Exit: Interest on Reserves and Segmentation in the Federal Funds Market. *Journal of Monetary Economics*, 58(5), pp. 415–431.

Bernanke, B. S. (2004). The Great Moderation. In: *The Meetings of the Eastern Economic Association*. Washington, DC. [online] Available at: www.federalreserve.gov/boarddocs/speeches/2004/20040220/

Bernanke, B. S. and Gertler, M. (1995). Inside the Black Box: The Credit Channel of Monetary Policy Transmission. *Journal of Economic Perspectives*, 9(4), pp. 27–48.

Bindseil, U. and Jablecki, J. (2011). A Structural Model of Central Bank Operations and Bank Intermediation. *ECB Working Paper*, 86(273), pp. 178–184.

BIS. (2005). Zero-Coupon Yield Curves: Technical Documentation. *BIS Paper*, (25).

Blinder, A. S. (1998). *Central Banking in Theory and Practice*. Cambridge: MIT Press, pp. 83–176.

Blinder, A. S., Ehrmann, M., Fratzscher, M., Hanan, J. D. and Jansen, D. (2008). Central Bank Communication and Monetary Policy: A Survey of Theory and Evidence. *Journal of Economic Literature, American Economic Association*, 46(4), pp. 910–945.

Brunner, K. (1981). *The Art of Central Banking*. London: Longmans, Green and Co.

Campbell, J. and Shiller, R. (1987). Cointegration and Tests of Present Value Models. *Journal of Political Economy*, 95(5), pp. 1063–1088.

Cas, S., Carrión-Menéndez, A. and Frantischek, F. (2011). The Policy Interest-Rate Pass-Through in Central America. *IMF Working Paper*, No. 11/240. [online] Available at: https://www.imf.org/external/pubs/ft/wp/2011/wp11240.pdf.

Chenery, H. and Syrquin, M. (1988). *The Development Style: 1950–1970*. Beijing: Economic Science Press.

China Securities Journal and PBOC. (2015). China has Basically Lifted Interest Rate Control. [online] Available at: http://www.cs.com.cn/sylm/cstop10/201510/t20151026_4825221.html.

Christiano, L., Eichenbaum, M. and Evans, C. (1999). Monetary Shocks: What Have We Learned, and to What End? *Handbook of Macroeconomics*, (1), pp. 65–84.

Engle, R. and Granger, C. (1987). Co-Integration and the US Term Structure. *Journal of Banking and Finance*, 18(1), pp. 167–182.

Estrella, A. and Hardouvelis, G. (1991). The Term Structure as a Predictor of Real Economic Activity. *Journal of Finance*, 46(2), pp. 555–576.

Estrella, A. and Mishkin, F. S. (1997). Is There a Role for Monetary Aggregates in the Conduct of Monetary Policy. *Journal of Monetary Economics*, (40), pp. 279–304.

Fama, E. (1990). Term-Structure Forecasts of Interest Rates, Inflation and Real Returns. *Journal of Monetary Economics*, 25(1), pp. 59–76.

Fan, W. (2002). *Study on China's Interest Rate Marketization*. PhD. Beijing: Graduate School of Chinese Academy of Social Sciences.

Fang, K. (2011). Roots and Rules of Financial Crisis and Economic Recession in Japan and the United States Based on Industrial Revolutionary Cycle Theory. *Journal of Financial Research*, (8), pp. 72–77.

Feyzioglu, T., Porter, N. and Takats, E. (2009). Interest Rate Liberalization in China. *IMF Working Paper*. [online] Available at: https://www.imf.org/external/pubs/ft/wp/2009/wp09171.pdf.

Fischer, S. (1987). Economic Growth and Economic Policy. In: *Growth-Oriented Adjustment Programs*. Washington, DC: World Bank.

Friedman, B. and Kuttner, K. (2010). Implementation of Monetary Policy: How Do Central Banks Set Interest Rates? *Handbook of Macroeconomics*, (3), pp. 1345–1438.

Friedman, M. and Schwartz, A. (1963). *A Monetary History of the United States 1867–1960*. Princeton, NJ: Princeton University Press.

Gali, J. and Gambetti, L. (2009). On the Source of the Great Moderation. *American Economic Journal: Macroeconomics*, (1), pp. 26–57.

Gigineishvili, N. (2011). Determinants of Interest Rate Pass-Through: Do Macroeconomic Conditions and Financial Market Structure Matter? *IMF Working Paper*, No. 11/176. [online] Available at: https://www.imf.org/external/pubs/ft/wp/2011/wp11176.pdf.

Goodhart, C. (1986). Financial Innovation and Monetary Control. *Oxford Review of Economic Policy*, (2), pp. 75–91.

Guan, Q. (2014). Which Red Lines That Have Restrained Reform Should Be Cancelled? [online] Available at: http://www.stcn.com/2014/1010/11765300.shtml.

Guan, T. (2012). Market-Based Exchange Rate Reform Has Gained Great Progress. [online] Available at: http://www.southmoney.com/waihui/waihuifenxi/201208/362870.html.

Guitian, M. (1997). Reality and the Logic of Capital Flow Liberalization. In: Hekman, C. R. and Sweeney, R. J. eds., *Capital Controls in Emerging Economies*. Boulder: Westview Press, pp. 17–32.

Hamilton, J. (1997). Measuring the Liquidity Effect. *American Economic Review*, 87(1), pp. 80–97.

He, D. and Wang, H. (2011). Dual-Track System of Interest Rate and China's Monetary Policy Implementation. *Journal of Financial Research*, (12), pp. 1–18.

He, D. and Wang, H. (2012). Dual-Track Interest Rate and the Conduct of Monetary Policy in China. *China Economic Review*, 23(4), pp. 928–947.

He, D. and Wang, H. (2013). Monetary Policy and Bank Lending in China: Evidence from Loan Level Data. *HKIMR Working Paper*, No. 16/2013. [online] Available at SSRN: https://ssrn.com/abstract=2346181

He, D., Wang, H. and Yu, X. (2013). Where Will China's Interest Rate Go: The Formation and Operation of Policy Interest Rate after the Marketization of Interest Rate. *New Finance Commentary*, (6).

Hellmann, T., Murdock, K. and Stiglitz, J. (1997). Financial Restraint: A New Analysis Framework. *Economic Herald*, 5, pp. 42–47.

Hester, D. D. (1969). Financial Disintermediation and Policy. *Journal of Money, Credit and Banking*, (8), pp. 600–617.

Hong, P. (2012). Why We Should Marketize Interest Rates. [online] Available at: http://blog.sina.com.cn/s/blog_9cc0e68401015h58.html

Hu, B. (2014). *Financial Repression and Interest Rate Liberalization in China*. Bloomington: Department of Economics, Indiana University Bloomington.

Hu, X. (2012). Market-Based Interest Rate Reform Involve Banks of All Sizes. [online] Available at: http://epaper.stcn.com/paper/zqsb/html/2012-03/30/content_354753.htm

Hu, X. and Yuan, J. (2011). Incremental Reform: Rational Choice of China's Interest Rate Marketization. *International Economic Review*, (6), pp. 132–146.

Huang, J. (2013). Improving the Regulation on the Ceiling of Loan-to-Deposit Ratio. [online] Available at: www.cf40.org.cn/plus/view.php?aid=7145

Huang, Y. and Wang, B. (2010). Cost Distortions and Structural Imbalances in China. *China and World Economy*, 18(4), pp. 1–17.

IBS. (1968). Recent Innovations in International Banking. *Bank of England Quarterly Bulletin*, June, pp. 209–210.

IMF. (1998). The Asian Crisis: Causes and Cures. *Finance and Development*, 35(2).

IMF. (2011). People's Republic of China: Financial System Stability Assessment. *Country Report*, No. 11/321.

Jappell, T. and Pagano, M. (1994). Saving, Growth, and Liquidity Constraints. *Quarterly Journal of Economics*, 109(1), pp. 83–109.

Jiang, Z. and Li, H. (2013). The Term Structure of Interest Rate as a Predictor of Macro-Economic Growth. *Chinese Review of Financial Studies*, (3), pp. 72–83.

Jin, Z. (2013). The Future of the International Monetary Framework. [online] Available at: file:///D:/Documents/Downloads/OMFIF-The-Future-Of-The-International-Monetary-Framework.pdf

Jin, Z. and Hao, H. (2015). Coordination of Interest Rate and Exchange Rate Policy Under International Monetary Policies. *Economic Research Journal*, (5), pp. 35–47.

Johnston, R. B. and Sundararajan, V. (1999). *Sequencing Financial Sector Reforms*. Washington, DC: International Monetary Fund.

Kang, S. (1989). The Far Reaching Effect of Western Financial Innovation. *World Economy*, (1).

Kang, S. and Wang, Z. (2010). Studies on the Risk Profile and Information of the Term Structure of China's National Bonds. *World Economy*, (7), pp. 121–143.

Kornai, J. (1980). *Economics of Shortage*. Amsterdam: North-Holland.

Kornai, J. (2009). Soft Budget Constrain Syndrome and Global Financial Crisis. *New Fortune*, (6), pp. 32–36.

Lardy, N. (2013). Enhancing China's Economic Growth by Marketizing Interest Rates. *21st Century Business Herald*, May 27.

Lau, L., Qian, Y. and Roland, G. (1997). Pareto-Improving Economic Reforms through Dual-Track Liberalization. *Economic Letters*, 55(2), pp. 285–292.

Lau, L., Qian, Y. and Roland, G. (2000). Reform without Losers: An Interpretation of China's Dual-Track Approach to Transition. *Journal of Political Economy*, 108(1), pp. 120–143.

Laurens, B., et al. (2005). *Monetary Policy Implementation at Different Stages of Market Development*. Washington, DC: International Monetary Fund.

Levhari, D. and Srinivasan, T. N. (1969). Optimal Savings under Uncertainty. *Review of Economic Studies*, 44(1), p. 197.

Li, B. (2014). New Issues in Monetary Policy: International Experience and Relevance for China. In: *Second Joint Conference of People's Bank of China and IMF*. Beijing.

Li, H. (2012). The Term Structure of Interest Rates as a Predictor of Forward Interest Rates. *Journal of Financial Research*, (8).

Li, H. and Su, N. (2017). Financial Innovation, Financial Disintermediation and Credit Money Creation. *Research on Financial and Economic Issues*, (10), pp. 40–50.

Li, R. (2013). How to Finish the 'Last Jump' in Interest Rate Reform. *Money China*, 31, pp. 74–77.

Li, Y. (2010). The Key Moment for China's PE Development. In: *2010 China's Private Equity Annual Conference*. Beijing.

Lian, P. (2014). *The Influence of Interest Rate Liberalization on China's Economy and Finance*. Beijing: China Citic Press.

Liang, Q., Zhang, X. and Guo, X. (2010). Cultivation of Benchamark Interest Rate in China's Financial Market: Based on the Empirical Analysis of Constructing a Complete Benchmark Yield Curve. *Journal of Financial Research*, (9), pp. 81–98.

Llewellyn, D. (1985). *The Evolution of the British Financial System: Gilbert Lectures on Banking*. London: Inst of Bankers, pp. 57–68.

Lu, Z. (2011). Market-Based Interest Rate Reform Can Neither Wait Nor Be Hurried. [online] Available at: http://finance.stockstar.com/SS2011012430181679.shtml.

Ma, J. (2010). *Protecting People's Money Pocket*. Heilongjiang: Heilongjiang People's Publishing House.

McKinnon, R. I. (1984). The International Capital Market and Economic Liberalization in LDCs. *The Developing Economies*, December, 22.

McKinnon, R. I. (1991). *The Order of Economic Liberalization: Financial Control in the Transition to a Market Economy*. Baltimore: Johns Hopkins University Press, pp. 3.

Miao, J. (2010). The Development and Future of China's Insurance Sector Management. *China Finance*, (3), pp.26–28.

Minsky, H. (1975). *John Maynard Keynes*. New York: Columbia University Press.

Mishkin, F. (2009). *The Economics of Money, Banking and Financial Market*. Boston: Pearson Education and Addison-Wesley, pp. 417–426.

Murphy, K., Shleifer, A. and Vishny, R. (1992). The Transition to a Market Economy: Pitfalls of Partial Reform. *Quarterly Journal of Economics*, 107(3), pp. 889–906.

Nelson, C. and Siegel, A. (1987). Parsimonious Modeling of Yield Curves. *Journal of Business*, 60(4), pp. 473–489.

PBOC. (2002). *China Monetary Policy Report*. Beijing: China Financial and Economic Publishing House.

PBOC, China Banking Regulatory Commission, China Securities Regulatory Commission, China Insurance Regulatory Commission, and State Administration of Foreign Exchange. (2012). The 12th Five-Year Plan for the Development and Reform of the Financial Industry. [online] Available at: www.gov.cn/gzdt/2012-09/17/content_2226795.htm

PBOC Operation Office. (2013). *2013 Selected Research Reports by PBOC Operation Office*. Beijing: Economic Science Press. pp. 23–25.

Perkins, D. H. and Rawski, T. G. (2007). Forecasting China's Economic Growth to 2015. In: Brandt, L. and Rawski, T. G. eds., *China's Great Economic Transformation*. Cambridge: Cambridge University Press.

Plosser, C. I. (2013). Forward Guidance. In: *Stanford Institute for Economic Policy Research's (SIEPR) Associates Meeting*. Stanford.

Posen, A. and Kuttner, K. (2004). The Difficulty of Discerning What's Too Tight: Taylor Rules and Japanese Monetary. *The North American Journal of Economics and Finance*, 15(1), pp. 53–74.

Reinhart, C. and Tokatlidis, I. (2005). Before and after Financial Liberalization. *Mpra Paper*, 5(3), pp. 231–271.

Research Group of World Bank and Development Research Center. (2013). *China in 2030*. Beijing: China Financial and Economic Publishing House.

Sa, Q. (1996). International Practices on the Relation between Interest Rate Marketization and High Interest Rates. *Studies of International Finance*, (1), pp. 41–45.

Saborowski, C. and Weber, S. (2013). Assessing the Determinants of Interest Rate Transmission through Conditional Impulse Response Functions. *IMF Working Paper*, No. 13/23. [online] Available at: https://www.imf.org/external/pubs/ft/wp/2013/wp1323.pdf.

Sachs, J. (1987). Trade and Exchange Rate Policies in Growth Oriented Adjustment Programs. In: *Growth Oriented Adjustment Programs*. Washington, DC: World Bank.

Sheng, S., etc. (2012). Promote China's Interest Rate and Exchange Rate Reforms and Capital Account Liberalization in a Coordinated Manner. *Research Report of PBC Survey and Statistics Department*. [online] Available at: http://roll.sohu.com/20120418/n340862998.shtml.

Sims, C., Stock, J. and Watson, M. (1990). Inference in Linear Time Series Models with Some Unit Roots. *Econometrica*, 58(1), pp. 113–144.

Smith, A. (1827). *An Inquiry of the Nature and Causes of the Wealth of Nations*. Edinburgh: University Press for Thomas Nelson and Peter Brown. pp. 331.

Song, W. (2009). *Study on China's Financial Disintermediation*. Beijing: China Renmin University Press.

Svensson, L. (1994). Estimation and Interpreting Forward Interest Rates. *NBER Working Paper*, No. 4871. [online] Available at: http://www.nber.org/papers/w4871.

Taylor, J. B. (1993). Discretion versus Policy Rules in Practice. *Carnegie-Rochester Conference Series on Public Policy*, (39), pp. 195–214.

Taylor, J. B. (2012). Monetary Policy Rules Work and Discretion Doesn't: A Tale of Two Eras. *Journal of Money Credit and Banking*, 44(6), pp. 1017–1032.

The Federal Reserve System. (2012). Federal Reserve issues FOMC statement. [online] Available at: https://www.federalreserve.gov/newsevents/pressreleases/monetary20121212a.htm.

Wan, X. (2014). Managing the Interest Rates Ceiling Is the Way to Provide Affordable Finance. *Shanghai Security News*. Oct. 22.

Wang, G. (2014). Three Paths for Interest Rate Reform. *Economic Research Information*, 7, pp. 26–29.

Wei, J. (2011). Transforming Economic Growth Path Is a Comprehensive and thorough Reform. *Academic Monthly*, 43(8), pp. 61–68.

Wei, S. (2013). Trade Liberalization and Embedded Institutional Reform: Evidence from Chinese Exporters. *American Economic Review*, 103(6), pp. 2169–2195.

Woodford, M. (2005). Central Bank Communication and Policy Effectiveness. *Proceedings: Economic Policy Symposium: Jackson Hole, Federal Reserve Bank of Kansas City*, (August), pp. 399–474.

Woodford, M. (2012). Methods of Policy Accommodation at the Interest Rate Lower Bound. *Proceedings: Economic Policy Symposium: Jackson Hole*, pp. 185–288.

Wu, X. (2013). Six Issues in Liberalizing Deposit Rates. *Cf40 Weekly*, (219).

Xia, B. and Chen, D. (2011). *China's Financial Strategy: 2020*. Beijing: People's Publishing House. pp. 38.

Xiang, W. and Li, H. (2014). The Characteristics of Money Market Benchmark Rate and Empirical Study of Shibor. *Economic Review*, 185(1), pp. 107–117.

Xie, P. (2013a). *Why China Should Re-Launch the Financial Reform*. Beijing: China Financial and Economic Publishing House.

Xie, P. (2013b). *How to Reform China's Financial Sector: 2013–2020*. Beijing: China Financial and Economic Publishing House.

Xu, G. (2015). Prerequisites and Strategies for Accelerating China's Interest Rates Liberalization. *CF40 Youth Forum*, (71).

Xu, J. (2003). Interest Rate Marketization Is an Incremental Reform. *International Finance News*, (4).

Xue, H. (2003). *Co-Movement of the Interest Rate and the Exchange Rate during the Dynamic Opening of the Financial Markets*. PhD. Beijing: Central Party School of the Communist Party of China.

Yang, T. and Zhong, Y. (2013). Concentration, Competition and Risk for Banks in China. *Journal of Financial Research*, (1), pp. 122–134.

Yao, Y. and Tan, H. (2011). Inflation Expectation in China's Financial Market. *Journal of Financial Research*, (6), pp. 61–70.

Yao, Y., Xu, G., Lin, N. and Wang, Y. (2015). Premise and Strategy of China's Interest Rate Marketization. *Financial Regulation Research*, (3), pp. 1–24.

Yi, G. (2008). The Development of Shibor as a Market Benchmark. In: *2008 Shibor Working Conference*. [online] Available at: www.bis.org/review/r080130e.pdf

Yi, G. (2009). 30-Year Course of the Market-Based Interest Rates Reform since the Reform and Opening Up. *Journal of Financial Research*, 343(1), pp. 1–13.

Yi, G. (2013). Trust the Market. *New Century Weekly*, (46).

Yu, Y. (2011). China Can Break Free of the Dollar Trap. *Financial Times*. [online] Available at: www.ft.com/content/2189faa2-bec6-11e0-a36b-00144feabdc0

Zhang, J. (2011). International Comparison and Experience of SME Financing. *China Finance*, (18), pp. 19–22.

Zhang, J., Gao, Y., Fu, Y. and Zhang, H. (2007). Why Does China Enjoy So Much Better Physical Infrastructure? *Economic Research Journal*, (3), pp. 3–17.

Zhang, J., Lei, Y., Zhu, H. and Wang, L. (2012). *Global Experience of Interest Rates Liberalization*. Beijing: China Machine Press.

Zhang, M. (2013). Incomplete Interest Rates Liberalization. [online] Available at: http://magazine.caijing.com.cn/2013-07-29/113099051.html

Zhang, X. (2011). Enhancing the Status of Shibor as a Benchmark Interest Rate in China's Money Market. *China Finance*, (12).

Zhang, X. and Hu, Y. (2010). Market Concentration, Competition and Monetary Policy Transmission Mechanism of Banking Industry: Based on the Experience of Chinese Banks. *Journal of Shanxi University of Finance and Economics*, 13(12), pp. 45–51.

Zhang, X. and Pan, L. (2013). Market Structure of China's Banking Industry and Relationship Lending of Small-and-Median Sized Corporations. *Journal of Financial Intermediation*, (6), pp. 133–145.

Zhang, Y., Xia, J. and Zhang, W. (2010). Top-Down Yardstick Competition and the Spill-Over Effect of Local Government's Fiscal Expenditure. *Zhejiang Social Science*, (12), pp. 20–125.

Zhou, K (2012). Market-Based Interest Rate Reform has Accelerated and the Banking Sector Needs to Change its Operation Strategy. *China Banker*, (9), pp. 10–15.

Zhou, L. (2007). Governing China' s Local Officials: An Analysis of Promotion Tournament Model. *Journal of Economic Research*, (7), pp. 36–49.

Zhou, X. (2004). Pushing Forward Interest Rate Liberalization Reform and Establishing Benchmark Yield Curve. *China Financier*, (1).

Zhou, X. (2006). Features and Characteristics of China's Monetary Policy. *Caijing*, (26), pp. 20–21.

Zhou, X. (2012). Major Features of China's Monetary Policy in the 21st Century. *New Century*, (46).

Zhou, X. (2013a). How to Understand the Convertibility of Capital Account. *New Century Weekly*, (3).

Zhou, X. (2013b). Major Characteristics of China's Monetary Policy in 21st Century. *China Finance*, (2).

Zhu, S. and Chen, J. (2003). Empirical Study on the Term Structure of National Bonds in Exchanges. *Journal of Financial Research*, 280(10), pp. 63–73.

Index

For Product Safety Concerns and Information please contact our EU
representative GPSR@taylorandfrancis.com
Taylor & Francis Verlag GmbH, Kaufingerstraße 24, 80331 München, Germany